Shakespeare and *The Faerie Queene*

Shakespeare and
The Faerie Queene

BY ABBIE FINDLAY POTTS

Professor Emeritus of English Literature
Rockford College

GREENWOOD PRESS, PUBLISHERS
NEW YORK

Copyright © 1958 by Cornell University

Reprinted by permission
of the Cornell University Press

First Greenwood Reprinting, 1969

Library of Congress Catalogue Card Number 69-14040

SBN 8371-1156-0

PRINTED IN UNITED STATES OF AMERICA

*In grateful recognition of
the teaching and counsel of*

GEORGE LYMAN KITTREDGE
who insisted that we know the text

JOSEPH QUINCY ADAMS
who taught us the facts

GEORGE PIERCE BAKER
*who never let us forget that
a play is a play*

Contents

	Preface	ix
I	Introduction: "The Rarer Action"	1
II	Shakespeare without Spenser	21
III	The Book of Courtesy as a Design for Comedy	35
IV	Legends of Friendship and Chastity	64
V	Courtly Code and Dramatic Action	84
VI	The Palace of Priam as a Bowre of Blisse	106
VII	Hamlet and Gloriana's Knights	128
VIII	*Measure for Measure* and the Book of Justice	150
IX	The Book of Holiness as a Design for Tragedy	174
X	Tutorial Action in the Late Plays	208
XI	Conclusion: Of Forms and Shapes	234
	Index	257

Preface

IF we are to make the most of Shakespeare's example in our own dramatic enterprises, we may well think of him not only as a playwright able to teach playwrights but also as a scholar with a message for scholars. Because he knew what he needed for his plays, he knew what to look for in the books he studied. We can scarcely equal his understanding of the essential form of our humanity, but we may profit by his willingness to relate dramatic form to the art of conduct. His action goes prudently to work because he has demanded from his agents, or characters, genuine choices for which they are themselves accountable. Moreover, the manifest improvement in his craftsmanship at the turn of the century can best be explained by the advance in his scholarship; it points to and shows traces of his reading of literature that deals with modes of conduct.

I began this investigation of Shakespeare's possible debt to *The Faerie Queene* because in my production of his plays for over a quarter of a century at Rockford College I became aware of his ethical premises as the chief constituent of his dramatic action and the distinguishing mark of his dramaturgy. If I were to prepare a stage picture appropriate for his text, the grouping and movement of the actors and their gestures and facial expressions should accord with the playwright's understanding of a code of behavior and thus reflect the inner even more than the outer habit of the time. Such pictorial ethics I found admirably substantiated in the cantos of Edmund Spenser. Here was a treasure house, if not a manual, for the dramatic artist of any century. When I had somewhat assimilated the wealth of these two writers in their hypothetical connection, I wondered why students of Shakespeare's dramatic poetry did not read Spenser's narrative poem more challengingly for the light it could shed on the action of the plays. Thus my own research was prolonged and in time augmented.

Working within the limits of one hypothesis, I have not been able to weigh my evidence with all other material bearing on the literary ancestry of each play or to decide that this or that and none other is the explicit source. My account of a single subsidiary of Shakespeare's art will later be evaluated and related to the whole matter of influence when scholars have more appreciatively examined the characteristic traits of his dramatic form. In certain instances, however, I have discussed alternative claims—notably in regard to *Troilus and Cressida* and in Chapter V, which allies Troilus and Hamlet with the courtiers of Castiglione. And I never forget that there are other sources.

The intense concentration on particulars demanded for this kind of study has saved me from what Sir Francis Bacon might call the "over-early and peremptory reduction" of those particulars into a facile summary; it has also deprived me of the doubtful pleasures of argument and pontifical assertion. Yet, wherever I have had strong convictions based on evidence, I have tried to be frank even as I was cautious. Because it must necessarily consider dramatic rather than epic form and emphasize the devices that shape a play for the stage—and hence for the auditor and spectator—this book does scant justice to Spenser's poem; but the wide range of comment on it in the Variorum edition of Edwin A. Greenlaw and his associates is accessible to my readers as it has been to me.

The text in *The Poetical Works of Edmund Spenser,* edited by J. C. Smith and E. de Selincourt (Oxford University Press, 1921), has been quoted with permission and checked by the text of the Variorum. For the convenience of the reader I use Arabic numerals in citing passages from *The Faerie Queene;* this is the form of reference in the appendixes of the Variorum. And I use Roman numerals for act and scene of Shakespeare's plays, referring with permission to the one-volume edition by George Lyman Kittredge (Boston: Ginn and Company, 1936). Mention of previous discussions of individual plays has been kept to a minimum, but I hope that I have not overlooked any significant contribution to my theme.

Along with the three scholars to whom this book is inscribed, I owe thanks to Professor Lane Cooper of Cornell University, who first called my attention to Aristotle's *Poetics* as important for understanding the drama of all centuries and countries. I wish to acknowledge the advice of Professor Alwin Thaler to continue my studies in a field where he himself had been long at work and the wisdom of Professor Oscar J. Campbell, who best knows the answer to his query why those who study Wordsworth's poetry go on to study Shakespeare's plays. Professor Marjorie H. Nicolson and Professor Hardin Craig wrote me painstaking and helpful letters when, many years ago, I was beginning to assemble my evidence; and I am also indebted to the comment of the late Tucker Brooke. I have not forgotten the cautions of two other wise scholars, George Lyman Kittredge and Joseph Quincy Adams, nor their counsel to persevere; and I hope that I have ever so little justified their wish to see such an investigation credibly set forth. Further, I owe a special debt for encouragement to Professor Northrop Frye, whose studies of literary form have been enlightening to us all.

My long and intermittent labor on the text of Spenser and Shakespeare has been assisted by many gifted students whose voices spoke great "lines" at countless rehearsals, thus dinning into my ears the evidence on which my book depends; by the hospitable librarians of the New York State Library at Albany and Russell Sage College Library at Troy, New York; and by the editors of the *Shakespeare Association Bulletin* and the *Shakespeare Quarterly*, who first printed in part and gave their permission for the reprinting of evidence that has here been expanded or revised as Chapters III and VII.

Janice Chilcott Merson has typed my thorny manuscript; Professor Vivian C. Hopkins gave suggestions for one of several revisions; Dr. Ruth Morris Bakwin has helped to make possible this publication of another of my studies of literary form; and again I am indebted to the wisdom and skill of the editors of Cornell University Press.

ABBIE FINDLAY POTTS

Troy, New York
April, 1958

Shakespeare and *The Faerie Queene*

CHAPTER I

Introduction: "The Rarer Action"

"WHAT'S to do?" asks the resolute invalid, Caius Ligarius, in Shakespeare's *Julius Caesar*. "What shall I do? Say what! What shall I do?" demands Ariel of Prospero. "My lord, it shall be done." From tyrannicide to benevolent magic, Shakespeare makes sure that the persons of his plays shall be doers of deeds. The imagined life of his fictitious men and women never fails to put us in mind of the responsible doings of actual men and women; his sprites and monsters do the deeds of responsible masters; and his ghosts seem always to obey the Ultimately Responsible Deed Doer.

Whatever degree of actuality is intended, the playwright shares this deed-doing obligation with Caius Ligarius and Ariel, as with the witches who do and do and do their "deed without a name." When, himself a kind of magician, he conceives his plot and while he arranges it, at every change of scene he meets the same old gerundive challenge: What am I to do about what is to be done, suffered, thought, felt, said, by the persons of my play? Even as he scribbles "finis" on his manuscript, he must still greet his actors with instructions about what they in their turn are to do about this, that, and the other histrionic matter. It is no wonder that after author and actors have together driven their play through the ears and eyes of a myriad audience into its collective consciousness thoughtful individuals will be heard saying in Shakespeare's own phrases, "Much ado about nothing" or "Masterly done" or "What's to do?" We have been excited or bored, amused or dismayed, to be sure; we may even have been emotionally cleansed or spiritually enlightened or aesthetically gratified; but those who wish to recreate themselves and others still think the good play is good because it stirs them to deeds of personal love or courage or propels them into attitudes of social justice.[1] And a bad play? Contrariwise.

At the crisis of this deed doing the critic also becomes dramatic. For him as for Ariel, in Prospero's words, "There's something else to do." Shall the play be ignored? Shall it be anatomized? Shall it be tagged with an epithet or two and shelved? Or shall it be helped along? And hence it comes about that the most dramatic criticism of dramatic art is such study and interpretation of a play as clarifies its agendum, its deed to be done, and thus helps young playwrights to forge yet-unwrought plays.

Remembering the advice given by the Clown to Cleopatra— "You must think this, look you, that the worm will do his kind" —and convinced that plays, like asps, do *their* kind, we may well decide that dramatic criticism is "not to be trusted but in the keeping of wise people." Yet the wisest critic will sympathize with Portia, who "can easier teach twenty what were good to be done than . . . follow [her] own teaching." And the boldest

---

[1] See Kenneth Burke on ritual drama as hub, in *The Philosophy of Literary Form* (Louisiana State University Press, 1941), pp. 103–132. Refer also to Philip Wheelwright, *The Burning Fountain* (Indiana University Press, 1954), pp. 123–217; Susanne K. Langer, *Philosophy in a New Key* (3d ed.; Harvard University Press, 1957), pp. 153–170; and Northrop Frye, *Anatomy of Criticism* (Princeton University Press, 1957), pp. 104–107.

Introduction: "The Rarer Action"

critic should heed Florizel's admirable statement of the concrete universal:

> What you do
> Still betters what is done.
>
> . . . . .
>
> Each your doing,
> So singular in each particular,
> Crowns what you are doing in the present deed,
> That all your acts are queens.

Shakespeare understood the heart of his own "mystery"; and to estimate his plays aright the scholarly critic will consider what he did to better what had been done.

Theseus' summary description of the poetic process at the beginning of Act V of *A Midsummer Night's Dream*, Hamlet's advice to the players, and Prospero's valedictory remarks are too well known to serve as more than a point of departure for these few hours with the *Concordance;* yet they, too, commend a poetic as distinguished from a solely aesthetic view of art. "The poet's pen" is a shaping pen. The player's art reveals nature to the "judicious." Unless we the auditors with our gentle breath fill the sails of Prospero's dramatic bark, en route from the magic isle to Naples, his "project fails." It is we who set Shakespeare's men and women "free."

In so doing, we may not disregard his rhythmic speech, his images, his diction—in which he is most like himself and least like anyone else—his quotable precepts and his profound characterization and his ingenious plots; but these constituents of a play in their several offices can furnish only partial values. According to Aristotle, whose observations are still helpful, tragedy (and, by inference, comedy) is an imitation of action, *mimesis praxeos*. To understand this mimesis we must investigate the technical devices necessary to the mimetic art: the organic or structural metaphors, the symbolic relationships, the myths and rituals determining form, and those archetypes which abide in all literary as in all human behavior.[2] But the researches of diplomatist, bibliographer, antiquarian, aesthete, mythologist, archetypologist, are frustrate without reference to this particular poet's dramaturgy, the identical craft whereby he wrought into mimetic form so wide a range of human affairs—from the merely wishful *Midsummer Night's Dream* to the highly effective *Winter's Tale*. Can Shakespeare's aims, choices, and method as a playwright be understood to illustrate an *agon* of which he himself is the protagonist, recapitulating the trials, discoveries, and, it may be, the victories of the dramatic life? Amid the comic folly and tragic waste in his works of art does the art itself emerge as an answer to the question of the invalid Caius Ligarius, "What's to do?"[3]

Or, if we prefer Latin derivatives—"act," "activity," "action" —throughout Shakespeare's text we find the same vital message. Among the "infinite doings of the world" (Camillo's words) there are many doers like the Dauphin in *Henry V*, for whom "Doing is activity, and [they]will still be doing." It is the disputatious Gravedigger in *Hamlet* who best states the case for dramatic art: "If I drown myself wittingly, it argues an act; and an act hath three branches—it is to act, to do, and to perform; argal [since Ophelia went to the water and the water did not go to Ophelia], she drown'd herself wittingly."

Wittingly. Hamlet himself does not stop with "actions that a man might play; [he has] that within which passeth show." Like him, Shakespeare was to evince in constantly clearer phrase through his great decade the more witting actions of human life.

---

[2] In his "Approach to *Othello*" (*Sewanee Review*, LXIV [1956], 110), Robert B. Heilman says: "When we follow up mimesis far enough, we come to archetype and symbol." Is it not also true that when we understand archetype and symbol well enough we are remanded to praxis, also by way of mimesis?

[3] "The end of life is a mode of action, not a quality"—τὸ τέλος πρᾶξίς τις ἐστίν οὐ ποιότης (Aristotle, *Poetics*).

Introduction: "The Rarer Action"

He would proceed from the command of his King Henry V ("Then imitate the action of the tiger") to the authority of his Hermione doomed to prison ("This action I now go on / Is for my better grace"). Most significantly, he would end his own dramatic enterprise with a plain speech from Prospero: "The rarer action is / In virtue than in vengeance." The mainspring of his works is the belief that action is more than activity, that it is the way to virtue. Thus he allies himself with Edmund Spenser, who in 1589 wrote to Sir Walter Raleigh about *The Faerie Queene*, "The generall end [of the book] is to fashion a gentleman or noble person in vertuous and gentle discipline."

Lest we be seduced, however, from scholarly research, also an action, into undramatic discussions of moral and social and political betterment, we must here define our enterprise in terms of Shakespeare's own experience. So doing, we add one more assumption about this dramatist's use of his learning to the rich literary data compiled by Professor Whitaker and his many industrious predecessors.[4] Such study is not less practical than the staging of his plays; it is the requirement for their good performance. Plots, heroes, heroines, doctrines, and maxims from antiquity; the hagiography, homilies, and ritual of the Christian Church; the figments of story, legend, and romance conveyed into England by Italian, Spanish, and French writers and their translators; the early plays and romances, the folklore, and the chronicles of Britain herself; schoolbooks and chapbooks; and always the behavior of the men and women he knew—such various wealth presented the young dramatist with his "matter." For his "manner" he might have observed the arrangement of Biblical events in the medieval cycles, the ups and downs in the plots of native moralities and popular comic or tragic stories, the classical patterns affected by university wits, and—not least—the protean mimicry of strolling players in courtyard

[4] Virgil K. Whitaker, *Shakespeare's Use of Learning* (San Marino, Calif., 1953).

and market place. Yet he emerges from his minor contemporaries in such a way as to suggest not only unique personal gifts but at its most urgent, as if he really believed it, a certain cultural prepossession, the faith that conduct, like playwriting, is an art and that there is no "good" playwriting or acting except in view of a theory of "good" conduct. Therefore we may not cease our search into the ethical codes of the Renaissance [5] if we are to furnish those overtones in his plays without which they fail to yield full encouragement to us in our own age, an age for which conduct seems predetermined or bequeathed or, if not that, something capricious, incalculable.

Important as they are, ethical codes and the systems of morality which they abbreviate are of less immediate value to the dramatist than are ethical actions.[6] These last he will consider most helpful when they have already been put into literary form with the proper literary agents or those picturesque figures, "coloured shows," through which allegory attempts to endear to the reader the necessary struggles of men and women. Fortunately, there was a book of ethical actions at hand for Shakespeare's profit and delight: *The Faerie Queene* of Edmund

---

[5] In Ch. V the reader will find one such study. See also Madeleine Doran, *Endeavors of Art* (University of Wisconsin Press, 1954), Ch. ix.

[6] Here, as ordinarily elsewhere, "action" is used in the sense of the Aristotelian term "praxis" and "agents" for Aristotle's "prattontes." If "action" is an intentional and effective process (what we assume Aristotle to mean by "praxis"), we must think of it as temporally and logically antecedent to "plot," which is the Aristotelian "mythos." Shakespeare's plot may be likewise described as the "synthesis" or "syntaxis" of "pragmata," particular events; but it is in his action itself, the "deed to be done" by his agents, that we find the propulsive force of his plays, their optative or imperative nature, their symbolic form. Plot as "psyche" of a drama is its unique shape rather than its ineffable soul; the Greek Lexicon allows this translation of ψυχή. The word "ethical" is used, with no suggestion as to better or worse, to indicate the effect of choice on character. It is not synonymous with "moral," meaning "without vice or sin." An "ethical action" may entail error or transgression even as it is a deed to be done toward virtue.

Introduction: "The Rarer Action"

Spenser, published in 1590–1596. That Shakespeare knew this book no scholar would presume to doubt, but that during the time when the comedy of humors was popular he depended rather on Spenserian virtues and vices to enrich and sharpen the ethical action of his own comedies is a hypothesis as yet unexplored.

The research called for in illustrating this hypothesis is massive, and it obliges the scholar to deal perceptively with evidence never to be considered apart from literary form. Such evidence must be sought within the frame of all known facts but is itself not susceptible of logical proof and cannot now be attested to by the author or his acquaintances. Furthermore, it concerns particular resemblances for which statistical handling is inappropriate, resemblances which are entangled with and not easily distinguishable from phrases, doctrines, images, and ideas anonymously current or present in other plays, poems, and discourses of known authorship. And even when striking parallels have been noted, singly or in groups, we are reluctant to assess and interpret them; the mind we are probing is beyond most others capacious and inclusive, pre-eminently able to fuse experiences of literature as well as impressions of men, women, and affairs.

One asks whether the result is worth the effort, whether any vivid adventure in scholarship or criticism can be shared with others who have not partaken of it. Strong convictions will not satisfy those who ask for indisputable facts. Yet it is high time that *The Faerie Queene* and the plays of Shakespeare should be set side by side [7] and scrutinized on the assumption

---

[7] Particular likenesses have already been noted by Joseph Q. Adams, in his *Life of Shakespeare* (Cambridge, Mass., 1923), p. 145, and Lilian Winstanley, in her eds. of *The Faerie Queene* (Cambridge, Mass., 1914 and 1915), Introduction to Bk. II, pp. xlii–xliii, and Introduction to Bk. I, p. lxxvii. See also F. M. Padelford, "The Women in Spenser's Allegory of Love," *Journal of English and Germanic Philology*, XVI (January, 1917), 78. In *Shakespeare Association Bulletin*, X (October, 1935), 192–

that they are mutually illuminating as works of literary art, not mere tandem records of the same historical epoch. Surely they have an aesthetic not less than a chronological relationship. Should this be granted, even if we fall short of proving actual kinship, we shall have gained from our study a more authentic picture of narrative-dramatic action as the two greatest writers of the English Renaissance understood it, long before the tradition of Shakespeare the Bard was shaped by critics with little knowledge of playwriting.

This book, then, is a study of ethical action as a comparable term in the art of Spenser and that of Shakespeare. Other scholars may fruitfully refer poetic structure to philosophical or psychological doctrines, to semantic theories, to fancied similarity with musical, pictorial, or sculptural art, even to personal impressions and racial myths and rituals. Here, however, we are to suppose that literary form becomes more reliably manifest when we compare a poem with poems of the same or similar kind. The evidence offered is literary evidence. As such, let us repeat, it

---

211, and XI (January, 1936), 33–40, Alwin Thaler summarized the observations of Renwick, Cory, Greenlaw, and others and made substantial additions of his own. More recently he has pointed out Spenserian echoes in *Romeo and Juliet* ("Mercutio and Spenser's Phantastes," *Philological Quarterly*, XVI [October, 1937], 405–407) and in *Much Ado* ("Spenser and *Much Ado about Nothing*," *Studies in Philology*, XXXVII [April, 1940], 225–235). In *SAB*, XVII (April and July, 1942), 103–111, 126–133, Abbie F. Potts discussed "Spenserian Courtesy and Temperance in *Much Ado about Nothing*" (Ch. III of this book); Charles T. Prouty commented on this article in *The Sources of 'Much Ado about Nothing'* (Yale University Press, 1950), p. 53. *Shakespeare and Spenser*, by W. B. C. Watkins (Princeton University Press, 1950), is a series of essays dealing with similarities in theme, character, imagery, and diction between the two poets. The author refers to their "kinship . . . in temperament, in permeating spirit, in poetic preoccupations, even in technique, . . . and in thematic development" (pp. 43–44). His observations and mine are now and then in accord; but my studies of similarities in situation and action have been independently pursued and were set down before I was familiar with his book. Professor Watkins in nn. 13 and 14 to Ch. II of his book lists "previous studies of the relation of Shakespeare to Spenser."

Introduction: "*The Rarer Action*"

does not logically prove the direct influence of *The Faerie Queene* on certain of Shakespeare's plays which are to be discussed; at best it gives us one probability. But the evidence leading toward the probability should not be without value for dramatist, archetypologist, scholar, and critic.

Our hypothesis can be briefly stated as follows: At the turn of the century, the better to enhance his plays written from 1599 to 1604, Shakespeare was studying *The Faerie Queene* of Edmund Spenser.

This hypothesis rests, first, and negatively, on the complete absence of analogies with *The Faerie Queene* in those plays which Francis Meres listed in *Palladis Tamia: Wit's Treasury* in 1598: *The Two Gentlemen of Verona, The Comedy of Errors, Love's Labour's Lost, Love's Labour's Won, A Midsummer Night's Dream, The Merchant of Venice, King Richard the Second, King Richard the Third, King Henry the Fourth, King John, Titus Andronicus,* and *Romeo and Juliet.* From Meres's list we may omit *Love's Labour's Won,* the identity of which is not established. For obvious reasons we need not discuss *King Richard the Third* or *Titus Andronicus;* nor would it be helpful to review the three Parts of *Henry VI* with Spenser in mind. The reader may rest assured that they are in no respect Spenserian.

In the following chapter, then, we shall study the ethical content and metaphorical structure of the other plays noted before 1598, with special attention to the series of history plays beginning with *King John* and including *Richard II,* I *Henry IV,* and II *Henry IV,* the last-named not separately mentioned by Meres. Except for a few faint echoes of the Book of Justice in II *Henry IV,* we shall find in all these plays no certain trace of Spenser's actions, his situations, his agents, or his diction. Nor does there seem to be anything of the sort in *The Taming of the Shrew* or in those three texts safely dated in 1598–1599: *As You Like It, Julius Caesar,* and *Henry V.*

With *Much Ado about Nothing,* however, Shakespeare's

comedy begins to acquire another dimension. In this play, in *Twelfth Night*, in *All's Well That Ends Well* and *The Merry Wives of Windsor* (both not yet exactly dated), in *Troilus and Cressida*, in the quasi-tragic *Hamlet* as set forth in the second quarto, and in *Measure for Measure*, there are many demonstrable analogies with the agents and actions of Spenserian allegory. The uncertainty about and anxious debate over the plays for which there would seem to be most frequent Spenserian cross reference may arise from Shakespeare's obvious effort to combine inherited plot and inner action; his ethical discoveries and attempted reversals do not always fit comfortably within the frame of the old story. In spite of the dexterous management of romantic and historical themes in his early plays, now, amid the somewhat embarrassing bounty of a new Spenserian ethics on the one hand and a new Jonsonian poetics on the other, he composes more tentatively, almost as if he has recognized the need for making a dramaturgic choice of his own toward a reversal or peripety [8] of still another kind.

[a] This word translates the Greek περιπέτεια. According to Aristotle as Englished by S. H. Butcher in the 4th ed. of *Aristotle's Theory of Poetry and Fine Art* (London, 1907), p. 41, it is "a change by which the action veers around to its opposite, subject always to our rule of probability or necessity." Lane Cooper translates ἡ εἰς τὸ ἐναντίον τῶν πραττομένων μεταβολή as "change in some part of the action from one state of affairs to its precise opposite" (in *Aristotle on the Art of Poetry* [New York, 1913], p. 35). Ingram Bywater's version (in *Aristotle on the Art of Poetry* [Oxford University Press, 1920], p. 46) reads, "the change from one state of things within the play to its opposite." Notice that the key word is πραττομένων—not the "deed to be done," but "doings." Such change from better to worse fortune Aristotle prefers for the specific emotional effect of Greek tragedy (Cooper, p. 42). In modern literature and criticism, however, what Shakespeare's Prospero calls "the rarer action . . . in virtue than in vengeance" depends on a peripety from worse to better ethical fortune, sometimes as the result of an outward disaster but always as the result of a new discovery. This extension of Aristotle's terms is illustrated in Kenneth Burke's studies of symbolic form. Philip Wheelwright (in "Mimesis and Katharsis: An Archetypal Consideration," *English Institute Essays*, 1951, ed. by Alan S. Downer [Columbia University Press, 1952], pp. 16–20), speaks of "the psyche's attempt at re-equilibra-

Introduction: "The Rarer Action"

Soon his mastery will be complete. Although in *Othello, King Lear, Macbeth, Coriolanus,* and *Antony and Cleopatra* any traces of Spenserian allegory have been overlaid, situations and actions comparable with crises in *The Faerie Queene* can still be detected; and they serve to remind us of the mythic and ethic substructure on which both poets have relied. Finally, beneath the dissimilar situations of *Pericles, Cymbeline, The Winter's Tale,* and *The Tempest* stretches the map of Faeryland. Now at last fables such as Spenser's "faithfull loues" rather than his "fierce warres" supply and direct the energies at work on a ship off Mitylene and in a temple of Ephesus, near Milford Haven, along the coast of Bohemia and in the Kingdom of Sicilia, or upon that magical uninhabited isle somewhere between Tunis and Milan. Ever more and more hopefully the Shakespearean hero and heroine have been conceived in the enchanting tradition of Spenserian romance rather than in the humorous fashion of Jonsonian comedy. For his mature delineation of character in process the playwright no longer needs colorful pictures of the virtues and vices, the excesses and defects; his genius can dispense with systematic morality and allegorical tourneys; but he has grown fond of Faeryland and delights to temper the allegorist's loyalty for what must go right with the dramatist's compassion for what has gone wrong. Evidence to follow will, let us hope, justify the consideration of these two poets in a fruitful literary relationship.

Our argument, therefore, is concerned secondarily with

---

tion . . . or krasis." Francis Fergusson (in *The Idea of a Theatre* [Princeton University Press, 1949], p. 148) relates even Ibsen and Chekhov to the *Poetics:* "They are imitating action according to the Aristotelian prescription: not a concatenation of event but a movement of the psyche." He speaks of "a change in the moral being of the protagonist by the discovery of the truth." M. C. Bradbrook (in *The Growth and Structure of Elizabethan Comedy* [University of California Press, 1956], p. 79) says that Shakespeare "evolved a new and subtler form of metamorphosis—an interior one." Shakespeare's growth as an artist follows upon the advance in his scholarship; and so it is with his dramatic agents, who do better as they learn better.

Shakespeare's possible indebtedness to *The Faerie Queene* but primarily with the narrative or dramatic devices and procedures shared by Spenser and Shakespeare as poets of ethical action.[9]

What in the tradition of *The Faerie Queene* would best serve a playwright? Reading Spenser's poem without regard for its fanciful and circumstantial embellishments—its heritage from Greek, Italian, and Celtic romance—a playwright would find it highly, if somewhat elaborately, articulate. It combined two factors essential also in a good play, responsible behavior and admirable endeavor. Moreover, Spenser's near-Aristotelian *ethos*[10] and his near-Christian *mythos* furnished a wider system of choices and a loftier view of enterprise than Shakespeare or any other English dramatist had known in the chronicles, biographies, tales, or narrative collections already under the eye and hand. Not least probably, a poet writing for the ear would observe the skill with which a pentametrical line had been made to carry anything sententious or spectacular into the very accents of melodious and cogent speech. Yet our discussion of this narrative poem as one hypothetical source of a series of plays most relies on what poem and plays obviously have in common: an action or actions and agents, with other devices relating the agents to the action, namely, characteristic choices according

---

[9] Fergusson, p. 230, quotes the authority of the Moscow Art Theatre for indicating the action of a play "by an infinitive phrase, e.g., in the play *Oedipus*, 'to find the culprit.'" But there is nothing infinitive about a dramatic action. Might it be better to invoke the Latin supine, an accusative verbal noun, or the Latin second periphrastic or gerundive, as in *Carthago delenda est*? We could then indicate the Shakespearean tragic action as follows: *Hamlet*, the time out of joint must be set right; *Othello*, Cyprus and Venice must be protected from the Turks, even from the Turklike Othello; *Macbeth*, Scotland must be fitly governed or—in the metaphor of Macbeth himself—purged "to a sound and pristine health."

[10] What Edwin A. Greenlaw has called "diffused Aristotelianism." H. S. V. Jones has described the process of diffusion in "The Faerie Queene and the Mediaeval Aristotelian Tradition," *JEGP*, XXV (July, 1926), 283-298.

Introduction: "The Rarer Action"

to appropriate codes, an ordeal, discoveries, and reversals. Aristotle and his followers have outlined the constituents of drama and epic so truly that we are never at a loss for significant terms, accepted with remarkable unanimity, even when they have been elaborated or modified by critics of different countries in different ages.[11]

Therefore, since epic and drama are both acknowledged to be imitations of action, we may preface the study of Spenserian and Shakespearean action with a brief reminder of the kind of action prevailing on the one hand in the literature interpreted by Aristotle and on the other in the literature deriving from the deeds and purposes of Jesus. Whatever the intermediary, both kinds of action can be found in *The Faerie Queene* and in Shakespearean drama.

Neither Greek tragedy nor the medieval mysteries—least of all *The Divine Comedy* of Dante—had been content with mere temporal sequence or mere changes of fortune; each involved its dramatic action in a distinctly characteristic way. The Greek searched backward through time for what was still true and complicated the search by persistent folly, or *hubris;* in a purgatorial ordeal the Christian stretched upward through time for what was forever holy and burdened his ascent with all the wicked ways, or *peccata,* of the rebellious spirit. Human blindness predominates in the disasters of the one and human disobedience in the transgressions of the other; the agents of antiquity, mistaking the will of the gods, must guess or infer their

---

[11] Among our contemporaries, the comments of Lane Cooper in *Aristotle on the Art of Poetry* and in *An Aristotelian Theory of Comedy, with an Adaptation of the "Poetics" and a Translation of the "Tractatus Coislinianus"* (New York, 1922); the discussions by Philip Wheelwright, Francis Fergusson, Reuben A. Brower, and Elder Olson, in *English Institute Essays, 1951;* the studies of Kenneth Burke already referred to and his *A Grammar of Motives* (New York, 1945) and *A Rhetoric of Motives* (New York, 1950); and the various references to Aristotelian theory in the publications of Northrop Frye, especially *Anatomy of Criticism.*

way back into piety, and Christians, disobeying the will of God, might, if they chose, be chastened into holiness. This is, of course, too tidy and simple a statement to do more than indicate the respective emphasis placed by dramatic writers of the two traditions on discovery and reversal—*anagnorisis* over *peripeteia* in antiquity; in Christendom, conversion over epiphany. At the cost of further simplification it may be said that in a Greek tragedy *anagnorisis* seems fundamental to, sometimes even sufficient for, the peripety; in plays written anno Domini the converted agent, although he profits by the discovery of truth on any level of meaning and value, must at least aim at or struggle toward his own redemption. The seer and the apprehensive chorus are the foreshadowing agents who supervise the protagonists of Greek drama, and their last word is wisdom; the martyr or crusader is the hero of Christendom, and salvation is his deed.

Before we abandon our antitheses, however, we may note that these diversities in dramatic action are characterized by two stylistic modes: dramatic irony and what we might call dramatic urgency. For the Greeks the man understating his knowledge, the ironical man (*eiron*), was representative; and irony (*eironeia*), whether self-depreciation or mockery of others, whether at work through implied contrast or understatement or double talk, was the familiar tool of both orator and poet.[12] In the field of dialectic it proceeded through appearance toward reality and in the field of epic and drama it invoked truth—little by little for reasons of suspense—to reconcile those misunderstandings in which agents and auditors alike had a proprietary interest. Dramatic irony, then, is primarily an affair of relative blindness and vision; even when it ends in a riddling obscurity, it tries to resolve tension through *anagnorisis*—recognition of identity, disclosure of events, discovery of principles.

[12] J. A. K. Thomson, *Irony* (Harvard University Press, 1927); G. G. Sedgewick, *Of Irony, especially in Drama* (University of Toronto Press, 1948).

Introduction: "The Rarer Action"

But the founder of the modern world, Jesus of Nazareth, although a gifted riddler, was more than an *eiron;* and in spite of their dependence on Greek ethics and their devotion to antiquity Spenser and Shakespeare could not undo fifteen Christian centuries. In Spenser's narrative poem and in Shakespeare's drama we come upon what the latter was to call the "urgent hour." [13] This concept of dramatic urgency does not supplant but rather completes that of dramatic irony. Instead of the classical *anagnorisis* and *peripeteia* which Aristotle considered a necessary or probable result of *previous* incidents, instead of the medieval testimony and dedication which directed effort out of this world into another, these greatest writers of the English Renaissance endorsed the need for amelioration of conditions in their own time and place. Instead of the backward look of blind or sinful man toward crimes of the houses of Atreus or Laius, or toward that disobedience of Adam without which theological conversion would be insignificant, Spenser and Shakespeare called into play all the drives toward futurity, optative and imperative. Now that the map of their world had been vastly widened and their calendar ominously extended, the total energies available to them and their fellows must be exerted for the maintainance of mundane order and spiritual identity. As Spenser had given fresh value to the oaths, vigils, temptations, and tourneys of formal knighthood, Shakespeare would endow his agents, however myopic and awkward, with the will to peer and strive manfully ahead toward what might or should be. This is the new mimesis of that modern world in which Spenser and Shakespeare have never yet been discredited.

Spenser supplies a good word—protensity—when he invokes Clio to recount the ancestry of Gloriana (3.3.4.8–9):

> Till that by dew degrees and long *protense,*
> Thou haue it lastly brought vnto her Excellence.

[13] *The Winter's Tale,* I.ii.465.

Whatever doctrinal secrets lurk in the phrase "by dew degrees," drama is the protensive art. Its life is in time, backward and forward; but in its nature it is more than a series of yesterdays and tomorrows. Neither the human spirit nor the art of poetry can compromise with regret or decay or anything else that time, unassisted, will bring in. The stakes seemingly lost to Greek wisdom and Christian faith were in the last decade of the sixteenth century still to be lost or won. From gods standing on their rights and saints standing on their testimony the action passed into the agency of mobile knights and ladies traveling up and down and all across the realm of the future, each with a commission.

This change had been prefigured in Dante's summary interpretation of the action leading from hell to heaven and in the anonymous mysteries, miracles, and moralities that mediated between the communal religion of the Church and popular diversion in the courtyard. Yet Dante speaks more effectively to us than he did to Spenser, and although Shakespeare was familiar with surviving religious performances, the cycles he knew were only shells to indicate where life had been. Not one of the actions of his tragic drama points explicitly to the texts of the medieval religious drama. *The Faerie Queene* is in no sense a theologico-religious poem—witness the great predominance of classical over Biblical allusions even in the Book of Holiness.[14] It was through certain by-products of the Church of the Middle Ages, through chivalry and courtiership, that the urgent message and example of Jesus reached those nonetheless Christian writers, Spenser and Shakespeare. Their kingdom of heaven, like His, was to be located on earth.

If, needing alternatives for Jonsonian humors, Shakespeare

---

[14] Consult Virgil K. Whitaker, *The Religious Basis of Spenser's Thought* ("Stanford University Publications in Language and Literature," Vol. VII, No. 3 [Stanford University Press, 1950]), and Frye, *Anatomy of Criticism*, pp. 194-195.

Introduction: "The Rarer Action" 17

opened a copy of *The Faerie Queene*, how could he have been unaware of the value for a playwright of Spenser's ethical assumptions? This was what he needed; here he would find justification for the behavior of the persons of his plays and authority for what they wished to accomplish or avoid. If thus through their choices they might elude the superimposed destiny of Jonsonian agents, they could the more intelligently help him in the making of his plots, whether they asked, with Sir Andrew, "What is 'pourquoi'? Do or not do?" or meditated with Hamlet, "To be or not to be." What was to be found in Spenser's poem, although indiscriminately derived from antiquity or the Middle Ages, would also serve his playwriting as a welcome alternative for previous mythological and theological statements of human destiny and as a relief from the vortex of romance and the unresolved crisis of history. Otherwise he might have continued to haunt the pages of Halle and Holinshed, Plutarch as translated by Sir Thomas North, and the several purveyors of Italian stories, without any hint from these as to how chronicles and biographies and *novelle* are shaped into proper tragedies. Again, and signally, the agents of *The Faerie Queene* must have suggested then to him as now to us actual courtiers about whom readers were gossiping and guessing, contemporary men whose propensities revealed the problems of every man, prince and clown alike; this would help to return drama to the people. The redemptive action of the poem might be fanciful; but its agents were demonstrably human, and its theatre was the soul of man.

However substantially Spenser's ethical images could in these ways enrich a playwright's agents or however strictly Spenserian ethical patterns could invigorate his action, there was accessible in *The Faerie Queene* an even more challenging lesson for any attentive reader. As an allegory it raised literary questions, questions of a formal nature; and these would have been provocative for a dramatist hitherto deferential mainly to his theatrical obligations. Watching Spenser's habit of composition in a narrative poem partaking of the traits of both romance and epic, noting his arguments and his ways of inclusion, exclusion, and emphasis, a man of the theatre who was also an avid reader and a poet would come to give more thought to the thematic side of his dramatic compositions. Seneca's plays, to be sure, were sententious; and the meditations or aphorisms of such as Montaigne, evoking thought, might help to universalize the characters of his dramatis personae or the import of his dramatic situations. But in Spenser's allegory chiefly he would find illustrated the proper relation between thought and character and between thought and plot—in short, between dianoetic form, with its maxims and persuasions, and dramatic form, with its choices and ordeals. In no other great poem of the time had the Aristotelian *dianoia* and *mythos* been so justly combined. Thus instructed, a writer familiar with *The Faerie Queene* might crown his native genius with the refinements of the literary art.

We cannot, of course, endow Shakespeare with our own critical insight; nor need we deprive him of our own good sense. The assumptions in which we have been indulging must remain a *petitio principii* until we have illustrated them more fully in later chapters. We can do no more than guess that he anticipated the delight acknowledged by John Keats in his *Sonnet to Spenser:*

> The flower must drink the nature of the soil
> Before it can put forth its blossoming.

This same metaphor of men as plants Shakespeare had already used in his own sonnets. There as the seasons passed he must come to grips with time, "the bloody tyrant" time, "never-resting" time, "wasteful" time, "devouring" time. But a sonneteer's method of transcending time by way of exquisite imagery and dauntless thought will not quite serve a playwright. Feelings and meditations may indeed seem to grow with the artist who entertains them; but comedies and tragedies are poems and must be made. The playwright cannot wait with Viola for time to untie the hard knots in human affairs. He will himself knot and unknot time and all temporal matters—literally, he complicates and explicates.[15]

How, then, would this appear in the business of plotting a play?

Much as the Great Dramatist, Jesus, assumed man's evil to be God's unaccomplished good, so Shakespeare represents his comic and tragic agents as handicapped by those vices or defects from which only their own struggles can deliver them. Thus he increases the tension between their temporal and their eternal states. And he has, as Christians and modern dramatists invariably must, taken sides with the unquiet sinners against the quiescent saints. Illustrating the kinds of bondage which they have only just recognized as pitiable and terrible or foolish and ridiculous, because of this recognition his persons have become newly responsible agents, and thus they join the rest of us in a hampering discomfort from which we all can be set free only as we attempt the deed which must be done by them and us. That they stand, and prompt us to stand, at the center of the universal ethical action of mankind reminds us of Spenser's fidelity to concepts of holiness and temperance and of his unvarying devotion to chivalric and courtly aims. His was no mere conviction; it was a passion.

Again, in their common belief that actions do not change, that they supervene their faulty agents, Shakespeare corroborates the practical wisdom of Spenser. Like Sirs Guyon and Calidore striving toward temperance and courtesy, like the sometimes unholy St. George and the inflexible but once disas-

---

[15] See the translation by L. J. Potts of the beginning of Ch. XVIII of the *Poetics* (in *Aristotle on the Art of Fiction* [Cambridge, England, 1953], p. 41): "Every tragedy consists in the tying and untying of a knot." Lane Cooper uses the words "complication" and "unravelling" for δέσις and λύσις (in *Aristotle on the Art of Poetry*, p. 60).

trously susceptible Artegall in the realm of picturesque concept, so also the intemperate Troilus and Hamlet, the discourteous Claudio and Leontes, the unholy because overcredulous Othello and Lear, the tyrannical and unjust Angelo, Macbeth, and Coriolanus in the realm of human emotion and motive—all have the authoritative task of relating what unfortunately *is* to what happily might be or might have been. Ophelia like Florimell, Viola like Amoret or Olivia like Briana, Desdemona or Hermione or Miranda like Una, Helena like Britomart, Imogen like Belphoebe—not to speak of a Cressida, a Lady Macbeth, and a Cleopatra mirroring Duessa—are entangled in a code that necessitates an ordeal. These heroines share with their collaborating heroes the tasks of discovery and reversal. They must bear witness, yes; but, further, they must lend a hand toward or against a properly hopeful solution. This does not mean that all will finally be sweetness and light or light or sweetness; it does mean that "by dew degrees and long protense" we get a bit nearer to that Court of Faery, that Excellence of Gloriana, which is so delicate a veil over the body of this life within the Kingdom of Heaven on earth.

If comedy, then, depends for its refreshing laughter on the hiatus between what we see in ourselves and what others see in us or between what we are and what we ought to be; if romance might well lose its fascination except for its desire to make the impossible probable; so modern tragedy would be feeble and plaintive—as it sometimes is—instead of pitiful and terrible without the conviction that man can help to redeem himself and that, at whatever cost, human life is thus potentially divine. This obligation upon us all is what Prospero means when he speaks of "the rarer action."

CHAPTER II

Shakespeare without Spenser

THE argument for Shakespeare's knowledge and use of Spenser's *Faerie Queene* in a series of plays beginning with *Much Ado about Nothing* gains force when we study the very different ethical constituent of the plays that precede it, especially the ones mentioned by Francis Meres in 1598. From these we select for brief analysis *The Comedy of Errors, Love's Labour's Lost, The Two Gentlemen of Verona, A Midsummer Night's Dream, The Merchant of Venice, Romeo and Juliet, King John, Richard II*, and *Henry IV*. Such a review has a positive as well as a negative value. We shall travel, not in an ethical Faeryland, but rather in the conventional world of a young playwright observing the surfaces and circumstances of conduct on his way to more profound and central matters.

The Comedy of Errors, adapted from the *Menaechmi* and *Amphitruo* of Plautus, elaborates an unreal situation without much regard for ethics. Bodily deformities and personal "defeatures" are glanced at; impatience and jealousy supply the only grounds for thoughtful laughter; and the comic effect results mainly from the arbitrary working of a capricious plot. *Love's Labour's Lost* is a clever exercise in the manner of John Lyly, depending rather on ingenious artifices and wordplay than on refinement of or progress in the character of its courtly agents. Its comic persons follow the tradition of the Italian *commedia dell' arte*, pointedly modified to suggest a ludicrous but amoral English equivalent. *The Two Gentlemen of Verona*, however, even as it violates the laws of probability which were also disregarded in its Spanish original, includes passages of real feeling such as real people might experience if the situations were credible. It is the least fantastic of the three early comedies, and it merits a careful examination.

The metaphors of *The Two Gentlemen* refer to water, ice, stone, steel, fire; stream, sand, sea, tide, cloud, moon, sun, star; bud and canker, sedge, root and flower; wasps, bees, honey, robin redbreast, fish, cock, spaniel, lamb, sheep, dog, ass, fox, lion, tiger, and also chameleon and leviathan. References to the body, which are at a minimum, have to do mostly with digestion: victuals, excess and surfeit—and pills. Beauty and deformity have merely a physical connotation. Love is blind love, and its effects are, according to fashion, progressively enfeebling. Implements and artifacts play almost no part, although Lucetta is compared to a writing tablet, and jewels are mentioned, along with the pearl, pure gold, and nectar of the sea; staff, glass, ink, waxen image, and puppet occur, as do weathercock, steeple, and tenantless mansion.

Patience is a virtue, but merely in a personal crisis; reason as controlling passion is rarely mentioned. Julia swears by her modesty, and Proteus is "constant to myself." Duty is recommended, but the paternal comment on a "peevish, sullen, froward, proud, disobedient, stubborn," daughter is hoary in the comic portfolio. According to Proteus, the "three things that women highly hold in hate" are "falsehood, cowardice, and poor descent." Even Silvia, the most vibrant person in the play, receives the baldly conventional epithets—"holy, fair, and wise is she," and "kind." She says of herself only that she is not so "shallow" and "conceitless" as to be seduced by Proteus' flattery. A good woman, it seems at this stage in Shakespeare's dramatic art, is either a "heavenly saint" or an "earthly paragon."

"Angel-like perfection" Valentine disavows for himself, but his praise of Proteus as "complete" is an easy enumeration of courtly traits "with all good grace to grace a gentleman." Proteus is the obvious denial of them. Flattery, slander, perjury, fraud, ingratitude, treachery, are considered unlovely but are freely indulged in without what would in actual life be their proper moral effects. Indeed, the whole conceptual range of the play is limited, and its conceptual lore is poorly organized: substance versus shadow, wit versus folly, honor versus love, constancy versus inconstancy. The constancy of Silvia and Valentine is such because Shakespeare will have it so; its reason for being is not made clear. Nor is the inconstancy of Proteus related to anything understandable in character or motive.

Now it is in their functions and offices that persons of a play stretch themselves to be at once most energetic and most like life; and here above all we detect the scarcely relieved conventionality of Shakespeare's ethical assumptions in *The Two Gentlemen*. Along with the shepherd and his sheep, the nurse and her babe, the pilgrim, the captain of the outlaws (who must be a "linguist" and skilled in "the tongues"), the musician with his "base" and "mean," his "concord" and "descant" and "burden," there are no allusions to persons and no dramatic agents from whom civility and policy—as Elizabethans understood those terms—can be expected at any cost to themselves. "Braggardism" and "sluggard[ism]" and "shapeless idleness" are deplored; but the training valuable to a young man seeking preferment implies no magnanimity toward others and no responsibility at court. The "perfect man" is his own good and to that end he must be "tried and tutor'd in the world." "Tilts, tournaments,

... sweet discourse, converse with noblemen," are intended for ornament and advancement, with no thought of future service. The borrowing and spending are all for personal gain, and the exchequer of words is meant to be rifled, with bankruptcy at the end of any and all word matches.

Further, let us glance at references in the play to the arts and fashions of its persons. The Duke is convinced that "Much is the force of heavenbred poesy"; but he is curious to hear mainly about the late fashion in wooing. The "degenerate and base" Thurio is shrewdly interested in "songs" and "wailful sonnets" and "dire-lamenting elegies." Proteus, however, allows that it will take "wit to plot [his] drift"; and the clowns have heard of parables, metamorphosis, "allycholly [melancholy]," and "malecontents." Julia in disguise says that she once took part in a "pageant of delight." And the dramatist himself employs as dramatic devices the old literary tricks: the oath, the letter, the picture, the ladder, itemization (later to be used in *Twelfth Night*), the exchange or gift of rings (later to be used in *The Merchant of Venice* and, still later, in *All's Well That Ends Well*), and the always-useful device of overhearing (later to be used to good effect in *Much Ado about Nothing* and *Troilus and Cressida*). The myths referred to in *The Two Gentlemen* are Hero and Leander (twice), Phaëton, Orpheus, and Ariadne and Theseus; none is structural. In another tradition we are reminded only of the prodigal son, Sts. Gregory and Patrick and Nicholas, Hallowmas and Pentecost, even Robin Hood's fat friar. These casual references have no close association with the agents or the action. Nor can we find any hint that Shakespeare's action or his agents profited by the publication in 1590 of the first installment of *The Faerie Queene* with its new kind of ethical beauty and the mythic resonance of a fairyland much richer than the forest on the frontier of Milan.

And the action? "Discipline" as mentioned by the Duke means experience in wooing and hence skill as a wooer. The penance of the inconstant Proteus is "but to hear / The story of [his] loves discovered." Marriage for both pairs of lovers is the peripety. And the action is still nearsightedly romantic: every Jill must have her Jack: every Julia, her Proteus; and every Valentine, his Silvia.

The next in order of Shakespeare's comedies are *A Midsummer Night's Dream*, *The Merchant of Venice*, and *The Taming of the Shrew*, the last-named not mentioned by Meres and, says Kittredge, scarcely to be identified as his *Love's Labour's Won*. Let us associate with them the early romantic tragedy *Romeo and Juliet;* and, regarding these four plays thus grouped about the years 1595–1596, let us pose the same question: Is there any clear evidence in them that Shakespeare was familiar with Spenser's *Faerie Queene?* Again the answer is no.

The prevailing metaphor of *A Midsummer Night's Dream* is nature—the earth, with its flora and fauna, and the heavens. With increasing skill Shakespeare relates natural imagery to the conduct of his total plot; but the fairyland scene depends exclusively on folklore and superstitious legend. The literary help he receives from Ovid and Chaucer is welcome; it is important further as an earnest that he will later discover the availability of Virgil and Spenser. The stage properties are, as it were, from the property room of Whitsun pastorals. Classical myth now includes Cupid and Venus by name, Phoebe, Aurora, Neptune, and the triple Hecate. And with an obvious increase in dramatic propriety over the play of the Nine Worthies included in *Love's Labour's Lost*, we have the play of Pyramus and Thisbe, preceded by a thoughtful passage on the transfiguration of minds into something of great constancy. Shakespeare's craftsmanship is improving; but Puck, the most canny and dynamic of the agents, is best pleased by things "that befall preposterously"; and in the "fond pageant" of the mortals he sees only folly. His action—and it is his action—is "No more yielding than a dream."

26   *Shakespeare and* The Faerie Queene

If Shakespeare, like Puck, is to "make amends ere long," he must amplify his ethical references as elaborately and truly as he has particularized the natural phenomena of his physical world. This we find him doing in *The Merchant of Venice*. Things are taking on symbolic value: hourglass, chapel, church, ducats, casement, candle and torch, cradle and roof, dram and scruple. References to the physical body of man increase, and the activities of mankind are used suggestively: acting, archery, divinity, education, horseshoeing, animal husbandry, law, music, road mending, lottery, enter the fabric of his play as revelatory tropes. Signiors, burghers, smiths, pages, prodigals and strumpets, runaways, saints, pilgrims, beggars, torchbearers, Christians, and Jews are aptly distinguished. His literary allusions show not only a widening range but a shrewder application: Janus, Sibylla, Jason, Diana, Hercules, Mars, the three Fates, Midas, Scylla and Charybdis, Endymion, Erebus, join the list of mythic or legendary figures; Nestor and Abram, gossip Report (Fama) and Hagar, Pythagoras and Jacob, Cressid and Medea, the Dardanian wives at Troy and Dido, Phoebus and Daniel—even the Nazarite—bear witness to Shakespeare's reading in classical and Biblical lore. He is considering human values in their ethical diversity, and we find him dropping a hint that he is interested in classical doctrines as to conduct. It is no mean happiness to be seated in the mean, he says.

And again the action? Bassanio must win Portia, Gratiano must win Nerissa, Lorenzo must win Jessica; and in these affairs Antonio must be saved from Shylock. That each of the eight is brought to understand himself a little better through his choices and decisions would suggest a kind of discovery; but the action in wooing is barely differentiated and rests on circumstance and well-nigh fortuitous choice. We are promised no improvement, not in the unregenerate Shylock, not even in the genial spendthrift and fortune hunter Bassanio.

The farcical *Taming of the Shrew* and the pathetic *Romeo*

and Juliet have in common their origin in well-known plots. What is more notable in the advance of Shakespeare's playwriting, they share a certain kind of doctrinary conclusion. Katherine instructs Bianca and the Widow in the proper behavior of wives toward husbands necessary to securing a happy marriage. Her word is "duty"; but although her obedience may not be contagious, she is permitted to indulge in ethical generalization. The lessons of magnanimity read to Capulets and Montagues by the Prince of Verona are widely pertinent. In short, both plays through their love affairs are concerned with the more important domestic and civic action. Yet neither play exhibits any trace of the dangers and hardships of the dedicated life to be lived in Spenser's Court of Faery. *The Taming of the Shrew* is even more ingeniously complicated for success than is *Romeo and Juliet* for failure; but the success and failure are brought about in superficial ways without awareness of underlying causes or firm management of relevant effects.

The histories obey an ethics of fact rather than an ethics of idea. Their situations are predetermined. Let us turn our attention first to the texts in which, if *The Faerie Queene* had been influential for Shakespeare's dramatic art about 1594–1596, Spenserian cross reference would be most likely, *King John* and *Richard II*. Both are concerned with the moral disintegration of kings of England; and both, the latter more effectively, ally personal with civic crisis.

King John exhibits the range and quality of allusion detailed in our analysis of its contemporaries, *A Midsummer Night's Dream* and *The Merchant of Venice*. The phenomena of nature and the seasons, flora and fauna, homely articles and familiar activities, furnish the metaphors. The major patterns, besides war and statecraft, are sailing and bowling. Antiquity is represented by the basilisk, Nero, the Amazons, Ate, and Mercury; Jewry, by Cain; and Christendom, by Good Friday, Ascension Day, and St. George swingeing the Dragon (which, however, shows no slightest reminiscence of Spenser's use of the legend). Bodily ills are important; humors abound; there is no penetration into the illnesses of the soul.

Richard II offers a contrast between ethical agents on the courtly level, with the royal action still predominant. Its burgeoning images, metaphors, and allusions markedly resemble those of the romances of 1595–1596. The titular hero is threatened by his lassitude and self-pity. Here would have been the perfect opportunity to consult Spenser's ethical pattern; but Richard is denied the compensatory and redeemable traits of the Redcrosse Knight or Sirs Guyon and Calidore, and he seems anxious only to "undo [himself]." "True chivalry" and "knightly trial" are invoked, and St. George and St. Lambert are mentioned; but hermitage and almsman, palmer and saint are incidental. There is notable reference to Eden, Adam, Eve, Abel, Cain, Abraham, Jewry, Mary, Jesus, Judas, Pilate, Golgotha, the Holy Land, May Day, and Hallowmas, and there are quotations from the New Testament; but none of this is in the vein of Spenser. Mars, Neptune, Phaëton, Troy, and the Tower built by Julius Caesar give scant suggestion of such classical agencies or actions as interested Spenser. To the contrary. What the playwright includes in this play to advance his art compares rather with the nonliterary substance of *A Midsummer Night's Dream* and *The Merchant of Venice;* he will amplify the scope of his allusions to seasonal matters, to vegetative and animal life, to the parts and operations of the body and the humors of it and its illnesses and death, and, notably, to artifacts and games and other such activities of men. The list of artifacts or tools is extensive: jewel, chains, plough, viol, harp, portcullis, wall, moat, sepulchre, book and blot, glasses, lamp, taper, clock and dial and bell, ink and parchment and map, scales and buckets, inn and alehouse and goblets, gown and scepter and walking staff, throne and carpet, and—highly significant—the ladder and mirror. Horsemanship, falconry, and hunting; pilgrimage; chess and bowls; music, dancing, acting, pageantry; the telling of tales and singing; and—again significant—gardening with grafting and pruning. These are what determine the play's metaphorical structure. Nevertheless the dramatic action is concerned less and less with what must be done outwardly; the King's "grief lies all within." He is finally brought to confront himself, not in a mirror, but in his own "still-breeding thoughts." This is indeed an accomplishment.

William H. Schofield [1] believed that Hotspur Percy owed something to Spenser's Hotspur Blandamour and suggested that Shakespeare was also familiar with the Book of Justice when he wrote *Henry IV*. His evidence shows a slight similarity in a few terms and phrases and some analogy in sentiment and political motive but, it seems clear, no such thoroughgoing study of this Book as we find amply illustrated in *Measure for Measure*. In both Parts of *Henry IV* the scenes are cluttered with immediate references to what has existed in time or exists in space. His regeneration is announced by the Prince at the beginning of Part I of the plays, and not until the final scenes of Part II are there strong indications that the agents are moved by personal or political principle. Yet just at this point we are prompted to look for Spenserian echoes, a few of which will be mentioned in following paragraphs.

Without passing judgment on the literary value of this whole series of history plays, in which Shakespeare is experimenting with the relation of plot to action and of action to historical fact, we may say that his main device is one of powerful characters opposed or juxtaposed. Thus he falls into the pattern of history itself: Richard versus Bolingbroke; King Henry IV versus Northumberland and the other rebels; Prince Hal versus Hotspur Percy; King Henry versus Prince Hal; the English Harry versus the French Dauphin; and, it may be most success-

[1] *Chivalry in English Literature* (Harvard University Press, 1912), pp. 209-212, 243-244.

fully, the King-to-be versus the Jack-who-has-been. Thanks to time and the weather, and in a natural metaphor, Hal emerges from the influence of Falstaff like the sun through "the foul and ugly mists / Of vapours that did seem to strangle him." The "reformation" so baldly prophesied at the beginning by the hero to be reformed forestalls any progressively heightened interest in the steps of his change from an "unthrifty son," a "wanton and effeminate boy," "as dissolute as desperate"—or so his father believes—to a right princely and kingly person. The action proper is surrendered to the various scenes and situations of it, which in their turn are presented chiefly for their humorous or ritual effect. The outcome is never in doubt, and we turn from what would have been a stirring royal game—the making of a king—to the lesser matter of who conquers whom. In Hal's words at the end of Act III of Part I:

> The land is burning; Percy stands on high;
> And either they or we must lower lie.

The crushing of rebellion in England and, later, the dynastic compromise in France are here and elsewhere explicitly stated as the outer action of the series; but although many ethical distinctions are drawn no persistent ethical action is represented. This is agglutinative drama, its parts cohering at the will or fancy of a dramatist who depends on historical fact or legend to unify what otherwise would be merely brilliant sketches of character, powerful monologues, or racy dialogues.

Nor in the representation of abstract qualities or conditions is there any sure trace of Spenserian nomenclature. Throughout *Richard II* the emphasis is all on treachery, treason, and traitors.[2] The contrasting virtues are loyalty, noblesse, and honor. Honor is the theme also of the Henries. The rites of knighthood are still medieval. To review them in a "history" of Shakespeare is

[2] I.i.11, 27, 39, 44, 57, 102, 144; iii.24, 39, 108, 114, 201; II.ii.57; iii.30, 60, 88, 109; III.ii.16, 47; iii.93; IV.i.54, 64, 135, 151, 246, 248; V.ii.72, 75.

Shakespeare without Spenser

to discover how far Spenser was ahead of his time in the charting of ethical action.

Psychologically, too, we are still in the fashion of humors, although the creator of Nym in *Henry V* is soon to subject them to comic treatment. "Courtesy" and "courtship" are suspect. "Justice" designs "the victor's chivalry"; but not until we reach the last scenes of II *Henry IV* is it conceived as an action in itself and hence comparable with Spenserian justice. Cowardice taints nobility; Richard upbraids himself for his cowardice. "Rage" is "deaf as the sea, hasty as fire"; "will doth mutiny"; but a "rash fierce blaze of riot cannot last." Young rulers are compared to "young hot colts"; they reveal none of the properly ethical and hence redeemable nature of a Spenserian hero. "Unkindness" and "shame" are to be censured; loyal peers are praised and rewarded, not for holiness, temperance, or justice, but for "worth," "nobility," and "honor." Rebellion is virtuous or vicious depending upon whether it is looked at by rebels or by loyal subjects. When Richard is "not himself," "degenerate," "sick . . . [from] surfeit," "bankrout," the "pernicious lives" of Bushy and Green are to blame for the "disfigured" lineaments of a "happy gentleman," and his nobles must intervene. He comes nearest to acknowledging his own share in his downfall when he compares himself to Phaëton or sees in himself "a traitor with the rest." Again, only late in his career does Prince Hal speak of his reformation as a choice, "the noble change that I have purposed."

In I *Henry IV* "action" still means a military plan or coup. Courtesy is a matter of scorn for Hotspur or a specious demeanor which King Henry confesses he "stole . . . from heaven." Honor and humors furnish the ethical scheme of the play in maxims and counsels too numerous to mention. Once only Hal asks pardon for his "intemperance"; hereafter he will be "more myself." His royal father threatens the Percies in the same phrase: "I will from henceforth rather be myself." Toward the end of II *Henry IV*, however, royal responsibility seems more thoughtfully considered—an acknowledgement, almost as an afterthought, that a rudimentary action has been at work. "Presume not that I am the thing I was," says the new King to the old Falstaff. In a kind of reversal he has "turned away his former self" and must advise that his fellows "reform" themselves.

Recalling that II *Henry IV* and *Much Ado*, with its frequent Spenserian parallels (pp. 39–54, were both entered upon the Stationers' Register in August of 1600 and made their appearance in print the same year, we should carefully inspect the former play for echoes of *The Faerie Queene*. Along with the increase in the cast of such names as Shallow, Silence, Fang, Snare, Mouldy, Shadow, Wart, Feeble, Bullcalf (which, however, reflect Jonsonian rather than Spenserian practice), there are a few Spenserian images.

First, the Gyant with the Scales in the Book of Justice and, second, Florimell's girdle, so hard to fit to Spenser's ladies in the Book of Friendship, may be glanced at in Part II of the play (III.i.45–51):

> O God, that one might read the book of fate,
> And see the revolution of the times
> Make mountains level, and the continent,
> Weary of solid firmness, melt itself
> Into the sea! and other times to see
> The beachy girdle of the ocean
> Too wide for Neptune's hips.

Again, the dying King imagines the licence "curbed" by him with a "muzzle of restraint" now to be set loose by the Prince; the "wild dog" will "flesh his tooth on every innocent." So the Blatant Beast escaped from Calidore. Finally, Hal accepts the crown under the guidance of the Chief Justice with an authority and humility not less admirable than the traits of Sir Guyon deferring to the Palmer Reason or Sir Artegall depending on the Iron Man, Talus. In the last serious passages of the play allusions to the "balance and the sword" are not distinctively Spenserian; but the frequent invocation of justice, rather than the honor of the earlier histories, marks a change in the ethical frame of reference, possibly due to Elyot's account as reported by Stow.

Should these few very faint analogies with situations in *The Faerie Queene*, of a sort not detected in the preceding histories, be buttressed by evidence of another kind,[3] we might then hazard a premise that the end of II *Henry IV* was composed or revised with Spenser in mind; but in that case questions of the relative dating of II *Henry IV* and *Henry V* would need to be raised against the clear statement in the Epilogue to the former play that the latter play is still to come. For in *Henry V* we shall find no echo of Spenserian agencies or actions, images or phrases. Tailoring, diceplaying, morris dancing, beekeeping, stock breeding, and husbandry are added to the gardening of *Richard II* and the bowling of Faulconbridge in *King John* as patterns suggesting political, social, or ethical truth. Horsemanship and falconry continue to point the moral. Distillation is found relevant for the plays, as earlier for the sonnets. Cupid, the Parcae, Jove, Phoebus, and Hyperion watch over the action —with Lucifer and Beelzebub. Henry's Ceremony joins Faulconbridge's Commodity as a whipping boy. None of this bears on the imperative life of the knights of *The Faerie Queene*. Therefore we might tentatively suppose that *Henry V* antedates

[3] Evidence like that recently discussed by Professor Hardin Craig (*PQ*, XXXV [April, 1956], 218–219) as to the Dering version of Shakespeare's *Henry IV*, which, he suggests, may antedate the quartos. It contains a Chief Justice "whose part is confined to one short formal speech." If or when a play of *Henry IV* was divided into two Parts and the theme of justice was emphasized in a revision shortly before the 1600 quarto of II *Henry IV*, Spenser's Book of Justice would have served the purpose well.

Much Ado, which in so many ways parallels Spenser's ethical actions and agents.

For the same reason—that it bears no resemblance to the Spenserian treatment of lofty matters—*Julius Caesar* may tentatively be assumed to antedate *Much Ado.* Although George Lyman Kittredge cross-refers to Spenser some few words, phrases, or allusions ("cast," "unicorn," "honey-heavy dew," "drawing days out," "mace," "my hair to stare"), these seem fortuitous or in common parlance. Like the habit of Antony, who says, "I only speak right on," Shakespeare's diction in this play is spare and forthright. Yet even where he permits himself ornament or hidden metaphor or structural comparison there is no clear indication that he has the ethical actions of Spenser's allegory in mind. Falconry, archery, horsemanship, racing, bear-baiting, and alchemy and augury support the dramatic pattern. Ate continues to preside and is joined by Erebus and Pluto, stock references. The animals are mostly unpleasant (hawk, ferret, owl, wolf-sheep, lion-hind, adder, unicorn, bear, elephant, "base spaniel fawning," ass, jade, dog, wasp and Hybla bee, ape, hound, cur). They are symbolic; but they are unassociated.

With *Much Ado* and *Twelfth Night* and with *All's Well* and *The Merry Wives* Shakespeare composes in a new vein. His actions are conceived in terms of such ethical codes, ethical aims, ethical discoveries, and ethical peripeties as also characterize *The Faerie Queene.* Although we cannot prove a chronology on evidence of the sort we shall adduce in this book, we may offer the hypothesis that these four plays follow *Henry V* and *Julius Caesar.* In the next chapter reasons will be given for the belief that *As You Like It* precedes both *Much Ado* and *Twelfth Night.*

CHAPTER III

The Book of Courtesy as a Design for Comedy

THE most disabling error of the playwright is the assumption that his persons are good or bad on the basis of unchangeable characteristics, as in the classical stereotypes, the moralities and allegories of the Middle Ages, the comedy of humors, or in our own day the drama of psychoses, traumata, or endocrine imbalance. Granted that such plays are easily imitated, often establish a tradition, and hence now and then survive, they rarely prevail; their plots lack a proper human motive and must be galvanized from the outside by the manipulation of doctrine or circumstance. Man's will and imagination have surrendered to Fate or Fortune. Fate and Fortune have surrendered to Nature. Nature surrenders to the Id.

Thanks in part to his dependence on historical fact or familiar legend for his histories, Shakespeare was learning how to represent men as men. His *Love's Labour's Lost* and *A Midsummer Night's Dream* had well-nigh exhausted the euphuistic influence of John Lyly, and he was engaged in exploiting current Italian and Spanish stories for their utmost effect, of laughter or tears.

His plots were articulate, but they had not grown from his characterization. His persons were lively enough, but they were still pawns, facing each other in a somewhat barren opposition: Tybalt versus Romeo, Shylock versus Antonio, Oliver versus Orlando. And his dramatic situations would still be imperiled or saved arbitrarily: Friar John was stayed in Mantua by the pestilence; Antonio's ships were reported lost by a convenient storm at sea and later, just as conveniently, reported safe; Orlando and Oliver met again thanks only to a fantastic device.

Meanwhile, there was a new dramatic fashion to be considered. In 1598, with the appearance of *Every Man in His Humour*, Ben Jonson, Shakespeare's associate and friendly competitor, had invested his scholarship and critical momentum in a novel version of an old theory that man is controlled by something other than his own conscious power and choice. According to this pseudopsychological premise, certain humors arise from an excess of body fluids, and a man is sanguine, phlegmatic, choleric, or melancholy because he has too much blood, phlegm, yellow bile, or black bile. A tempting but perilous prospect for the comic writer! For none of the refinements and amplifications of this premise—not even when seemingly justified by its truth to life—could atone for its fundamental shortcomings. It was undramatic in that it represented the traits of human beings and societies as predetermined and static. The rewards and punishments bestowed upon those coerced into absurd behavior indicated no proper growth, no suitable redress. Ridiculous lapses and defects might bring about a welcome change of social controls, but they brought no real deliverance for the persons on the stage and no satisfying relief for those in the audience. In spite of Jonson's learning and authority and his effort to represent "deeds and language such as men do use," his drama lacks propulsion because it assumes ethical truth to be no more than unregenerate "nature."

This is alien to Shakespeare's understanding of men and their conduct, and in mirroring nature he successfully avoided Jonson's pattern.[1] However foolish the choices of his agents, however swift or incredible the peripety of his actions, he was not content with "abominable" imitations alone, or with perfunctory answers. The proper ordeal must be ended in the soul itself. There the feature of virtue as well as the image of vice would be clearly recognized. If, then, audiences were becoming impatient with shallow romantic pleasantry or harsh records of dynastic change, how might he suggest to them a world of good and evil, a real world, across the boundaries of history and above the miry terrain of humors?

In short, how would he, how did he, get from the causeless and effortless changes in fortune of *As You Like It* to the intense personal challenges of *Much Ado* and *Twelfth Night?* A review of the characterization and situations of *As You Like It* reveals no shred of evidence that the Forest of Arden derives from Spenser's Faeryland or that those persons escaping court to follow their fancy under the greenwood tree (where there is no enemy but winter and rough weather) suffer from the human tensions of *The Faerie Queene*. On the other hand, there are very few passages of *Much Ado* and *Twelfth Night* without echoes of the tourneys and journeys to which Spenser's agents had dedicated or doomed themselves.

So delightfully is *As You Like It* phrased in the terms of its pastoral and courtly traditions, so wholesome are the young lovers and so folksy the clowns, that many readers do not notice and few will regret the absence of the ethical dimension. When Dame Fortune turns her wheel, we watch its revolution without

---

[1] At this point readers should review Professor Northrop Frye's comparative study of Jonson and Shakespeare as comic writers, in his *Comic Myth in Shakespeare* ("Transactions of the Royal Society of Canada," Vol. XLVI, Ser. iii [June, 1952], sec. 2, pp. 47–58). The evidence to follow, although permitting a less authoritative generalization, supports his argument.

anxiety; and we are pleased that no one has a mission. To gratify us further we have an abundance of explicit similes and a widely extended although not very structural pattern of metaphors: horsemanship and animal husbandry; the sports of wrestling, hunting, archery, falconry, tilting, and dueling; also acting, versifying, philosophizing, and wooing; and, throughout, those seasonal tropes previously helpful in *A Midsummer Night's Dream*. That all this is aggregated rather than organized is not out of keeping with the title. What formal symmetry the play exhibits beyond its opposition of country to court and its clever pairing of lovers arises from the old contrasts of fair versus honest, Fortune versus Nature, wit versus folly, and duty versus meed; from the antitheses, formal and material, into which many of the long speeches are arranged, set pieces of wisdom and wit uttered by Orlando (I.ii; II.iii), Rosalind (III.ii), Touchstone (III.iii), and Phebe (III.v). The climaxes of Jaques (IV.i), Rosalind (IV.i), and Touchstone (V.iv) sparkle on the surface of the action but do not influence it.

The fun in antitheses, climaxes and anticlimaxes, synonymous bombast, and responsive love chanting need not be discounted; that is how we like it when Shakespeare furnishes it. Yet such comic artifices will scarcely accredit or interpret those more human persons who may not remain in the Forest of Arden or join the repentant usurper and Jaques in the "religious life" but must go out upon another kind of countryside where wrestling of another sort awaits them and where snakes and lionesses are less easily put to rout. There the heirs apparent of dukedoms will find themselves in a place indeed very like Spenser's Faeryland, commissioned as were Spenser's knights and ladies to rule the realm within themselves. At least that is how Shakespeare henceforth liked it. Self-rule or self-misrule, self-condemnation and self-redemption, were now to give firmer shape to his comic plots. In a series of witty and willful plays beginning with *Much Ado* and extending through *Measure for Measure* we discover

The Book of Courtesy 39

that the persons of his comedies are provided with weightier purposes and involved in more varied ethical situations. This allies them with, even though it may not derive them from, those agents of Spenser undergoing the tests and pursuing the aims of courtesy, chastity, temperance, and justice. The playwright was not yet quite ready for tragedy proper; but these plays, which again and again reveal Spenserian likeness, have tragic implications, that is, they take it for granted that the agents of drama bear full responsibility and that the action of drama rests on the principle of freedom to choose, the Greek *proairesis*. Our prior concern, therefore, will be the ethical status of the dramatis personae of *Much Ado* and *Twelfth Night*, viewed against the behavior of Spenser's persons, who, although abstractly named and allegorically intended, are never deprived of personality.

Ethos in *Much Ado about Nothing*

It was toward Spenser's Book of Courtesy, conceivably, that Shakespeare might have looked for an alternative to humors. There grows not a "fayrer flowre" in "the sacred noursery / Of vertue" than the "bloosme of comely courtesie"; and at Court there was no more courteous knight than Calidore, who had been charged with the pursuit of the "Blatant Beast" (6.1.10.6-8):

> Now God you speed (quoth then Sir Artegall)
> And keepe your body from the daunger drad:
> For ye haue much adoe to deale withall.

Much ado in dealing with the Blatant Beast, who stigmatizes and lightly or falsely accuses, could indeed be punningly translated into *Much Ado about Nothing* as pronounced "noting"; this meaning of "note," although now obsolete, was familiar in the language of Shakespeare's day. We shall have somewhat less ado to deal with the bountiful evidence [2] indicating that the

[2] The following discussion of *Much Ado* is revised from an article first printed in the *SAB*, XVII (April and July, 1942), 103-111, 126-133, and

action of this play parallels that of the Book of Courtesy in its concern with the cure of incivility, disdain, scorn, and slander.

Two Ladies Disdain: Mirabella and Beatrice

Benedick calls Beatrice "Lady Disdain," and Hero alludes to the "disdain and scorn" which ride sparkling in her eyes. These are the attributes of Spenser's "Ladie" Mirabella, who also misprized love and her wretched lovers. Brought to the bar of Cupid's court and there doomed by him to suffer penance, Mirabella must ride through the world upon a "mangy iade" (6.6.16.8; 6.8.22.7–8),

> With these two lewd companions, and no more,
> *Disdaine* and *Scorne*.

With Spenser's disdainful "Ladie" Shakespeare's Beatrice has much else in common. According to Hero (III.i.54–56),

> She cannot love,
> Nor take no shape nor project of affection,
> She is so *self-endeared*.

"By'r lady," says Margaret tauntingly to Beatrice (III.iv.82–87), "I am not such a *fool* to think what I *list;* nor I *list* not to think what I can; nor indeed I cannot think, if I would think my heart out of thinking, that you are in *love, or* that you will be in *love, or* that you can be in *love*." These garrulous phrases make an excellent parody of Mirabella's doctrine (6.8.21.1–5):

> But let them *loue* that *list, or* liue *or* die;
> Me *list not* die for any *louers* doole:
> Ne *list* me leaue my *loued* libertie,
> To *pitty* him that *list* to play the *foole:*
> To *loue* my *selfe* I learned had in schoole.

---

entitled "Spenserian Courtesy and Temperance in *Much Ado about Nothing.*" All italics in passages quoted from Spenser or Shakespeare are mine, unless otherwise noted.

The Book of Courtesy

Both Ladies Disdain are tearful (IV.i.256–258):

> Benedick. Lady Beatrice, have you wept all this while?
> Beatrice. Yea, and I will weep a while longer.

Mirabella had wandered "two whole yeares, . . . / Wasting her goodly hew in heauie teares"; when questioned, "then bursting forth in teares . . . a while she stayd" (6.7.38.1–3; 6.8.19.1–2). Further, Benedick's remark about the "base (though bitter) disposition of Beatrice" may be illuminated by reference to the "base" kindred of Mirabella, whose beauty and scorn were regarded as inconsistent with her position. Beatrice, we remember, is a ward in the house of her uncle; she must apologize to him for household duties left undone.

The impeachment of Beatrice, carried on, as was the ordeal of Mirabella, in the metaphor of Cupid's love court, ends with the humiliation of Lady Disdain. She is presently summoned by Margaret ("A Baylieffe errant forth in post did passe" to attach Mirabella); she hears herself accused of disdain, with pertinent evidence; she cannot answer, of course, being hidden (Mirabella did not plead or answer), but she accepts the verdict in legal phrase: "Stand I condemned for pride and scorn so much?" She promises to tame her "wild heart" to the "loving hand" of Benedick (Mirabella's "stubborne hart, which loue before disdayned, / Gan stoupe, and falling downe with humble awe, / Cryde mercie"); and, finally, the scene which was prefaced by an allusion to Cupid's crafty arrow is concluded with a reference to Cupid's methods (III.i.105–106):

> If it prove so, then loving goes by haps;
> Some Cupid kills with arrows, some with traps.

This image and rhyme are found also in the Spenserian Mask of Cupid (3.12.11.5–9):

> A net in th' one hand . . . that Mishap;
>   . . . . .
> For whom he could not kill, he practizd to entrap.

Beatrice is not only a Lady Disdain; she is "the infernal Ate in good apparel." Ate's two-parted tongue reappears in Shakespeare's play as a sobriquet, my Lady Tongue, and constitutes Beatrice's jest about Benedick as reported by Don Pedro: " 'Nay,' said I, 'he hath the tongues.' 'That I believe,' said she, 'for he swore a thing to me on Monday night which he forswore on Tuesday morning. There's a *double* tongue; there's *two tongues.*' " This banter (II.i.264, 284; V.i.167–171) closely accords with the Spenserian description of Ate (4.1.27.6–9):

> Her lying *tongue* was *in two parts* diuided,
> And both the parts did speake, and both contended;
> And as her tongue, so was her hart discided,
> That neuer thoght one thing, but *doubly* stil was guided.[3]

And Beatrice provokes Benedick to challenge Claudio as Ate had provoked Paridell to challenge Blandamour, rendering them "Forgetfull each to haue bene euer others frend" (4.2.14.9).

Still another Spenserian figure, Sclaunder, may have helped to characterize Beatrice. Sclaunder's words (4.8.26.3–8) were "like the *stings* of Aspes,"

> *noysome breath*, . . .
> And breathed forth with blast of bitter *wind*.

"If her breath were as terrible as her *terminations*," cries Benedick of Beatrice, "there were no living near her; she would infect to the North Star" (II.i.256–258). "Foul words is but foul *wind*, and foul *wind* is but foul *breath*, and foul *breath* is *noisome*," agrees Beatrice in another passage of the play (V.ii.52–54); "therefore I will depart unkissed." Sclaunder had been represented (4.8.24–25) as pouring out

---

[3] The editor of the Shakespeare Variorum, Dr. H. H. Furness, concedes that Shakespeare "might" have heard of Ate from Spenser and cites Wright to the same effect.

The Book of Courtesy

>   streames of poyson and of gall
> Gainst all, that *truth or vertue* doe professe. . . .
>
> Her nature is all goodnesse to abuse,
>
>   . . . . .
>
> Ne euer Knight so bold . . .
>   but she would striue
> With forged cause them falsely to defame;
> Ne euer thing so well was doen aliue,
> But she with blame would *blot,* and of due praise depriue.

Beatrice, says Hero, spells all her wise, noble, rarely featured lovers backward. The "fair-faced" are womanish, the "black" are foul *blots* made by "Nature" (III.i.59–70). She

>   never gives to *truth and virtue* that
> Which simpleness and merit purchaseth.

Nor is Benedick much better until he, too, has been chastened by the operation of love. It would seem that, at the beginning of the action, both lovers-to-be are equally dominated by the barking, biting, scratching, vile-tongued Blatant Beast. Beatrice would rather hear her dog bark at a crow than a man swear he loved her; Benedick congratulates the gentleman who might thus escape a predestinate scratched face. A parrot with the tongue of Beatrice is better than a beast with the tongue of Benedick; Benedick will hang upon Claudio like a disease. Says Beatrice to the Messenger, "He is sooner caught than the pestilence, and the taker runs presently mad. God help the noble Claudio!" Was not the Blatant Beast (6.1.8.7–9) sent into this wicked world likewise

> To be the plague and scourge of wretched men:
> Whom with vile tongue and venemous intent
> He sore doth wound, and bite, and cruelly torment?

When we see Beatrice emerge from these disdainful, contentious, and slanderous habits into a Beatrice who, according to

Benedick's taunt, might have had her good wit out of the *Hundred Merry Tales*, we are reminded of Phaedria (2.6.6.4–5), who

> greatly ioyed merry tales to faine,
> Of which a store-house did with her remaine.

Beatrice, the pleasant-spirited lady with little of the melancholy element in her, may be compared with Pleasance; in her birth under a dancing star she is another "sweet Cherefulnesse" (4.10.50.6–9):

> Whose eyes like twinkling stars in euening cleare,
> Were deckt with smyles, that all sad humors chaced,
> And darted forth delights, the which her goodly graced.

The real and final Beatrice, however, may stand beside Britomart without disadvantage to either. Both anxiously inquire about their absent lovers; both "missay" these same absent lovers most cruelly; both are offered herbs to cure their lovesickness. Both fall in love unawares, Britomart by swallowing "the hidden hooke with bait," Beatrice by greedily devouring "the treacherous bait." Most important, both devote themselves to seeing justice done. Thus each advances an ethical action.

Two Victims of the Blatant Beast: Serena and Hero

The discipline of Beatrice is only less important to the action of the play than the tragic catastrophe narrowly averted from Hero. Now the ordeal of Hero at the altar—not present in Bandello but surely an incident of value in *Much Ado*—has a counterpart in the ordeal of Serena at the altar, directly following the story of Spenser's Ladie Disdaine in his Book of Courtesy. The denouements differ, but the well-nigh intolerable suffering of an innocent woman serves a like purpose in either case; emotions of pity if not of terror are similarly aroused.

The cause of Hero's suffering, the scandalous report of her

The Book of Courtesy

unchastity, had been allegorically set forth by Spenser in a previous adventure of Serena. And we may compare Hero trying on her rebato and discussing her gown (III.iv) with Serena making "a garland to adorne her hed" (6.3.23.8; 24.1–4):

> All sodainely out of the forrest nere
> The Blatant Beast forth rushing vnaware,
> Caught her thus loosely wandring here and there,
> And in his wide great mouth away her bare.

Serena, like Hero, had fallen into a "drery swound" (6.3.27–28). Thence, like Hero, she had been borne

> to some place of rest . . .
> Where she in safe assuraunce mote abide,
> Till she recured were of those her woundes wide.

Such is the plan of the Friar for Hero; and in various other ways the Friar who comes to Hero's aid resembles the experienced Hermit of sage counsel who received the scandal-bitten Serena into his little "chappell."

The actual rescue of Hero is accomplished by Dogberry's Watch. These rustics, and Dogberry in particular, accord well with the "saluage man" who came to the rescue of Serena in canto 4—"by fortune, passing all foresight." Even Dogberry's paronymous use of language may be derived from the "confused sound / Of *senselesse* words" of the salvage man, "which *nature* did him teach." "To be a well-favoured man is the gift of fortune," says Dogberry, "but to write and read comes by *nature*." The salvage man's appropriation of warlike arms to "put them all about himselfe vnfit" certainly matches the antics of the Watch with bill and lanthorn, to whom Dogberry says, "You are thought here to be the most *senseless* and fit man for the constable of the watch. Therefore bear you the lanthorn."

And chief in Spenser's delineation of the salvage man was his mercy. He (6.5.2.5–6)

> Yet shewd some token of his gentle blood,
> By gentle vsage of that wretched Dame.

Right at this juncture in the Spenserian story we find a discourse on gentle blood "wrapt / In sad misfortunes foule deformity." Might we have here an explanation of the obscure jest about "Deformed" in Shakespeare's scenes with the Watch? Borachio says, "The fashion of a doublet, or a hat, or a cloak, is nothing to a man.... Seest thou not what a deformed thief this fashion is?" At which one of the Watch whispers, "I know that Deformed. 'A has been a vile thief this seven year; 'a goes up and down like a gentleman."

While Borachio, who knows that villainy is villainy in a man whatever the fashion of his doublet, thus speaks of the deformed thief fashion to Conrade, who knows only that the fashion is the fashion, both villains are captured by Dogberry's Watch. A third villain, Don John, escapes. Together these three illustrate the characteristics of the three conspirators of the Book of Courtesy, who found the Blatant Beast the fittest means to work their villainy (6.5.13–14):

> The first of them by name was cald *Despetto,*
> Exceeding all the rest in powre and hight;
> The second not so strong but wise, *Decetto;*
> The third nor strong nor wise, but spightfullest, *Defetto.*

Roughly, this corresponds to the functions of Don John, Borachio, and Conrade. "Only to despite them I will endeavor anything," says Don John. Borachio lays the deceitful plan. Conrade, "Master Gentleman Conrade," is he not Deformed, Defetto? However we construe "Defetto"—physical deformity, grotesque apparel, or mental defect—Conrade fits. He is the scab that follows the itch; he was born under Saturn; for him "the fashion is the fashion," and while insisting on his own specious gentility he deforms Dogberry with the memorable epithet "ass." In confronting Conrade and Dogberry, Shakespeare in his turn illustrates for eye and mind the difference between the Deformed that goes up and down like a gentleman, and the deformity of a salvage man, who yet by gentle usage saved a wretched dame. Whether or not he remembered Spenser's images and phrases, Shakespeare used the term "deformed" with the Spenserian connotation.

Beyond these similitudes there exists one still closer. Don John *is* the Blatant Beast. "I am trusted with a muzzle and enfranchis'd with a clog. . . . If I had my mouth, I would bite; if I had my liberty, I would do my liking" (I.iii.34–38). Unfortunately Don John in another way resembles the Blatant Beast, who broke his iron chain "And got into the world at liberty again" (6.12.38.8–9). Hero will be the next victim of "biting error," as her father calls it. The propriety of her forgiveness of Claudio after the insult at the altar—a step difficult for the modern reader to condone—can be supported by several Spenserian analogies: first, the power of the Blatant Beast to break into the sacred church, to foul the altars, and to cast down the images; second, the real danger existing for the Spenserian knight in such fair-appearing ladies as Duessa and the false Florimell; third, the deceptive report of his lady's unchastity which abused even the Knight of Holiness. He, too, cruelly left his Una (1.12.21.2–3), her father's

> onely daughter deare,
> His onely daughter, and his onely heyre.

And Una would forgive him because (1.3.30.7–8)

> true is, that true loue hath no powre
> To looken backe; his eyes be fixt before.

Although there is little in Hero's situation to arouse terror in the beholder, the kind of pity we give to Serena and Una, even to Pastorella, Florimell, and Amoret, she richly deserves.

Two Knights of Courtesy: Calidore and Claudio

Claudio a knight of courtesy? And yet is courtesy not a trait obviously perverted rather than lacking in him? The Messenger's announcement of success in battle represents him doing "in the figure of a lamb the feats of a lion," as did Calidore (6.1.2. 3–4, 7–8):

> In whom it seemes, that gentlenesse of spright
> And manners mylde were planted naturall;
>
> . . . . .
>
> Nathlesse thereto he was full stout and tall,
> And well approu'd in batteilous affray.

Claudio visits Leonato, the father of a fair daughter, Hero; Calidore visited Meliboe, the reputed father of a fair daughter, Pastorella. Leonato's paternity is jokingly challenged; Meliboe was not the real father of Pastorella. Leonato's guests apologize for burdening his hospitality: "You embrace your *charge* too willingly"; Calidore feared that "the burden of so bold a guest" would "*chargefull*" be (6.9.32.1–2).

In his wordless admiration of Hero, Claudio resembles Calidore, "vnwares surprisd in subtile bands / Of the blynd boy" (6.9.11.6–7). Like Pastorella, that "Diamond of rich regard," Hero prompts Claudio to ask, "Can the world buy such a jewel?" Both Claudio and Calidore surrender war thoughts for soft and delicate desires. When Claudio's intemperance and jealousy become evident—faults from which Calidore was free —he is another Coridon; and the scenes of revelry in the Book of Courtesy parallel those in *Much Ado*. Calidore danced with Pastorella, and Coridon bit his lip; but Calidore courteously yielded to Coridon and placed Pastorella's flowery garland on him, whereupon "Coridon woxe frollicke, that earst seemed dead." Don Pedro dances with Hero, and Claudio sulks; Don Pedro, however, graciously restores Hero to Claudio after some

The Book of Courtesy

scoffs from Benedick about willow garlands for a discarded swain; then Claudio is joyful. Beatrice's gibe about Count Claudio's civility—the trait of a courteous knight—also occurs during the first jealous seizure. He is "neither sad, nor sick, nor merry, nor well; but civil count—civil as an orange, and something of that jealous complexion" (II.i.303–306). Beatrice well knows what Malvolio will soon be trying so hard to learn: that it is the function of the three Graces (6.10.23.7–9) to

> teach vs, how to each degree and kynde
> We should our selues demeane, to low, to hie;
> To friends, to foes, which skill men call Ciuility.

Her demeanor toward Don Pedro is jokingly civil: "Hath your Grace ne'er a brother like you? . . . Your Grace is too costly to wear every day. But I beseech your Grace, pardon me. . . . By your Grace's pardon." These remarks with Leonato's pun—"His Grace hath made the match, and all grace say Amen to it!"—are reminiscent of Spenser's lines close by the stanza on civility and the three Graces (6.10.26–27):

> For which the Graces that here wont to dwell,
> Haue . . . graced her so much to be another Grace.
>
> Another Grace she well deserues to be,
> In whom so many Graces gathered are.

It is during Claudio's first jealous seizure, too, that the resemblance becomes apparent between the intrigue of *Much Ado* and the Spenserian story of the intemperate Phedon in the Book of Temperance. Phedon's friend, Philemon, had persuaded a handmaid, Pryene, to array herself in the clothes of her mistress, Claribell, the betrothed of Phedon. Then Phedon was abused with false evidence of Claribell's unchastity. He slew Claribell, poisoned Philemon, and pursued Pryene to kill her. From the time of Langbaine (1691) until Professor Thaler's recent study [4]

---

[4] "Spenser and *Much Ado about Nothing*," SP (April, 1940), 225–235. See also Charles T. Prouty, *The Sources of 'Much Ado about Noth-*

this Spenserian episode has been debated as one source of *Much Ado*; to the evidence should be added the name taken by the disguised Don Pedro: "My visor is Philemon's roof." This speech would naturally be glossed by reference to the story of Baucis and Philemon; under the circumstances, however, the Spenserian Philemon has additional propriety in *Much Ado*.

Indeed, Claudio is transformed into a Phedonlike, furious, and intemperate character by the operation of forces well known to the student of Spenser's lovers. When he says (II.i. 185–186), "Let every eye negotiate for itself / And trust no agent," and when Benedick exclaims over him (II.i.209–210), "Alas, poor hurt fowl! now will he creep into sedges!" we may recall Doubt, in the Mask of Cupid, who "lookt askew with his mistrustfull eyes." To Phedon, impatient for the rites which marriage make, "that day too farre did seeme." "Time goes on crutches," says Claudio, "till love have all his rites." Neither Phedon nor Claudio can keep his own counsel; and Phedon's tormentor, the Spenserian Furor, like Claudio, in rage (2.4.7. 4–9)

>   strooke more often *wide*,
> Then at the aymed marke, which he had eide:
> And oft himselfe he chaunst to hurt vnwares,
> Whilst reason blent through passion, nought descrie,
> But as a blindfold Bull at randon fares,
> And where he hits, nought knowes, and whom he hurts, nought cares.

Hero refers to Claudio's insults in this figure (IV.i.63): "Is my lord well that he doth speak so *wide?*" Benedick reproves him for the same fault (II.i.202–207): "So they sell bullocks. . . . Ho! now you strike like the blind man! 'T was the boy that

ing' (Yale University Press, 1950). Kerby Neill, in his "More Ado about Claudio: An Acquittal for the Slandered Groom" (*Shakespeare Quarterly*, III [April, 1952], 91–107), carefully scrutinizes the sources of this play. Although he does not cite Bk. VI of the *F.Q.*, his conclusions leave room for, even invite, my hypothesis that Shakespeare intends an action for the cure of discourtesy even more than intemperance.

The Book of Courtesy 51

stole your meat, and you'll beat the post." The temperate Guyon himself (2.4.2.6–7) needed the help of reason,

> when strong passion, or weake fleshlinesse
> Would from the right way seeke to draw him *wide*.

If Guyon erred, if the loving Scudamour believed the worst of his lady, Amoret, when Ate reported her falsely, if the Redcrosse Knight "burnt with gealous fire" and his "eye of reason was with rage yblent," if he too would have slain his lady in his "furious ire," all knights beware! Only in the "antique age" before "faire grew foule, and foule grew faire in sight" might one trust one's lady. This much may be said to mitigate our scorn of Claudio as a credulous and discourteous hero.

Two Vainglorious Knights: Braggadochio and Benedick

Scarcely more usual than Claudio as a knight of courtesy would be the comparison of Benedick to the vainglorious coward knight. Yet in this guise he is humorously represented by Beatrice to the Messenger; and his own friends, Don Pedro and Claudio, say that he avoids quarrels with great discretion or undertakes them with a most Christianlike fear. In Act IV, chiefly, Beatrice drives Benedick to challenge Claudio by the most outrageous insults: "It is a man's office, but not yours! . . . Oh that I were a man! . . . O that I were a man for his sake! or that I had any friend would be a man for my sake!" The attempted flight of Beatrice from Benedick when he has met her charge of unmanliness with offers of love may be compared with the flight of Belphoebe from Braggadochio under the same circumstances. Claudio's jeering answer to Benedick's challenge—"He hath bid me to a calf's head and a capon"—suits Braggadochio's "capon's courage." The wise horse of Guyon bearing the foolish Braggadochio (2.3.46.5–6), who

> had not trayned bene in cheualree,
> Which well that valiant courser did discerne,

gives point to Beatrice's scoff at Benedick for having only wit enough to bear as "a difference between himself and his horse." Braggadochio's "pleasing vaine of glory" and "flowing toung" are recognizable in Benedick. And the fate of Spenser's boaster, a shaven beard and the jests and gibes of all, is matched by the jests and gibes of Don Pedro and Claudio at the newly shaven lover Benedick.

Undoubtedly the most striking analogy between the two boasters appears when each shrouds himself in the greenery and creeps into a bush: "I will hide me in the arbour," says Benedick; there he lurks while the jokers play their prank. "Stalk on, stalk on," whispers Claudio, "the fowl sits." Emerging later to re-establish himself in his own esteem, Benedick presents exactly the picture of Braggadochio (2.3.36.1, 5–9):

> As fearefull fowle
> . . . . .
> Seeing at last her selfe from daunger rid,
> Peepes foorth, and soone renewes her natiue pride;
> She gins her feathers foule disfigurëd
> Proudly to prune, and set on euery side,
> So shakes off shame, ne thinks how erst she did her hide.

This prank, whereby Benedick is cozened into a lover, follows the general order of the early part of Spenser's Mask of Cupid. When Don Pedro and Claudio enter, Benedick exclaims, "Ha! the Prince and Monsieur Love." Then, while the evening "is hushed on purpose to grace harmony" (Claudio), here, as in the Mask (3.12.3–6), there issues a "ioyous fellowship . . . / Of Minstrals, making goodly meriment" (Balthasar and the musicians, to joke of "notes" and "nothing"),

> The whiles a most delitious harmony,
> In full straunge notes was sweetly heard to sound.

Cupid's prologue, "a graue personage" with "count'nance sage" by his "liuely actions . . . gan bewray / Some argument of

The Book of Courtesy

matter passioned." Likewise Leonato, "the white-bearded fellow," gives weight to the prank; Benedick cannot think it a gull when Leonato says of Beatrice, "There was never counterfeit of passion came so near the life of passion as she discovers it."

Yet Benedick is not merely a disdainful braggart; when finally he emerges from his comic prepossession, he exhibits the nobler traits of knighthood. In this regard his career runs parallel to Prince Arthur's (1.9.10.1-5):

> That idle name of loue, and louers life,
> As losse of time, and vertues enimy
> I euer scornd, and ioyd to stirre vp strife,
> In middest of their mournfull Tragedy,
> Ay wont to laugh, when them I heard to cry.

As Prince Arthur defended the aged Reason against the taunts of Cymochles and Pyrochles, so Benedick arrives to rebuke Don Pedro and Claudio for their behavior to Leonato. And the reverberant joke on Benedick as the "savage bull" echoes the simile applied to Arthur himself when he conquered Cymochles and Pyrochles (2.8.42):

> As saluage Bull, whom two fierce mastiues bayt,
> . . . . .
> . . . with his dreadfull hornes them driues afore,
> . . . . .
> So rag'd Prince Arthur twixt his foemen twaine.

Prince Arthur at last overcame Disdaine and Scorne (6.8.12.1-4)

> As when a sturdy ploughman with his hynde
> By strength haue ouerthrowne a stubborne steare,
> They downe him hold, and fast with cords do bynde,
> Till they him force the buxome yoke to beare.

Not less surely does Don Pedro's prophecy for Benedick's reformation come true: "In time the savage bull doth bear the yoke."

Although Prince Arthur had not yet found, might never find, his Queen of Faeryland, Benedick wins his woman of all graces. Our literary quest of disdainful ladyship and discourteous or vainglorious knighthood relates the heroes and heroines of *Much Ado* to Mirabella, Braggadochio, Serena, and Coridon; but it permits them also to claim descent from Britomart, Arthur, Una, and Calidore, the nobler representatives of chivalric habit. Deformed has little value in literature unless behind him shines the Form. This principle of Spenser's narrative art, so contrary to Jonsonian humors, will now become the pattern of Shakespeare's dramatic action. Henceforth he will deal in a more confident way with what Jonson would call "the time's deformity."

Ethos in *Twelfth Night*

Even as Spenser's disdainful or slanderous agents provide us with a commentary on the transformation of Bandello's *novella* into this most effective English comedy, we may tentatively cross-refer certain additional persons from the Book of Courtesy to his play *Twelfth Night, or What You Will*. Barnabe Riche's adaptation of another Italian *novella* into the story of Apolonius and Silla, Julina and Silvio, furnished as complete a plot for *Twelfth Night* as Lodge's *Rosalynde* had furnished for *As You Like It;* but this time what we like has become what we will, to the great advantage of the action, ethically invigorated by its concern for Spenserian civility. Orsino and Viola, Olivia and Sebastian, and their associates—Malvolio, Feste, Sir Toby, Sir Andrew, Maria—are all set to work to ameliorate incivility in one another. The Duke, having bidden Cesario, "Be clamorous and leap all civil bounds," can yet call Olivia "uncivil lady." Malvolio, himself "sad and civil" in the estimation of his mistress, warns Maria not to give means for this "uncivil rule" of Sir Toby, Sir Andrew, and Feste. When Olivia accuses Cesario of having been "saucy" at her gates, he retorts, "The rudeness that hath appear'd in me have I learn'd from my entertainment." This

The Book of Courtesy

is substantiated by Malvolio's behavior toward him and by the unwarranted challenges of Sir Toby and Sir Andrew. In all such mutual recrimination the twins Viola and Sebastian serve as the happy mean, justifying Spenser's argument (6.2.1.1–4):

> What vertue is so fitting for a knight,
> Or for a Ladie, whom a knight should loue,
> As Curtesie, to beare themselues aright
> To all of each degree, as doth behoue?

Briana-Maleffort-Calidore and Olivia-Malvolio-Cesario

Since courtesy is the "roote of ciuill conversation," let us study this gentlest of the comedies with the help of Spenser's Knight of Courtesy, Sir Calidore, the prototype of Shakespeare's Cesario. Calidore (Cesario) must deal with Briana (Olivia), her seneschal Maleffort (Malvolio), her dwarf (Feste), and her accomplice Sir Crudor (Sir Toby).

In the episode of the uncivil Briana and Crudor (6.1), both of whom were to be "restored" by Calidore, there was a "lewd" custom requiring as toll from all who passed by Briana's castle the shorn locks of the ladies and the shaven beards of the knights, with which a mantle would be lined for the wedding of Briana and Crudor. To that end, Maleffort, Briana's "Seneschall," was the executor of "her wicked will." Calidore slew Maleffort and upbraided Briana as one who broke the "bands of ciuilitie" —"No greater shame to man then inhumanitie" (6.1.26.9). Briana then took from her hand "a ring of gould" and bade her "Dwarfe" carry it to Crudor, begging his aid. When Crudor appeared, he, too, was defeated by Calidore and then compelled to marry Briana without her dowry of locks and beards. Briana was "All ouercome with infinite affect, / For his [Calidore's] exceeding courtesie" and invited everyone to "goodly glee and feast" at her castle (6.1.45–46).

The toll of locks and beards to line a mantle, a device which may have reached Spenser from the Castle of the Beards in the prose *Perceval le Gallois*,[5] plays no dramatic part in Shakespearean comedy but is faintly discernible in Beatrice's foolery about beards, the bearded, and the beardless, in Benedick's loss of a beard gone to stuff tennis balls, in his name "my Lord Lackbeard," in the excellent head of hair Sir Andrew might have exhibited—had he but followed the arts—instead of the hair actually hanging upon him "like flax on a distaff." Viola is "almost sick for" a beard. Sir Andrew "will hang like an icicle on a Dutchman's beard" in the north of Olivia's opinion unless he redeems himself by "some laudable attempt either of valour or policy." And Feste puts on a gown and a beard for his scourging of Malvolio.

The shameful demands made at Briana's castle, however, and Calidore's arguments for amending the incivility and boorishness of Briana and Crudor are very close to the discourteous behavior of Olivia, the unjustified attacks of her retainers, and the arguments used by Cesario (along with Sebastian's resolute courage) in dealing with these deformities. Briana with "scornfull pryde / And fowle entreaty . . . indignifyde" Calidore when he sought admittance; but Calidore was one (6.2.3.2–4) whose

> euery deed and word . . .
> Was like *enchantment,* that through both the eares,
> And both the eyes did steale the hart away.

He finally prevailed on her and Crudor "Strangers no more so rudely to intreat" (6.1.40.7). Thus he pointed the way for Cesario's success with Olivia and her complete surrender (III.i.122–124):

> I did send,
> After the last *enchantment* you did here,
> A ring in chase of you.

---
[5] Spenser Variorum, VI, 365–366.

The Book of Courtesy

Spenser's Maleffort was slain too early to do more than offer the first syllable of his name, and his nature, to Malvolio; but he had despitefully bound a passing squire, as Malvolio has put Cesario's captain "in durance." For the further delineation of Olivia's Steward and Clown Shakespeare might well have remembered Disdaine and Scorne, who attended on Mirabella. Disdaine was "sterne, and terrible by nature." His looks were "dreadfull" (6.7.42),

>   and his fiery eies
> Like two great Beacons, glared bright and wyde,
> Glauncing askew, as if his enemies
> He scorned in his ouerweening pryde;
> And stalking stately like a Crane, did stryde
> At euery step vppon the tiptoes hie,
> And all the way he went, on euery syde
> He gaz'd about, and stared horriblie,
> As if he with his lookes would all men terrifie.

The costume of Disdaine—a "Iacket quilted richly rare / Vpon checklaton"—justifies Malvolio's equally fantastic and elaborate cross-gartering upon yellow stockings. But the terrifying looks of Disdaine are never changed into the smiles of Malvolio. When overthrown by Prince Arthur and graciously permitted to arise (6.8.25–26), in spite of his cracked leg (again refer to the appearance of cross-gartering on Malvolio's stockings),

>   being vp, he lookt againe aloft,
> As if he neuer had receiued fall;
> And with sterne eye-browes stared at him oft,
> As if he would have daunted him withall:
> And standing on his tiptoes, to seeme tall,
> Downe on *his golden feete* he often gazed,
> As if such pride the other could apall.

Except for Olivia's intercession, Shakespeare would have visited upon the unregenerate Malvolio the punishment Mirabella barely warded off from Disdaine.

Spenser called Disdaine's companion, Scorne, "the fool." Scorne whipped and reviled and flouted his victim, and in such wise he is paralleled by the antics of Feste, both with the disdainful Olivia and the "stubborn and uncourteous" Malvolio. Although Feste is much more than a Spenserian figure of retribution, he lends to the plot against Olivia's Steward its justifiable castigation. Malvolio is scourged almost out of his five wits; and, in lieu of the shaving of his beard, his nails will have been pared (IV.ii.140). When Olivia exclaims, "Alas poor fool, how have they baffled thee!" (V.i.377), she seems to allude to such a punishment as that of the discourteous Turpine (6.7.27.2–5), soon to be hung by the heels

> And baffuld so, that all which passed by,
> The picture of his punishment might see,
> And by the like ensample warned bee.

In Sir Turpine and his wife, Lady Blandina, we may next see prefigured the unlovely extremes that Sir Toby and Maria will carry into Illyria from some such place as Faeryland. As the name Turpine indicates, Spenser's knight was base, of "rude speach," "a rude churle" who "laught and mockt"; Sir Toby is also "rudesby," and his threats to Cesario are "as uncivil as strange." The plausible Lady Blandina, who knew "how to please the minds of good and ill" and could "allure such fondlings, whom she trayned / Into her trap vnto their owne decay" (6.6.41–42), may have helped Maria to her ingenious plot against Malvolio. Malvolio, like Sir Turpine, is finally "baffuld"; Sir Toby has to send for the surgeon. But Shakespeare has so well refurbished the purely romantic knight and lady that they would not know themselves, nor can we clearly recognize any particular romance through the endearing comic circumstance with which he endows the wedded Sir Toby and Maria.

Calepine in love with Serena is a nobler figure than Sir Andrew wooing Olivia; but both knights have been dishonored in

The Book of Courtesy 59

their challenges, and in the combat between Turpine and Calepine the latter was chased round about "like a wilde goat" and must seek refuge "behinde his Ladies backe." Here is more than a hint for the ridiculous conflicts of Acts III and IV of *Twelfth Night* and for Sir Andrew's craven behavior.

Into these encounters Antonio strides, like a Prince Arthur to the punishment of Turpine, and Sebastian deals blows upon Sir Toby and Sir Andrew as effectively as did Calidore upon Maleffort and Crudor. Without such timely succor the fortunes of Olivia cannot be satisfactorily repaired. And yet the inner action, the rarer action, is not so much miraculous wedlock [6] as it is the chastening of incivility. Olivia, who in the beginning flouted the Duke and his messenger, is at the end heard to say (V.i.324-327):

> My lord, so please you, these things further thought on,
> To think me as well a sister as a wife,
> One day shall crown th' alliance on't, so please you,
> Here at my house and at my proper cost.

Tristram and Sebastian; Sir Bruin and Orsino

Shakespeare's inherited story was not much concerned with civility, but it did demand a husband for each of the two heroines. How might the playwright associate these husbands with his "rarer action"? Riche's Silvio became Sebastian and his Apolonius was renamed Orsino. Now Spenser's Tristram and Sir Bruin were to be met with in the second and fourth cantos in the Book of Courtesy, closely following the story of the uncivil Briana. Here we shall tentatively suggest, first, that Spenser's sylvan Tristram of the darts and "borespeare" reminded Shake-

---

[6] For a recent interpretation of Shakespeare's comedies as actions to be concluded by marriage, see Geoffrey Bush, *Shakespeare and the Natural Condition* (Harvard University Press, 1956). Read also Susanne K. Langer's discussion of comic form in *Feeling and Form* (New York, 1953), Ch. 18.

speare of St. Sebastian of the arrows and hence of a new name for the Silvio of Riche's story. Secondly, we shall point to the bearish behavior in Orsino, "little bear," which inclines us to believe him kin to Spenser's Sir Bruin. Both Tristram and Sir Bruin are deficient rather than deformed and would suggest lovers not quite sophisticated into courtliness; they are novices in love.

First, then, to Tristram, son of Meliogras of Lionesse. When Tristram was challenged by Sir Calidore to discover his estate, he said that he had come "into the land of Faerie" to be "trayned . . . in gentle thewes," and he begged to "beare armes, and learne to vse them right." Calidore dubbed him knight, gave him the arms he had won, and then bade him farewell. "So taking courteous leaue, they parted twayne." Several characteristics of Shakespeare's Sebastian accord pleasantly with Spenser's Tristram. Each is dearly loved by an older man; each is questioned as to his parentage; each has avoided "ydlesse"—witness Sebastian's desire (III.iii.19, 22–24) to see the relics of this town and

> satisfy [his] eyes
> With the memorials and the things of fame
> That do renown this city

—an urban equivalent of Tristram's zeal for self-improvement in the "seemely leres" of the "forrest greene." Both Tristram and Sebastian are resolute, gracious, humble; both Sir Calidore and Antonio are justified in their "dear affection"; and the gifts of armor (to Tristram) and a purse (to Sebastian) at separation will not prove unmerited. Finally, there is a special propriety in the frank joy each novice feels, the one at the armor betokening knighthood, the other at the pearl betokening wedlock. Tristram (6.2.39.3–5), feeding his eyes "with the faire sight"

> Of the bright mettall, shyning like Sunne rayes;
> Handling and turning them a thousand wayes,

The Book of Courtesy 61

helps us to understand Sebastian's lyrical outburst (IV.iii.1-4):

> This is the air; that is the glorious sun;
> This pearl she gave me, I do feel't and see't;
> And though 'tis wonder that enwraps me thus,
> Yet 'tis not madness.

Sebastian goes off with Olivia and the Priest to his marriage with joy as full as Tristram's when he went off with the "Ladie" whom he had rescued from her discourteous knight.

Orsino appears in the action as infrequently as does Sebastian, and less cogently. Olivia is in need of rescue from his importunate wooing, and there is no gainsaying his bearishness. He is indeed a veritable little bear for honey:

> Give me excess of it, that, surfeiting,
> The appetite may sicken, and so die.

Although the honey of music is Orsino's "food of love" in peacetime, he has recently come home from a successful war against the pirates, comparable with the victory of Sir Bruin over the "great Gyant, called Cormoraunt, . . . by yonder foord." His intemperate surrender to his desires "like fell and cruel hounds" and his command to Cesario to "leap all civil bounds" (I.i.22; I.iv.21) are not lovely traits. Still more bearish are his rage at Cesario, who seems to come between him and Olivia, and his threat to kill out of "savage jealousy," sacrificing the lamb that he loves to spite another. Strongly indicative of his ursine nature also is his rebuke to Cesario in the words, "O thou dissembling cub!" He has been deceived as to the sex of his page as completely as Sir Bruin was deceived about the paternity of his son. What will his cub be, he asks, "When time hath sow'd a grizzle on [his] case" (V.i.168).

But enough of bears, grizzly or otherwise. Viola loves him, even if she is too good for him. And his persistence in love, though misdirected, puts him in the category of Scudamour and hence leads us to a few words about Viola as Amoret. That each is a twin (Viola of Sebastian and Amoret of Belphoebe) does not further concern us; but both have in notable degree the womanly quality Spenser illustrated when finally he revealed Amoret to Scudamour. Amoret sat "euen in the lap of Womanhood," and about her were goodly Shamefastnesse, sweet Cherefulnesse, sober Modestie, comely Curtesie, soft Silence, and "submisse" Obedience. In her despair later, when chained to her "brasen pillour" (3.12.30.9), she has given us a kind of preview of the disastered heroine of *Twelfth Night*, "like Patience on a monument, / Smiling at grief" (II.iv.117–118). Spenser probably would have recognized his Amoret in Shakespeare's Viola. Amoret is no more a Britomart or Belphoebe than Viola is a Helena or Imogen; but Spenser's womanly woman helps us to understand Shakespeare's womanly woman, despite the latter's long disguise.

Scudamour won Amoret too easily in the 1590 edition of Books I–III of *The Faerie Queene*. In 1596 Spenser raised the stakes, and Amoret must be lost again before she might really be won. Such discipline the confines of *Twelfth Night* do not permit for Orsino. But he and all the others—except for the ill-willed Malvolio and Feste, singing *carpe diem*, death, the goodman devil, and the wind and the rain—get what each wants or wills. And all of them—may we say thanks to the kind of enchantment Calidore worked on Briana?—will be invited by Olivia to a party given "at [her] house and at [her] proper cost."

These are mythic resemblances and not to be precisely equated. They do not characterize persons as explicitly as in *Much Ado*, but they do underlie comparable situations. If *Much Ado* is, as scholars believe, prior to *Twelfth Night*, Shakespeare's lessons in playwriting were leading him from persons seen in relation to an ethical action to situations framed in accordance with an ethical action. As yet his main agents, even Viola and Feste, are not fully responsible, not so much so as Helena and the Mistresses Page and Ford will be in the next two plays we consider. For Viola a plot like this is "too hard a knot . . . t'untie"; time must untangle it. And for Feste, too, as for his many kinsmen of today preoccupied with the death wish, it is still "the whirligig of time" which brings in his revenges. "But that's all one, our play is done." Ahead of us we see other plays, with ethical actions more masterfully concluded and by agents still further removed from the danger of doctrinal humors or other arbitrary limitations on their desires and will power. With the help of Edmund Spenser, or so the evidence encourages us to suggest, Shakespeare was holding up his end in the friendly competition to which Ben Jonson's comedy of humors had challenged him.

CHAPTER IV

Legends of Friendship and Chastity

AT THE beginning of the tenth canto of his Book of Friendship Spenser approves the truth of a very old saying:

> True he it said, what euer man it sayd,
> That loue with gall and hony doth abound,
> But if the one be with the other wayd,
> For euery dram of hony therein found,
> A pound of gall doth ouer it redound.[1]

Shakespeare also glances, skeptically, toward it in the last lines of Act V of *All's Well That Ends Well:*

> All yet seems well; and if it end so meet,
> The bitter past, more welcome is the sweet.

With the Blatant Beast temporarily in chains, then, let us assume that Shakespeare turned from his investigation of Spenserian courtesy and civility to review the piteous stories "Of louers sad calamities of old" in Spenser's Books of Chastity and

---

[1] See p. 133 for the help given by this passage in emending the "dram of eale" image in *Hamlet,* I.iv.36–38.

Friendship. What are sometimes called the problem comedies—of which *All's Well* is the notable instance—seem less enigmatic when studied in the light of love's pageants played "diuersely" in "diuerse minds" (3.5.1) throughout the Book of Chastity; and the precarious balance between Discord and Concord in the Book of Friendship lends new significance to the peripety of all Shakespeare's plays, comic or tragic, written in the first decade of the new century.

To such matters Helena possibly refers when she interrupts her word combat with Parolles on "virginity." Now that young Bertram has left home, she fears (I.i.180–189), he will have in Paris

> a thousand loves,
> A mother, and a mistress, and a friend,
> A phoenix, captain, and an enemy,
> A guide, a goddess, and a sovereign,
> A counsellor, a traitress, and a dear;
> His humble ambition, proud humility,
> His jarring concord, and his discord dulcet,
> His faith, his sweet disaster; with a world
> Of pretty, fond, adoptious christendoms
> That blinking Cupid gossips.

Whether or not Shakespeare thought of the third and fourth Books of *The Faerie Queene* when he set down this list, no present-day student of Spenser's allegorical patterns will fail to recognize in it various important "loues" from Faeryland and those abstractions multifariously displayed at the Temple of Venus, or at the House of Busirane when the Mask of Cupid swept by. Witness in the first place Cymoent (Cymodoce), *mother* of Marinell; Amoret, *mistress* of Scudamour; Britomart, *friend* of Amoret; Belphoebe, the *phoenix* for Timias' "turtle Dove"; the "cruell" *Captain* of the "raskall rout" besieging the House of Alma or the "lustfull" *Captain* threatening Pastorella; Ate, the sign of Discord, *enemy* of all, or Marinell, "loues enimy"; the Palmer Reason, *guide* of Sir Guyon; Diana and Venus, *goddesses;* Gloriana, *sovereign;* Glauce, the *counselor* of Britomart; Duessa as the false Florimell, the *traitress;* and Florimell herself, at last the *dear* of Marinell. Witness in the second place the following adoptious christendoms [personifications?], gossips of Cupid: Doubt, Delay, Daunger, Loue, Hate, Concord, Peace, Friendship, Womanhood, Shamefastnesse, Cherefulnesse, Modestie, Curtesie, Silence, Obedience; and Ease, Fancy, Desyre, Feare, Hope, Dissemblance, Suspect, Grief, Fury, Displeasure, Pleasance, Despight, Cruelty. Witness Cupid himself, whom Helena sees "blinking," possibly because Spenser had permitted him " a while vnbind" his blindfold eyes before "blinding him againe." Then followed Reproach, Repentance, Shame, Strife, Anger, Care, Vnthriftihead, Losse of Time, Sorrow, Chaunge, Disloyaltie, Riotise, Dread, Infirmitie, Pouertie, Death—all of them rich in facial and gestural hints for a dramatist evolving a new kind of comedy. Such variations on the themes of chastity and friendship would indeed be much more helpful than humors.

That Shakespeare set to work about 1600–1602 on what some scholars believe to be a revision of the *Love's Labour's Won* attributed to him in 1598 by Francis Meres is further borne out, in regard both to its likely date and its certain theme, by the appearance in *All's Well* of such devices, situations, and actions as Spenser earlier employed in his legends about love's labor lost or won. Those passages of *All's Well* not indebted to the story of Beltramo of Rossiglione and Giletta of Narbon (from Boccaccio by way of William Painter) bear a marked resemblance to the misogynous career of Spenser's Marinell as influenced by three resolute ladies: Cymoent or Cymodoce, his overanxious mother; the overzealous Florimell, who loved him unrequitedly and calamitously through almost two Books of *The Faerie Queene;* and, most significant, the somewhat overbearing Britomart, who outmaneuvered and wounded him with dire results for his health and peace of mind.

Legends of Friendship and Chastity

The hero and heroine of *All's Well* will therefore be reconsidered in the light of Spenser's woman-ridden Marinell and the Virgin Knight, whose own happiness must be so long delayed. In his new version of an old situation Shakespeare could profitably have associated these two well-known allegorical agents of *The Faerie Queene* for a novel dramatic effect; and we can show further that the Countess, Lafeu, Parolles, and Lavache—all added to the story by Shakespeare—have recognizable Spenserian prototypes.

The action of the play is restorative. The King of France and Bertram are both to be healed: the former of a fistula, the latter of an emotional injury akin to what is in our jargon called a trauma. If the evidence to follow be pertinent, we may succeed in relating the dramatic therapy of *All's Well* more closely to the devices necessary for relieving the tensions of *Much Ado* and *Twelfth Night* as already discussed; and in discussions yet to come we may, by further reference to Spenser's argument, discover that *The Merry Wives*, *Troilus and Cressida*, the second quarto of *Hamlet*, and *Measure for Measure* are most closely allied as dramas of therapeutic action. All seven plays, under Shakespeare's hand in swift succession through even fewer years (1599–1604), concern ethical disproportion and its attempted cure by dedicated agents. Beatrice, Cesario, Helena, the Mistresses Page and Ford, Thersites and Ulysses, Hamlet, and Vincentio—with varying degrees of success in various difficult situations—are commissioned by the dramatist to attack evil as deformity or illness. Their respective procedures cohere best in an ethical doctrine very like that supporting *The Faerie Queene*.

This is not to consider them as so many physicians making so many case studies of so many diseases, although Shakespeare himself frequently compares their operations to diagnostic and medicinal practices. Rather, they will be accredited as agents of actions within what Spenser calls "the sacred noursery / Of vertue" (6.Prol.3.1–2). We are to take the word "heal" as only one of the images in the wholesome process; but it would enfeeble both our argument and our evidence to forget the timeless function of the dramatic poet at the center of all this holy making—his revelations as diagnoses, his code as a prescription, his ordeal as a regimen, and his relief of troublous feelings as an end in view. Aristotle's father is reputed to have been a physician; and a doctrine of *katharsis* and *krasis* is to be expected from his son, author of the *Poetics*.[2] Shakespeare was quoting Aristotle in 1602 (*Troilus and Cressida* II.ii.166). Although he may not have known *katharsis* or *krasis* by those names, he was undeniably aware of their nature and relationship and understood his own English tongue well enough to acknowledge the part that healing plays in holiness.

Marinell and Bertram; Britomart and Helena

Marinell, son of "the famous Dumarin," now dead, was lord of a rich strand strewn with gems and rings.[3] When his mother, the sea nymph Cymodoce, heard from Proteus that her boy should have much ill of a woman, that "A virgin strange and stout him should dismay, or kill" (3.4.25–26), she sedulously protected him from womankind.

> Yet many Ladies faire did oft complaine,
> That they for loue of him would algates dy:
> Dy, who so list for him, he was loues enimy.

The wound inflicted by Britomart on this heir of gems and rings, this haughty son of an apprehensive mother, was first probed by "the lilly-handed Liagore," who "whylome had learned skill / In leaches craft, by great Appolloes lore" and who thus reminds us of the daughter of Gerard of Narbon and her aptitude for the art of healing. From Liagore's first aid in his emergency Marinell was taken to Tryphon, the "soueraine

[2] See Wheelwright's essay, "Mimesis and Katharsis."
[3] This is only one of the references to "rings" in his sources, but possibly it inclined Shakespeare to emphasize the device in his plot.

Legends of Friendship and Chastity 69

leach" at Neptune's court. Seemingly cured by Tryphon, he must remain for a long time "with the Nymph, his mother, like her thrall" (3.4.12–44; 4.11.7; 12–18).

> [She] sore against his will did him retaine,
> For feare of perill, which to him mote fall.
>   . . . . .
> Yet durst he not his mother disobay.

In these circumstances we recognize a pattern for Bertram's restive conduct when sent by his mother as an "unseasoned courtier" to Paris, henceforth to be the ward of the King of France (II.i.27–28):

> I am commanded here and kept a coil with—
> 'Too young,' and 'The next year,' and ' 'Tis too early.'

Bertram's departure by stealth from the Court of France to enter the Florentine Wars is, then, comparable with Marinell's escape from the solemn feast of the sea gods to wander by himself. Each aspirant for independence immediately gets into trouble: Bertram falls in love with Diana; and thus he imitates Marinell, who, overhearing the complaint of Florimell, prisoner of Proteus, that "the cause of all her care / [had] come of [Marinell] for using her so hard," fell in love with the woman he had previously scorned (4.12.12.4–5):

> His stubborne heart, that neuer felt misfare
> Was toucht with soft remorse and pitty rare.

This time neither Liagore nor Tryphon knew how to help him; his mother must send for "Apollo King of Leaches." Apollo came, and in a few stanzas Florimell was released, the lovers were united, and Marinell's "engrieued mind," having been successfully probed, was healed. With similar speed in the final passages of *All's Well*, Helena's suffering and loyalty and those incisive challenges of the King which Shakespeare added to the old story cure the ailing Bertram. Metaphorically speaking, his arrogance is lanced and his festering lies and evasions are cleaned away. As a soldier and a father he is at last on his wholesome own.

Such reminders of thraldom, initial shock, and the growing pains characteristic of emotional dependence in Marinell's career suggest to us, as possibly three centuries ago to Shakespeare, a Bertram more sinned against than sinning.[4] Marinell and Bertram are both obviously immature and inexperienced; the dignity of both has been impaired; and each wants to achieve self-respect.

Bertram, it may be confessed, stumbles into military success and fatherhood most awkwardly. Except for Helena's single-minded, daring substitution of herself for Diana, he would have wasted himself and his seed in the brothels of Florence, Diana would have been dishonored, and the Countess would have had no grandchildren. We need not condone a device unacceptable in the therapy of our own day; but we may say that Helena is not the daughter of a great physician for nothing. Her cure of the King of France is the lesser instance of her healing power. Without her, *All's Well* would lack its "rarer action," the healing of Bertram's soul.[5]

Helena is not a plaintive Florimell, although her face, too, is washed in brine. At this point in his remodeling of the play or story Shakespeare might recall that Britomart, no mere victim like Florimell, wept as copiously. Britomart, he would observe, disclosed her love only after she had been repeatedly and per-

---

[4] See in *Sh.Quart.*, VII (Winter, 1956), 21–31, A. H. Carter's article to the same effect on other evidence, "In Defense of Bertram."

[5] The healing of the King and the marriage of the Clever Wench are necessitated also by the old stories which Professor W. W. Lawrence has disentangled from the play in his admirable chapter on *All's Well* in *Shakespeare's Problem Comedies* (New York, 1931). Lawrence (p. 65) quotes Edward Dowden as follows: "Helen is the providence of the play; and there is 'no hurt done,' but rather healing—healing of the body of the French king, healing of the spirit of the man she loves."

Legends of Friendship and Chastity

sistently exhorted to do so by Glauce, her foster mother. This situation is closely paralleled in that scene of *All's Well* (I.iii) where Helena's foster mother, the Countess of Rossillion, with comparable difficulty elicits from her foster daughter a confession of love for Bertram.

Does Shakespeare's Countess of Rossillion, then, owe her place in the action to Spenser's Glauce, loving, faithful, ingenious, wise? For what may well be an affirmative answer let us review the quest of Britomart and Glauce to find Artegall.

Britomart had seen in the magic globe of glass which Merlin gave to her father, King Ryence, the features of an unknown knight, shining "as Phoebus face out of the east." Helena speaks of the "bright radiance and collateral light" of Bertram as beyond her "sphere"; but in her "heart's table" also, a "heart too capable / Of every line and trick of his sweet favour," she has drawn "His arched brows, his hawking eye, his curls" (I.i. 99–107).

Moreover, the close friendship between Britomart and her father resembles Gerard of Narbon's relationship with his daughter Helena. And Glauce's apprehension as to Britomart (3.2.30.7–9)—

> What vncouth fit . . .
> Hath . . .
> Chaunged thy liuely cheare, and liuing made thee dead?

—is matched by the anxiety of the Countess for her foster daughter Helena in the first scene of the play—"The tyranny of her sorrows takes all livelihood from her cheek." In each case the loving concern of the older woman validates both the ordeal and its outcome; yet Glauce's herbs, charms, counsel, "And choisest med'cine for sicke hart's reliefe," her "thrise three haires . . . trebly breaded in a threefold lace," were as unavailing to comfort the woe of Britomart as is the triple assurance of the Countess to Helena—"I am a mother to you"; "I say·I am your mother"; "I say I am your mother" (I.iii.144, 148, 160). Both foster daughters are under a sterner compulsion; each must seek her fortune abroad by her own wit and skill. In such a venture, however, each has the encouragement and blessing of her foster mother: Britomart was accompanied by Glauce to the Cave of old Merlin; and although Helena goes alone to the court of the invalid King of France, there, in lieu of the Countess, she has the aged counselor Lafeu to introduce and to abet her. Merlin explained the marital destiny of Britomart as mother of "a famous Progenie"; the King of France marries Helena to Bertram.

Britomart and Glauce next retired to frame "diuerse plots" and "to maske in strange disguise" (3.3.51.9) for their search of the destined lover. Their disguise was martial; Helena's is religious. Britomart became a warrior; Helena becomes a pilgrim. To this end Britomart stole the armor of Angela, Helena borrows the bed of Diana—again by necessary deference to the old story. Meanwhile, Britomart had succored Amoret, and Helena has succored Diana; and in so doing both heroines have undergone conflict with lust—the vile Ollyphant and the enchanter Busirane or the lecher Parolles and the foolish, wanton boy Bertram, respectively. The bitterest trial for each heroine is that she must learn of the hero's surrender to another woman (Radigund, Diana) in an enslavement which can be ended only by the complete risk of herself (in combat, Britomart against Radigund; by co-operation, Helena with Diana). As a result, each hero is delivered from the false position into which he has been led by his overconfidence and weakness. The particular kind of courage displayed by Helena may best be likened to Britomart's at her encounter with Busirane, the type of lust. If such comparisons seem to blur the outlines of the old "bed-trick" unduly, we may soften disapproval of Helena by noting that even Britomart had been wounded by the "murdrous knife" of Busirane (3.12.32–33).

> Vnwares it strooke into her snowie chest,
> That little drops empurpled her faire brest.

Shakespeare gives the name Diana to the previously unnamed maiden who furthers Helena's plot; and without Diana's connivance this plot would indeed have failed. Britomart, too, swore by Diana. So marked an association and the frequent references to virginity and the virgin encourage us in our hypothesis that Shakespeare's Helena owes her dauntless spirit to Spenser's Virgin Knight. Finally, their relation in the mind of the playwright appears highly plausible when, listening with the ears of the Countess' steward, we overhear Helena saying, "Dian [was] no queen of virgins, that would suffer *her poor knight* surpris'd without rescue in the first assault or ransom afterward" (I.iii. 119–122).

Bertram is the poorer for his friend Parolles, who seems to be the last sad remnant of the progeny of Spenser's Sir Paris—Parius, Paridas, Paridell, and, we may now add, Parolles. As a Frenchman, Parolles can be translated into the man of many words; as a villain in an English play he must be studied in connection with the Spenserian Paridell or, even more closely, with the Spenserian Braggadochio.

The attempt of Parolles to vitiate Helena's mind in their otherwise insignificant conversation about "virginity" is not so successful as was Paridell's rape of Hellenore, but it exhibits Shakespeare's power to change into winged words the "false belgardes . . . let fly" at Hellenore by her unpleasant lover. "Not my virginity yet," says the incorruptible Helena; and here a break in the text (I.i.179) suggests that Shakespeare might be reminding himself that his action must concern itself rather with false friendship and faithful love than with romantic seduction. In this play it is the boy Bertram who is egged on into foolish and wanton behavior by his unworthy friend Parolles and who must be rescued by his unvalued wife Helena.

Parolles is a coward like Paridell, who refused encounters with Britomart or with the bold Sir Ferraugh at the tournament of the girdle. Parolles scorns old Lord Lafeu as Paridell had scorned Glauce, disguised as an old squire. Parolles, faithless to Bertram, repeats the conduct of Paridell with his "profest" friend Blandamour. Parolles is always at the center of the turmoil, on his way in or out of a situation; Paridell likewise had flitted about the broils in the "chaos" of the ninth canto of the Book of Friendship. Nevertheless, although Paridell was not invited to the wedding of Marinell and Florimell, Parolles is summoned to assist at the reunion of Bertram and Helena.

That other rascal, Braggadochio, may also contribute to the rascally Parolles—Braggadochio of the "flowing toung" and "great brauery, / As Peacocke, that his painted plumes doth prancke" (2.3.4.6; 6.3–4). Parolles confesses himself "braggart" (IV.iii.370–372). He is likewise loquacious. He has "scarfs and bannerets" about him (II.iii.213–214), his soul is "in his clothes" (II.v.48), and he is a "jackanapes with scarfs" (III.5.88). His conduct throughout parallels that of Braggadochio: he begs off from his various encounters as impudently as did Braggadochio from Satyrane's "tourneyment" in the Book of Friendship or the "turney" at the wedding of Florimell and Marinell in the Book of Justice; even more distinctively in his word combats with Helena and with Lafeu he recalls Braggadochio's conversation with and attack on Belphoebe and his overbearing treatment of old Malbecco.

If Bertram is to be rescued from his dishonorable course, the disclosure of Parolles' villainy must be officially made. To that end Shakespeare gives us his incomparably skillful Act IV, where, thanks to the device of the French lords, Bertram with his own eyes sees Parolles in his true color, his "snipt-taffeta . . . saffron," as Lafeu phrases it. The whole laughable episode of the unmasking of the false friend may be postulated as an expansion into Shakespeare's restorative merriment of the "vncas-

Legends of Friendship and Chastity

ing" of Braggadochio by Artegall and Talus amid the jests and gibes of the guests at the wedding of Marinell and Florimell. Moreover, pending the outcome of Helena's knightly enterprise to secure Bertram's ancestral ring and a legally begotten son for him, Act V will swiftly advance to a solution comparable with those ceremonies in which Marinell was no longer a reluctant bridegroom and Florimell was no longer a neglected bride and (5.3.40) their friends were left

> in pleasure and repast,
> Spending their ioyous dayes and gladfull nights,
> And taking vsurie of time forepast,
> With all deare delices and rare delights,
> Fit for such Ladies and such louely Knights.

Spenser helps us to infer that *All's Well* really ends well.

Somewhere on the margin of all the gaiety Lafeu's daughter Maudlin lacks a husband, and the Clown, Lavache, is still "out o' friends." Like Britomart's Glauce, Lafeu has matchmaking propensities: he brings Helena to the King and so to Bertram, and when Helena is reported dead he offers Maudlin to Bertram. He is a whimsical person, a kind of benevolent Pandarus, to whom he compares himself in the words, "I am Cressid's uncle" (II.i.100). Lavache and Isbel, "foul-mouthed" though the Clown be, represent the merely sensual man and woman. They are much less monstrous than Ollyphant and Argante, "vile and vitious," of Spenser's Book of Chastity, and when considered against these monsters they illustrate Shakespeare's power to humanize even the lustful.

Thinking of Lafeu as a kind old uncle of Cressida and of Lavache as a milder Thersites, joking about Helen instead of inveighing against her (I.iii.74–75)—

> 'Was this fair face the cause,' quoth she,
> 'Why the Grecians sacked Troy?

—we are led to consider the relative dates of *All's Well* and *Troilus and Cressida*. It seems probable that a Lafeu and Lavache would precede a fully characterized Pandarus and Thersites; and this may indicate to the reader that Shakespeare will soon begin a more thoroughgoing study of the matter of Troy.[6] Parolles' sobriquet, "little Helen," for Helena of *All's Well* is a hint that the playwright has big Helen in mind, and Parolles may have pointed him back to Paris by way of Spenser's Hellenore and Paridell.

Ollyphant and Falstaff; Malbecco and Master Ford

But before we investigate what goes on in the Palace of Priam we should attend the banting of that "greasy knight," Sir John Falstaff, at the hands of those two virtuous wives of Windsor Meg Page and Alice Ford. This is a veritable antimask in the series of redemptive comedies with which we have been dealing. Although there are frequent echoes of *A Midsummer Night's Dream* in *The Merry Wives of Windsor*, Falstaff is more deeply involved with his antlers than Bottom with his asshead. The rogues of *Henry IV* and *Henry V* are up to their old tricks, but a fiercer light beats upon them; and the comic power they exhibit, lacking its contrast with and support from loftier human agencies, falls back instead on the thorny principles of right and wrong. In the words of Sir Hugh Evans, the Welsh parson trained to make fine moral distinctions, the peripety will supply "admirable pleasures and fery honest knaveries" (IV.iv.80–81).

Several reasons incline us to date *The Merry Wives* later than *Henry V* (1599). The caricature of Welsh speech furnished by Sir Hugh is a burlesque of its properly comic effect in the person of Fluellen; the habits of Corporal Nym—understatement and reference to "humors"—have proliferated mon-

---

[6] See Abbie F. Potts, "*Cynthia's Revels, Poetaster*, and *Troilus and Cressida*," *Sh.Quart.*, V (Summer, 1954), 297–302.

Legends of Friendship and Chastity

strously; the echoes of French idiom we hear from Doctor Caius are not so appropriate and not so witty as in the delightful lesson given by Alice to Katherine in *Henry V;* and something of the same kind of dramatic corruption has befallen the Sir John of *Henry IV*—he, too, has grown monstrous. No longer is he a scapegoat in the holiday representation of Misrule or Carnival, to be assimilated into a nobler action as its relief from tension or as its comic counterpart.[7]

Falstaff's first resurrection occurs in I *Henry IV* (V.iv) and is brought about through his own roguery. His second resurrection into the triple ordeal of *The Merry Wives* he owes, it is said, to the royal request of Gloriana. She wished to see him in love. Small wonder that Shakespeare exhibits him in that corner of her realm dedicated by Spenser to the tourneys between chastity and unchastity. Now in his own person as a monster threatening the courts of love he can be put to rout only by those latter-day knights of chastity Mistress Page and Mistress Ford. He must be subjected to lustration and tribulation, to bucking and drubbing, and then to a final ordeal by "trial-fire" in the very presence of the Queen of the Fairies.

When, on the receipt of his improper letter, Mistress Page says she would "rather be a giantess, and lie under Mount Pelion" than embrace him (II.i.81–82), we may cross-refer her image to the vile and vicious "Geauntesse Argante," daughter of those Titans who "heaped hils on hight, / To scale the skyes." Her sire was Typhoeus; her mother, Earth. And with her twin brother Ollyphant she had been "mingled . . . yfere" in the womb of Earth ere both "into the . . . world were brought" (3.7.47–50). Mistress Page would rather be such a one—located by Spenser in the metaphorical vicinity of Mount Olympus—

---

[7] See C. L. Barber, "From Ritual to Comedy: An Examination of *Henry IV*," in *English Stage Comedy*, ed. with an introduction by W. K. Wimsatt, Jr., *English Institute Essays*, 1954 (Columbia University Press, 1955).

than yield to the Falstaffian "mountain of mummy." Moreover, when Falstaff barely escapes in the hat, muffler, and gown of the gigantic Mother Prat, witch of Brainford, two monstrosities are allied to furnish a Shakespearean comic equivalent of Spenser's Titanic twins. That Mother Prat is assumed to have entered Sir John's chamber for no good reason recalls the unpleasant pairing of Ollyphant and Argante.

May it not be that Sir John, whom Master Ford calls a "monster" (III.ii.82, 93), was associated in Shakespeare's mind with Ollyphant, who "surpassed his sex masculine, / In beastly vse" (3.11.4.3–4) and was fearful of none but Britomart, "the flowre of chastity"? Sir John's blasphemous invocation of Jove the bull and Jove the swan and faults "done first in the form of a beast" makes him an unrepentant successor of Ollyphant. If he is to be invited to the wedding party of Anne Page and Master Fenton, he will need a monstrous pinching to chasten his monstrous lechery (V.v.97–98):

> Fie on sinful fantasy!
> Fie on lust and luxury!

The routing of the bestial Ollyphant by Britomart, the Knight of Chastity, and Satyrane was followed by the deliverance of Amoret from the House of Busirane, to which we may compare the rescue of Anne Page from the House of Page and a loveless marriage. Both these episodes of Spenser's third Book follow a story of jealousy that to some degree parallels the aberration of Shakespeare's Master Ford. Spenser's Malbecco would "no straunge knight host, / For peeuish gealosie"; and Master Ford, likewise, is suspicious of Sir John Falstaff. Among the many husbands in literature jealous of friend or priest or courtier or wayfarer, Malbecco is a most likely prototype for the husband of Alice, the merry wife of Windsor. Both have money, "mucky pelfe," with which to bribe; both "watch warily," depending on locks and keys; and both are represented as "mad," Malbecco to

Legends of Friendship and Chastity
79

the point of deformity and Master Ford, the "peaking cornuto," "horn-mad," as a less abstract case of "lunatics" (3.10.54.5; 60.8; III.v.71-72, 156; IV.ii.130). However, Malbecco's suspicions were confirmed; Ford's jealousy debases only himself.

Malbecco's faithless wife, Hellenore, inhabited a forest haunted by "huge monsters." There in the "greene-wood" frequented by the "iolly Satyres" (cf. Herne the Hunter under his oak tree) Hellenore reigned as their "May-lady," garlanded and dancing "liuely." Dame Quickly in Windsor Park is also a mistress of ceremonies and indeed the very queen of fairies and satyrs and hobgoblins. Into such a situation came the "biggelooking" Braggadochio, his wily Trompart, and Malbecco, whose moneybags they were stalking. This resembles and may have suggested Falstaff's initial purpose of getting at Master Ford's moneybags and the collusion of Falstaff and Ford disguised as "Master Brook" to buy Falstaff's lewd services with a bag of money—"spend all I have!" "Want no money, Sir John. You shall want none."

> Now when amid the thickest woods they were,
> They heard a noyse of many bagpipes shrill,
> And shrieking Hububs them approaching nere,
> Which all the forrest did with horror fill:
> That dreadfull sound the boasters hart did thrill,
> With such amazement, that in haste he fled,
> Ne euer looked backe for good or ill,
> And after him eke fearefull Trompart sped;
> The old man could not fly, but fell to ground halfe ded.

This exciting kind of crisis in the forty-third stanza of Spenser's tenth canto reappears in the satyr drama enacted under Herne's Oak in Windsor Park. There, too, we hear the equivalent of Spenser's "shrieking Hububs," and we see Falstaff—but not the jealous Ford—on his face in dread of the satyr Evans, the hobgoblin Pistol, and the tormenting fairies.

The arrangement of abstractions in a situation to deplore both lust and jealousy is a fairly close allegorical picture of what came to be the necessary complication in Shakespeare's burlesque on lust and jealousy. Spenser considers jealousy to be dehumanizing. Malbecco, after further discouragements which do not concern us here, "forgot he was a man"; and lust also is unhuman, monstrous. Yet in both sad cases Shakespeare's comic genius has intervened. The cornuto, alias Master Brook, comes off more cheaply than did Malbecco from the devices of Braggadochio and Trompart and from his own self-torment; and as a braggart the monstrous Falstaff is spared, although he richly deserves, the kind of disgrace meted out to Braggadochio in the Book of Justice (5.3.37–38): his horse lost, his beard shaven, his shield reversed, his sword broken, his arms blotted out, and his armor "sperst." Sir John must surrender his horse: "He hath enjoyed nothing of Ford's but his buck basket, his cudgel, and twenty pounds of money which must be paid to Master Brook. His horses are arrested for it."[8] Instead of a shaven beard he will henceforth wear the muffler of Mother Prat, and instead of his broken sword he has been unforgettably supplied with the antlers of Herne the Hunter. Is it too much to say that the tenth canto of the Book of Chastity helped Shakespeare to the fifth act of *The Merry Wives?*

Shakespeare does not burden Mistress Ford with the character and fate of Hellenore. It is Dame Quickly who takes up the role of a May lady or "Queen of all the Fairies," originally intended for Nan Page by her mother (IV.iv.71). Meanwhile, thanks to this substitution, Nan will slip away to marry Master Fenton, the main action Shakespeare intends. In it Dame Quickly is the main agent: "This is my doing, now. 'Nay,' said I, 'will you cast away your child on a fool, and a physician? Look on Master Fenton.' This is my doing." She lends an ear, a willing palm, and

---

[8] The episode of the stolen horses Shakespeare evidently lacked time to articulate with the main plot of his farce.

Legends of Friendship and Chastity 81

a bit of encouragement to all three of Anne's suitors; but "speciously [especially]" for Master Fenton she is "as good as [her] word" (III.iv.99–102, 112–113). There seems little question that Shakespeare meant the ritual speeches in the last scene of the play to be spoken by her.

As a cause of laughter the Falstaff of *The Merry Wives* is far different from the Falstaff of *Henry IV*. He is not less shrewd in his roguery; but he is more aware that his behavior is vicious, more willful in the pursuit of his evil ends. He has mistaken the nature of good and evil and is properly enlightened as to his own stupidity. The justice of his escape with mere bucking, drubbing, and pinching we might question, were it not that the playwright spares him and us further embarrassment by hurrying us on to that other and main concern, the outwitting of the scheming parents, Meg and George Page. Their plan to force the affections of their daughter must be thwarted if we are to settle back into our proper selves. In the words of the happily and chastely married Fenton (V.v.233–243):

> Hear the truth of it.
> You would have married her most shamefully,
> Where there was no proportion held in love.
> The truth is, she and I (long since contracted)
> Are now so sure that nothing can dissolve us.
> Th' offence is holy that she hath committed,
>
> . . . . .
>
> Since therein she doth evitate and shun
> A thousand irreligious cursed hours
> Which forced marriage would have brought upon her.

This is a peripety beyond praise.

It is easy to hear these echoes of the antimask of the Book of Chastity in Shakespeare's version of a similar episode; but we should look a little deeper to recognize in his Act V a less ridiculous, even a more sobering, pattern: Windsor as the surrogate for royalty, Sir John as the travesty of knighthood, and the go-between Quickly as the burlesque of fairy queendom, even to her "floral charactery" of "Honi soit qui mal y pense." The playwright has given the "peaked cornuto" and the "dissembling knight" every chance to escape their morally proper end. That is his right as a comic poet. But each makes love to disaster and is only a shade more ludicrous than painful. Dame Quickly, however, he bolsters up into the purveyor of good doctrine and the doer of a good deed, and he redeems her with a right good will.

That he does intend good doctrine and redemption we may infer from speeches like the following. The "dissolute disease" of the Knight "will scarce obey this medicine"—cleansing in a buck basket—says Mistress Page (III.iii.204). "I would not ha' your distemper in this kind," says Page to Ford, "for the wealth of Windsor Castle" (III.iii.230–232). And, finally, we may be sure of the therapeutic metaphor at work in Shakespeare's mind for both *All's Well* and *The Merry Wives* when he permits the Host of the Garter to speak of parson and doctor as "soul-curer and body-curer" (III.i.100). In a previous play Falstaff has died cold from the feet up—"as cold as any stone"; but in the purgatorial afterlife of *The Merry Wives* he shows some signs of amendment (V.v.127–135):

And these are not fairies? I was three or four times in the thought they were not fairies; and yet the guiltiness of my mind, the sudden surprise of my powers, drove the grossness of the foppery into a receiv'd belief, in despite of the teeth of all rhyme and reason, that they were fairies. See now how wit may be made a Jack-a-Lent, when 'tis upon ill employment!

This disclosure, discovery, recognition, or epiphany—whatever term we prefer for the Greek *anagnorisis*—Sir John shares with us all, even though we are not too hopeful that his peripety will be "the decay of lust . . . through the realm" (V.v.152–153).

Legends of Friendship and Chastity 83

Whether *The Merry Wives* derives from an archetypal ritual or a self-conscious discipline, its playwright has driven the comic catharsis of the play as far as it can well go. This is the ultimate in comedies. It is good-by to the laughable Pistols, Bardolphs, Nyms, Quicklys, and Sir Johns of London tavern or Windsor Forest.[9] With an extravagant bow toward the everyday and holiday life of well-nigh irredeemable rogues and rascals, the playwright returns to that ethical realm where every hour is an "urgent hour," whether it strike on the plains of Troy, on the battlements of Elsinore, or in the prisons of Vienna.

[9] Watkins, p. 293, notes Henry J. Todd as mentioning a resemblance between Braggadochio and Falstaff, but he himself thinks that Braggadochio and Trompart are closer to Stephano and Trinculo.

CHAPTER V

Courtly Code and Dramatic Action

A DEPENDABLE study of dramatic form as Shakespeare understood it will consider the laws, rules, or codes (*nomoi*) in view of which the choices of his agents are made. Otherwise, analyses of character and conduct may disregard his purpose and hence misrepresent his action. For the court plays especially, where the costly reversal takes place in the formal, or what we should now call the professional, behavior of prince or courtier, we need detailed instruction about decorum from pertinent treatises. The one treatise most helpful in elucidating these court plays, *The Book of the Courtier*,[1] has again and again been cited to show that Shakespeare's persons illustrate ideas of courtliness; here, rather, we shall retrace Castiglione's argument as bearing

[1] Baldassare Castiglione, *Libro del Cortegiano* (Venice, 1528), tr. by Sir Thomas Hoby as *The Book of the Courtier* (London, 1561). References in my book are to the page numbers of the Everyman ed. (E. P. Dutton and Co., New York, 1928) with an introduction by W. H. D. Rouse, D. Litt., and critical notes by Professor W. B. Drayton Henderson. The spelling has been modernized in passages which I quote from Hoby's text.

Courtly Code and Dramatic Action 85

upon agents in an action. Interpreters of the Prince of Troy and the Prince of Denmark above all will find Hoby's translation of *Il Cortegiano* valuable for the light it sheds on dramatic form and on the correct meaning and value of the widely debated actions of these agents.

That Spenser knew *The Courtier* need not lead us to infer that Shakespeare knew it only through its echoes in *The Faerie Queene*. Such analogies with Spenser's poem as we shall point out in Chapters VI and VII (on *Troilus and Cressida* and on *Hamlet*) will be found qualitatively distinct. Troilus and Hamlet cannot be properly estimated in terms of a single source.

These two dramatic agents emerged at the same time from Shakespeare's experiments in playwriting; and, with their friends and ladies, they illustrate at its most artful that fabric of court life from which during the years 1600–1604 he was deriving images and situations and actions for his dramas of professional responsibility and crisis. His two princes, however, are not mere examples of a fairly well assimilated Italian code of manners and statecraft; what Shakespeare has done to make Troilus and Hamlet more than pawns in two familiar stories is to involve each young courtier in a particular discipline necessary for the education of a prince. Similarly, Cressida and Ophelia, the traditional wanton and the traditional forlorn maiden, are placed by the dramatist in a frame far different from that in which their destinies had earlier been set forth; their new function as ladies of the court explains much in their behavior that a group less sophisticated than the courtiers at Urbino might find strange, even reprehensible; their dramaturgic value to Shakespeare lies not so much in their personal quality, fair or flawed, as in their conformity or nonconformity to code.[2] In either play the hero-

[2] See Theodore Spencer, *Shakespeare and the Nature of Man* (New York, 1942), pp. 111–121: "In *Troilus and Cressida*, almost more elaborately than anywhere else, Shakespeare sets up a standard of conduct which the main action of the play violates. . . . [The play] describes in

ine is necessary to the courtly ordeal of the hero; she is his partner in a situation through which he must be made independent of her if he is to be what courtly auditors would not fail to recognize as the ideal prince in the ideal state.

That Troilus and Hamlet are courtiers Shakespeare himself does not allow us to forget. Pandarus represents Troilus to Cressida as the "prince of chivalry," seasoned with the "spice and salt" of courtiership; Agamemnon refers to the men of Troy as "ceremonious courtiers." Ophelia allows Hamlet "the courtier's, scholar's, soldier's, eye, tongue, sword"; and Claudius calls him "our chiefest courtier." The court where Helen prevailed in the Palace of Priam furnishes a setting for satire, Gertrude's court frames a tragedy; but courtly and princely conduct in either will be thwarted or abetted according to well-known rules by friends as conventionally varied in their excesses and defects as Paris and Aeneas in Troy and Laertes, Rosencrantz, Guildenstern, and Osric in Denmark. All these courtiers, and Troilus and Hamlet as well, are under continual ethical criticism from other agents; and in no previous plays of Shakespeare do we find young men counseled by mentors so persistently homiletic as Ulysses and Thersites among "the Grecian tents" or the Ghost and Polonius on the battlements and in the arras-hung chambers of Elsinore.

---

a new way the difference between man as he ought to be and man as he is." In the New Variorum ed. of *Troilus and Cressida*, ed. by H. N. Hillebrand and T. W. Baldwin (Philadelphia, 1953), pp. 539–540, the editors quote Spencer's passage; Professor Baldwin himself says (p. 388): "We still need to work out what might be called the Elizabethan interpretation of the classical characters." The only reference to *The Courtier* in the New Variorum ed. is quoted from W. B. Drayton Henderson, "Shakespeare's *Troilus and Cressida* Yet Deeper in Its Tradition," in *Essays in Dramatic Literature, The Parrott Presentation Volume*, ed. by Hardin Craig (Princeton University Press, 1935), p. 152. There Erasmus' *Praise of Folly* is classed with "Plutarch's *Lives*, Castiglione's *Book of the Courtier*, Machiavelli's *Prince* . . . , and, later, Montaigne's *Essays* in its usefulness to Shakespeare." Refer also to the discussion in Kenneth Burke's *A Rhetoric of Motives* (New York, 1950), pp. 221–233.

Shakespeare's action in *Troilus and Cressida* is to be a discipline in love and war for the womanish and impatient Prince of Troy, as Pandarus openly warns him: "He that will have a cake out of the wheat must needs tarry the grinding, . . . the bolting, . . . the leavening, . . . the kneading, the making of the cake, the heating of the oven, and the baking. Nay you must stay the cooling too, or you may chance to burn your lips" (I.i.15–26). Pandarus' gustatory figure becomes an explicit command from the shrewd Ulysses, "Patience . . . patience . . . patience." And before the first act of *Hamlet* is over, the soulsick and sententious Prince of Denmark learns that he is born to set right a "time" which, in the simple language of the repair man, "is out of joint" (I.v.189–190). This rarer action to be performed by either hero transcends Troilus' vengeance upon Diomedes and Hamlet's revenge for the murder of his father. Although its rich implications are easier to recognize than to trace to sources, it seems, at least, that Shakespeare must have breathed deep of whatever courtly doctrine was in the air.

In this chapter *Troilus and Cressida* and *Hamlet* are reviewed together in the light of *The Courtier*—chiefly its fourth book, where Bembo sets forth courtiership as a progress from sensual to reasoning love and from reasoning to understanding or angelic love. Our evidence will serve to substantiate further the assumptions of Professor W. B. Drayton Henderson and others, and it helps to explain the comment of Miss Spurgeon about Shakespeare's metaphors.[3] It is presented here, however, not so

---

[3] W. B. Drayton Henderson's note on Castiglione and English literature, which precedes the text of *The Courtier* in the Everyman ed., suggests that "without Castiglione we should not have Hamlet." He refers to Hamlet's "physical strength, courage, and comeliness" and to his skill in fencing as usual traits of "the perfect prince of the north"; and he indicates further that Hamlet's scholarship, knowledge of puns and jests, retorts courteous and discourteous, ironies, faith in friendship and skill in music, a "certain recklessness," and his reverence for womanhood are "peculiarly of Castiglione's school." See also Caroline F. E. Spurgeon, *Shakespeare's Imagery and What It Tells Us* (Cambridge University Press, 1935), p. 320: "*Troilus and Cressida* and *Hamlet* are very closely

much to delineate the courtiers in question or to annotate their words and images as to reveal one important device in Shakespeare's craftsmanship. His knowledge and conscious use of code permit him to intensify the respective ordeals of his two heroes and thus to enhance both plots for his sophisticated auditors, gentlemen of the Court and gentlemen of the Inns of Court.

Troilus and Cressida as Courtly Agents

The author of *The Courtier* not infrequently illustrates his points from the story of Troy. Out of the Trojan horse, he says, there never issued so many great men and captains as from Urbino. To support the exemplary conversations at the Italian court Ulysses is represented as Homer's model "in passions and sufferances"; Achilles, "in practices." Again, "the beauty of women is many times cause of infinite evils in the world, hatred, war, mortality, and destruction, whereof the razing of Troy can be a good witness." We are told that the Trojan resistance against the Greeks was prolonged by the help of the Trojan women; these were present at the arming of their lovers, watched them from the walls and towers, and rewarded them with their praise—all three womanly functions important in *Troilus and Cressida*.[4] But of the courtly woman more later.

When Sir Frederick Fregosa has won the approval of the Duchess of Gonzaga for a discussion of "the perfection of courtiership," Lord Cesar speaks of courtly grace as "a sauce to everything," and Count Lewis refers to it as honey. The comparison of courtiership to the pleasures of taste is frequent in the early pages of *The Courtier:* "Lovers sauce their sorrows with sweetness"; from "subtlety in writing" the reader "tasteth the

---

connected in their imagery." Miss Spurgeon's analysis of the metaphors of *Troilus and Cressida* shows them to be mainly gustatory; and Professor Richard D. Altick discusses *"Hamlet* and the Odor of Mortality" (*Sh.Quart.,* V [Spring, 1954], 167–176).

[4] *The Courtier,* tr. by Hoby, pp. 258, 299, 308, 234.

pleasure that consisteth in hard things"; musical accomplishment is like a "savor"; certain jests "must be seasoned" with deceit; the holy name of friendship is to be tasted; the kiss of a lover is "savory"; and in music "the *seasoning* of the whole must be *discretion*." [5]

The gustatory metaphor prevails also in *Troilus and Cressida*. So Pandarus describes to Cressida the savor or taste of Troilus (I.ii.273–278):

Why, have you any *discretion?* . . . Do you know what a man is? Is not birth, beauty, good shape, discourse, manhood, learning, gentleness, virtue, youth, liberality, and such-like, the spice and salt that *season* a man?

Castiglione had enumerated the traits of the courtier in wellnigh the same order: "nobleness of birth" (p. 33), "beauty of phisnomy" (p. 38), "a good shape" (p. 40), "manly activity" (p. 41), "a good grace . . . in speaking" (p. 49), "to speak and to write well" (p. 54), "a good scholar" (p. 45), "the knowledge and learning of virtue" (p. 68), "beside goodness . . . letters" (p. 68), [of Francis I] "liberality" (p. 68), "a gentle and loving behavior in his daily conversation" (p. 105). "Praise us as we are tasted," says Troilus hopefully to Cressida, for whom his "imaginary relish is so sweet / That it enchants [his] sense" (III.ii.98, 20–21). Their love, like the courtiership of Castiglione, is at first a matter of gusto; will gusto suffice?

In spite of his salt and spice, Prince Troilus has many of the flaws against which Castiglione warns the courtly lover. He does not well "dissemble his desires, jealousies, afflictions, and pleasures"; in talking to Cressida he "ruffle[s]" like a subtle rhetorician—witness his high-sounding similes (III.ii), mocked by Cressida with equal subtlety. For somewhat of sensual love the courtier is excused if it lead him to do worthy acts for the favor of his lady; but he must not brag or boast, as both Aeneas and

[5] *Ibid.*, pp. 29, 43, 45, 27, 51, 76, 102, 168, 120, 181, 102.

Troilus remind themselves. Troilus does brag, however; and in his behavior at the departure of Cressida with Diomedes he sorely and repeatedly transgresses the code:

Some . . . whensoever they have opportunity to speak with the woman they love, lament and bewail so bitterly, and covet many times things so impossible, that through their unreasonableness they are loathed of them. Other, if they be pricked with any jealousy, stomach the matter so grievously, that without stop they burst out in railing upon him they suspect, and otherwhile it is without trespass either of him, or yet of the woman. And will not have her speak with him, nor once turn her eyes on that side where he is. . . . Because the fear that a lover declareth to have otherwhile lest his lady forsake him for the other, betokeneth that he acknowledgeth himself inferior in deserts and prowess to the other.[6]

Except for the fact of her infidelity when the fortunes of war make her a reluctant collaborator, Cressida conforms to the lady whom those at Urbino would commend to the perfect lover. She is circumspect, discreet; she decorously considers whether she ought to accept or to feign ignorance of the love of Troilus. She lets herself be urged and has a touch of shyness; she listens unwillingly to Pandarus' insinuations about Helen. She is "not squeamish" and has a "ready liveliness of wit." Like the ideal lady of Urbino in Hoby's translation, Cressida displays "a tenderness, soft and mild, with a kind of womanly sweetness in every gesture of hers, that in going, standing, and speaking whatever she lusteth, may always make her appear a woman without any likeness of man." She might well seem to Troilus one of those courtly women "that in their countenance, in their speech, and in all their gestures have about them all handsomeness, all fair conditions, all knowledge, and all graces heaped

---

[6] *Ibid.*, pp. 248, 249, 250. This is the matter of Shakespeare's Act IV, scene iv. "Be thou but true of heart" pleads the "godly jealousy" of Troilus, calling his own merit in question. He cannot dance or sing or talk or play at subtle games, as can the Greeks.

Courtly Code and Dramatic Action 91

together like one flower made of all the excellencies in the world."⁷ In the first scene of the play he represents her as inciting love by "her eyes, her hair, her cheek, her gait, her voice, . . . her hand" and its "soft seizure."

We recall that the Chaucerian Criseyde, too, is womanly rather than mannish (I.282-287), has soft hands (III.72), and wins love by "her moving and her chere" (I.289). Chaucer could not say whether she failed to understand that Troilus loved her or whether she feigned ignorance—"oon of the tweye!" (I.492-494). One feint of the courtly woman he failed to mention; but we notice that Castiglione allows a woman who is "somewhat fatter or leaner than reasonable size, or wanner, or browner," to help herself as best she may;⁸ and the Shakespearean Pandarus, in referring to Cressida's hair as "somewhat darker than Helen's" and to Cressida as "fair" or not, echoes this permission: "She has the mends in her own hands."

Like the Lady Elizabeth Gonzaga and the Lady Emilia Pia at Urbino, Helen and Cressida are members of a group in which preoccupation with love is the important business of polite men and women—a situation keenly parodied by Shakespeare in the first scene of the third act of *Troilus and Cressida*. Witness the regnant Queen and her ladies, the elaborate compliments paid to them, their insistence on having their own way, and their warning that it is "a *sour* offence" "to make a *sweet* lady sad"; and witness chiefly the mock account of the generation of love, in which, as for certain jocose courtiers at Urbino, its origin is not celestial but earthly and hence to be likened to eating and the pleasures of taste.⁹

Granted that Troilus is a sensual lover and that Cressida is not,

---

⁷ *The Courtier*, pp. 190, 191, 189, 242-243. Ulysses to the contrary; but there were suspicious courtiers at Urbino as well.
⁸ *Ibid.*, p. 194.
⁹ The Chaucerian Criseyde and Antigone talk about love (II.877 ff.); and there is a Chaucerian hint for the origin of love: "They wenen al be love, if oon be hot!" (II.892).

as Hoby translates it, "too reverend and awesome," causing courtiers to turn from her to "garish and enticeful women"; granted even that she is one of those women "that with a sharpness of wit, and with art it seemeth in their beauty that they hide a thousand crafts"; [10] if we are to discover in Troilus any new vision or new power as the outcome of his courtly ordeal, we may profitably review the action of Book IV of *The Courtier*, where Bembo encourages the sensual lover to advance from sensual to reasonable, even to angelic, love (p. 303):

[From knowledge arises beauty, and love covets beauty.] And because in our soul there be three manner ways to know, namely, by sense, reason, and understanding: of sense, there ariseth appetite or longing, which is common to us with brute beasts; of reason ariseth election or choice, which is proper to man; of understanding, by the which man may be partner with *Angels*, ariseth will.

Again we are reminded of a distinction between medieval and Renaissance ideas of love in Shakespeare's sources. The native beauty of the Chaucerian Criseyde was "angelik" (I.102-105), but "it sit her naught to be celestial / As yit" (I.983-984); Chaucer makes only a twofold distinction in "love's hete": "celestial, or elles love of kinde" (I.979). A hint that Shakespeare may be thinking rather of the Neoplatonic pattern of a Bembo, and thus admitting the triple nature of love, occurs in Troilus' vivid gustatory phrase, "Love's thrice-repured nectar" (III.ii.23). As a courtier in love, he knows the parlance of such; but, like the courtiers at Urbino, he suspects that angelic love is a joy "too fine, / Too subtile-potent, tun'd too sharp in sweetness / For the capacity of [his] ruder powers" (III.ii.24-26); and thus he represents the sensual lover yet unable to achieve "understanding" in love; his proper action, winning the "cruel battle . . . within" him or, as Pandarus says, having "a cake out of the wheat" (I.i.3, 15), is to develop that "reason" ·vhence ariseth

[10] *The Courtier*, p. 242.

Courtly Code and Dramatic Action 93

election or choice. Where the Chaucerian Troilus was pathetic, the Shakespearean Troilus will be dramatic.[11]

To the sensual lover waiting in the orchard comes Pandarus with Cressida. The courtly dialogue about the fountain of their love, in which Cressida espies "more dregs than water" (III.ii. 72), parallels Master Bembo's discussion of angelic love and heavenly beauty, which makes us "*drunken* with the bottomless fountain of contentation . . . that giveth a *smack* of the right bliss unto whoso *drinketh* of the renewing and clear water thereof."[12] Cressida has recognized in Troilus, then, the lesser love of beauty that is "guided with the judgment of sense," so that the soul "falleth into most deep errors, and judgeth the body in which beauty is discerned to be the principal cause thereof." The resultant errors are either satiety or a "blind opinion" of contentment, "as the diseased . . . dream they drink of some clear spring, yet be they not satisfied."[13] Troilus has fallen into the second of these errors; Cressida's rebuke is in agreement with Bembo's advice to lay aside this "blind" judgment of the sense: "Blind fear that seeing reason leads [i.e., led by seeing reason], finds safer footing than blind reason stumbling without fear." Troilus reminds her that the only monstrosity in love is the inadequacy of execution to will, of act to desire;

---

[11] Another echo of Castiglione's angelic love as explained by Bembo comes from Aeneas when he arrogantly delivers the challenge to the Greeks (*Troilus and Cressida*, I.iii.233-239):

"Agamemnon: This Troyan scorns us; or the men of Troy
                Are ceremonious courtiers.
"Aeneas: Courtiers as free, as debonair, unarm'd,
                As bending angels. That's their fame in peace.
                But when they would seem soldiers, they have galls,
                Good arms, strong joints, true swords; and, Jove's accord,
                Nothing so full of heart."

[12] *The Courtier*, p. 322. Master Bembo permits a smack of the lips even to angelic love in the enjoyment of heavenly beauty.

[13] *Ibid.*, pp. 304-305.

and to her retort that vows are a hundredfold more perfect than is performance he opposes the promise of one yet confident of his kind of love. Bembo would say that, in his subjection of reason to desire, Troilus exemplifies a defect in courtliness. Pandarus and Cressida in the orchard scene (III.ii) consider him laughable, and in the tent scene (V.ii) he is for the same defect scorned by Ulysses and Thersites.

Throughout the play Cressida's eyes lead her heart (III.ii.74) and sway her mind (V.ii.104–110); even when she "taste[s]" her grief and cannot "brew" her affection "to a weak and colder palate" (IV.iv.3, 7), she performs clear-sightedly, shrewdly, reasonably. The "single famish'd kiss" of the lovers when she must go to the Greeks is "distasted with the salt of broken tears" by Troilus (IV.iv.49–50); but Cressida's "seeing reason" looks with two eyes and soon with one eye—"Ah! poor our sex" (V.ii.109)—will look on Diomedes. The strain put upon Troilus' sensual and Cressida's reasoning love by their impending separation is the main ordeal of Shakespeare's courtly action. Can sensual, even reasoning, love suffice the courtier?

The more skeptical courtiers at Urbino had no high opinion of the faith of a woman. Unico Aretino and the Lord Gaspar Pallavicin would not have been surprised at Cressida's surrender to things as they are. They would have shared her increasing irritation at the warnings of Troilus; they would have approved the enterprise of Diomedes; and they would have judged her behavior when "kiss'd in general" by the malapert Greeks (IV.v.21) as her part of the recommended merry device [14] which the courtly lady expects and disregards in offers of love. Not improbably they would advise her that Diomedes was the better man.

Along with his painful discovery that Cressida's faith is "o'er-

---

[14] *Ibid.*, p. 238. The Lord Julian concedes (p. 240) that "infinite women," coveting "nothing so much as to be beautiful, . . . do their best to win them as many [lovers] as they can."

Courtly Code and Dramatic Action 95

eaten," reduced to "greasy relics" (V.ii.156–160), Troilus is helped by Ulysses to a reversal. The hungry lover who at the beginning of the action could not "tarry the grinding" or the bolting, the leavening, the kneading, the making of the cake, the heating of the oven, the baking, the cooling (I.i.15–26), with Ulysses as interlocutor goes through the ordeal of Cressida's infidelity into a self-control dramatically effective just because it is so hard won (V.ii.36–115):

—You are moved, Prince. . . . I beseech you go.
—Behold, I pray you!
—Nay, good my lord, go off. . . .
—I prithee stay.
—You have not patience. Come.
—I pray you stay. . . . I will not speak a word!
. . . By Jove, I will be patient. . . .
—You shake, my lord, at something. Will you go? . . .
—Nay, stay. By Jove, I will not speak a word. . . .
—You have sworn patience. . . .
—I am all patience. . . .
—My lord!
—I will be patient; outwardly I will. . . .
I did swear patience. . . .
—All's done, my lord.
—It is.

In courtly terms this outward patience is "continence," not yet "temperance." If to the reader Troilus' passion, like the "extreme passion" that the courtier feels when he sees his beloved "cherishing and making of" another—as Hoby translates it (p. 254)—seems too swiftly and easily controlled by the reasons of Ulysses, nevertheless actors of even moderate skill and power would convince us that this scene is the peripety of Shakespeare's dramatic action. After the change in fortune, after Troilus learns that "still sweet love is food for fortune's tooth" (IV.v.293), he takes himself in hand. He submits his sensual love to the reasonable discipline of the older courtier, Ulysses; and he returns to his duties as a prince of Troy and a warrior. Surely this is what the dramatic poet intends.

Yet the Trojans are "incontinent" not only in love but also in statecraft and war. As Troilus is seduced by desire, so Paris is seduced by honor; together they prevail against the reasonings of Hector and the warnings of Helenus in the second scene of the second act; as a result Helen is not surrendered, and the war, which is, in Priam's words, a "cormorant" with a "hot digestion" (II.ii.6), proceeds to its disastrous end. On the contrary, in the Greek camp Ulysses attempts to overcome the jealousies of the younger warriors by his shrewd and reasonable policy. Shakespeare's delineation of these two kinds of captaincy illustrates the discussion of the Lords Octavian and Julian in Book IV of *The Courtier* (p. 271):

> Which . . . would you esteem the valianter captain, either he that hazardeth himself in open fight, and notwithstanding vanquisheth his enemies, or he that by his virtue and knowledge weakeneth them in bringing them in case not able to fight, and so without battle or any jeopardy discomfit them? [Cf. Achilles' tactics with Hector, and Diomedes' with Troilus.] . . . He . . . that overcometh with most surety. . . . Continency may be compared to a captain that fighteth manly, and though his enemies be strong and well appointed, yet giveth he them the overthrow, but for all that not without much ado and danger. But temperance free from all disquieting is like the captain that without resistance overcometh and reigneth. And having in the mind where she is, not only assuaged, but clean quenched the fire of greedy desire, *even as a good prince in civil war dispatcheth the seditious inward enemies, and giveth the sceptre and whole rule to reason,* so . . . maketh [the mind] quiet and full of rest, in every part equal and of good proportion.

Now Ulysses is to the Greek state what reason is to the man, and hence his services to Agamemnon and Achilles completely illustrate the political duty of the courtier and the rational end of his courtiership. First, a courtier must purchase the good will

Courtly Code and Dramatic Action

and favor of his prince "that he may break his mind to him, and always inform him frankly of the truth of every matter meet for him to understand, without fear or peril to displease him" (as Ulysses with Agamemnon). He must "dissuade him from every ill purpose" and try to "set him in the way of virtue" (as Ulysses with Achilles). He must have not only goodness but ready wit, pleasantness, wisdom, and knowledge in letters (witness the book from which Ulysses quotes to Achilles). He must recommend to his prince justice, liberality, courage, and meekness. Castiglione's courtier is thought of as a cunning doctor; he rewards and promotes the good and finds "wisely a *remedy*, and sometime with rigor, that the evil and seditious wax not great: the which thing is easier to be stopped before they come to it, than *to pluck them down again after they are once aloft*" (pp. 286–287). When the Shakespearean prince, Agamemnon, asks the Shakespearean courtier Ulysses "what is the *remedy*" for a discordant and unjust state, he receives a similar reply: "Ajax employ'd *plucks down* Achilles' *plumes*" (I.iii.386). Again, the courtier is a gardener seeing beautiful flowers and fruits spring daily in the mind of his prince (p. 273), but corrupt princes "sow debate and strife" (p. 278). Likewise, Ulysses fears the "seeded pride" of Achilles, which must be "cropp'd" ere, "shedding," it "breed a nursery of like evil" (I.iii.316–319).

Associated with Ulysses in the plan to unify the Greek forces is Nestor, whose frequent reference to his disabilities reminds us of Castiglione's old courtier, past his time for music, festivals, games, arms, and other personal accomplishments. The Shakespearean Patroclus and Achilles find him laughable; Lord Gaspar in *The Courtier* says, "Peradventure boys would mock" such a one "behind his back" (p. 302). With him, too, the gustatory metaphor is in evidence. He begins "to relish" the advice of Ulysses and "will give a taste of it forthwith / To Agamemnon" (I.iii.388–390). To Thersites he is a "stale old mouse-eaten dry cheese" (V.iv.11).

Again, is not Patroclus the foolish courtier (Thersites calls him "fool positive") who, finding himself in more than common favor, becomes intoxicated? Is Ajax the "very dolt" who, when favored, becomes grotesque? "Blockish" is an epithet used by both Hoby and Shakespeare—a fine hint for the shrewd inflating given Ajax by the other courtiers of Agamemnon and for the "pageant" of Ajax enacted by Thersites. Pandarus, with his turn for song (III.i.125-136), may well be the courtier of the lesser accomplishments or (pp. 265-266) one of

> those naughty and wicked courtiers that make their honest and pleasant manners and their good qualities a cloak for an ill end, and by mean[s] of them seek to come in favor with their princes for to corrupt them, and to cause them to stray from the way of virtue, and to lead them to vice.

And, finally, what of Thersites, whose speech is chiefly of bad tastes and diseased bodies? Is he not such an unappreciated frank philosopher as Castiglione sketches with irony (p. 264)?

> But in case a grave philosopher should come before any of our princes, or whoever beside, that would show them plainly and without any circumstance the horrible face of true virtue, and teach them good manners, and what the life of a good prince ought to be, I am assured *they would abhor him at the first sight, as a most venomous serpent, or else they would make him a laughing stock, as a most vile matter.*

The graces and flaws of such an array of courtiers Shakespeare might easily validate from his personal experience of men and women and affairs. But a treatise in which graces and flaws are related to a courtly code to be obeyed or disobeyed suggests choice, and choice brings on an ordeal, and an ordeal successfully undergone is the very working of a plot. *The Courtier*, then, would furnish a kind of dramatic propulsion helpful to the dramatist seeking agents for an ethical action within the old tale of the Trojan War. The Prince of Troy—and the Prince of Denmark in that other script Shakespeare was revising

—were courtiers. Let them play the dramatic game according to the very sternest rules of courtiership.

Hamlet as Courtly and Princely Agent

We have noted the tropes of Prince Troilus to be sensuous, with particular reference to the sense of taste. In what sort will Prince Hamlet's imagination work? At certain violent moments he refers to his mother and Claudius in unpleasantly sensual terms, but Hamlet is a poet or maker rather than a voluptuary. Adapting the pastime of Castiglione's courtier, likening people "to coffers, to stools," he compares himself to a carpenter making a mousetrap or a joiner obligated to set right an unjointed joint stool (I.v.189–190). This echoes one of the most significant metaphors in *The Courtier* (pp. 156, 277): "Therefore ought the prince not only to be good, but also to make others good, like the carpenter's square, that is not only straight and just itself, but also maketh straight and just whatsoever it is occupied about."

Given this theme (the prince as one who makes others good), let us trace Hamlet's attempts thus to repair the state. First, he will accept the responsibility of one to the manner born; he will not avoid the test of arms. Although of studious tastes, he has been "in continual practice" and is reputed eager to try his skill against Laertes. In this he runs true to courtly form, a trait used advantageously by the dramatist in persuading him to action. According to Castiglione (pp. 31–32, 35–36),

If a [gentleman] swerve from the steps of his ancestors, he staineth the name of his family. . . . Truth it is, whether it be through the favor of the stars or of nature, some there are born indued with . . . graces, . . . some . . . un*apt* and *dull*. . . . But to come to some particularity, I judge the principal and true profession of a courtier ought to be in feats of arms; . . . the *fame* of a gentleman that carrieth weapon, if it once take a *foil in any little point* . . . *doth* evermore continue *shameful* in the world.

The Ghost and Hamlet agree (I.v.31–32): "I find thee *apt;* / And *dull*er shouldst thou be. . . ." Also, we may compare the form of Castiglione's *"fame . . . foil in any little point . . . doth . . . shameful"* with that of the debated passage (I.iv. 36–38): "The dram of eale / Doth . . . scandal. . . ."

Secondly, Castiglione's doctrine of the will as regnant over reason and sense allows us to suggest that the invigoration of the Prince's will is the main reversal in the action of *Hamlet;* it arises out of the "understanding" of man as "partner with Angels" (p. 303). With this in mind, we can the more easily resolve the crux in the interpretation of Hamlet as man of thought versus man of action. Castiglione's "reason [of which] ariseth election or choice" is not the final accomplishment of a courtier. Witness Master Bembo's appeal for the knowledge that covets supersensual and superrational beauty. Nor is reason the final argument with Hamlet, for whom Claudius and Gertrude are two human illustrations of the merely reasonable. "You cannot speak of reason to [Claudius] the Dane / And lose your voice" (I.ii.43–45); Gertrude's will has been seduced by the witchcraft of wit (I.v.43–46), has been pandered by reason (III. iv.88); and even the philosophy of Horatio cannot content the Prince of Denmark, who ends his scholarly course in agreement with the Neoplatonic assumptions of Bembo. He distinguishes "thinking too precisely on the event" from "godlike reason" (IV.iv.38); he admires a "prince, / Whose spirit, with divine ambition puff'd, / Makes mouths at the invisible event" (IV.iv. 48–50); he defies "augury" and comes to believe in a "special providence," in an "ordinant" heaven (V.ii.230–235, 48)—in short, in "a divinity that shapes our ends, / Rough-hew them how we will" (V.ii.10–11). It is princely conclusions of this sort, angelic rather than human or brutish in Castiglione's triple scale, that arouse Prince Hamlet's princely "will"; and the tyrannicide that follows would be by Castiglione adjudged "so profitable to the world, that whoso doth it, deserveth a far greater

Courtly Code and Dramatic Action 101

reward, than whatsoever is meet for a mortal man" (pp. 289–290).

Throughout his effort to achieve "understanding" love Hamlet has been the richer for a friend; and Horatio is the pattern of friendship as the courtiers at Urbino understood it. "Without this perfect friendship, men were much more unlucky than all other living creatures"; Sir Frederick calls it "so great a *felicity*."[15] May this not be the felicity to which Hamlet refers in his last command as Prince of Denmark, his farewell words to his friend Horatio (V.ii.357–360)?

> If thou didst ever hold me in thy heart,
> Absent thee from *felicity* awhile,
> And in this harsh world draw thy breath in pain,
> To tell my story.

Finally, and chiefly, we come to the Shakespearean courtier as counselor. As Ulysses counsels the Greeks shrewdly, so for the Danes Hamlet illustrates, even beyond the duties of action and reason, that "understanding" love which prompts the advisory procedures of courtiership. A courtier must "dissuade [his prince] from every ill purpose" and "set him in the way of virtue"—attempted by Ulysses with Achilles and by Hamlet with Gertrude. He must have not only goodness but ready wit, pleasantness, wisdom, and knowledge in letters. Whereas Ulysses quotes to Achilles Castiglione's Neoplatonic doctrine of value and beauty (p. 261), Hamlet also comes into a difficult situation "reading on a book" (II.ii.193–207). The "words, words, words" read by Hamlet and curiously challenged by Polonius evidently describe old age, for the Prince translates his author into a slanderous vocabulary which he applies to the old courtier Polonius, with his grey beard, wrinkled face, thickening eyes, and weak hams. We recall from the beginning of

---

[15] *Ibid.*, p. 120. Cf. by contrast the sensual and unreasoning friendship of Achilles and Patroclus in *Troilus and Cressida;* in *Hamlet,* the extravagant Osric and the self-protecting Rosencrantz and Guildenstern.

Book II of *The Courtier* the discussion of old age, how old men "all of them commend the times past" or, as Hamlet says, "like a crab . . . go backward." After counseling Polonius as to the care of his daughter, Hamlet takes leave of him with the words, "These tedious old fools!" Castiglione takes leave of his discourse on old age as "perhaps too tedious" (pp. 86, 91).

What will an old courtier say to a young one? Castiglione turns from the discussion of old age to recommend that a gentleman is "not only to set his delight to have in him *self* parts and excellent qualities, but also to order the tenor of his life after such a trade, that the whole may be answerable unto these parts, and see the *self* same to be always and in every thing such, that it disagree not from it *self*." At the beginning of Act II Polonius will deliver into the ears of Laertes this same Stoic doctrine—to thine own *self* be true—along with other general rules for the courtier: Castiglione's lowliness, sober mood, little speaking, avoidance of curiosity [affectation], "handsome and cleanly" garments, "respect in the first beginning of . . . friendships."[16]

With his friends, too, Hamlet exercises the traditional privileges and duties of the courtier as counselor. Toward Rosencrantz and Guildenstern, until they deceive him, he exhibits what the courtly treatise would describe as "a familiar gentle

---

[16] *Ibid.*, pp. 94, 95, 117, 119. Another analogue is, of course, the one in Lyly's *Euphues*, ed. by M. W. Croll and H. Clemens (London, 1916), pp. 13–17.

Readers interested in Shakespeare's Polonius should note the similar procedure of Sir Frederick in *The Courtier:*

"Afterward let him consider *what* the thing is he doth or speaketh, *the place where* it is done, in presence of *whom,* in *what time, the cause why* he doth it, his *age,* his profession, the end whereto it tendeth, and the *means* that may bring him to it: *and let him apply* himself *discreetly* with these advertisements to whatsoever he mindeth to do or speak."

"What . . . how . . . who . . . what means . . . where . . . wherefore . . . and let him ply his music" is Polonius' instruction to Reynaldo at the beginning of the second act. In the same vein he expostulates for Gertrude "What majesty should be, what duty is, / Why day is day . . ." (II.ii.87–89). When at her request he abandons his "foolish fig-

Courtly Code and Dramatic Action

behavior, with a soft and lovely kindness"; and to the players, for whom he quotes Sir Frederick's advice to the musicians—"The seasoning of the whole must be discretion"—he gives highly technical suggestions about diction, gesture, and bearing, similar to these parts of the doctrine of Count Lewis of Canossa (pp. 288, 102, 56–57):

A good voice, not too subtle or soft . . . nor yet so boisterous and rough, as in one of the country, but shrill, clear, sweet and *well framed with a prompt pronunciation,* and with fit manners, and gestures, which . . . consist in certain motions of all the body, *not affected nor forced, but tempered* with a mannerly countenance and with a moving of the eyes that may give a grace and *accord with the words,* and . . . signify also with gestures, the intent and affection of the speaker. But all these things were in vain and of small account, if the sentences expressed by the words should not be fair, witty, subtle, fine and grave *according to the matter.*

Again, it is as vital to Hamlet as to Laertes and Polonius that Ophelia be protected and her affections strictly reserved; in the numerous references to flowers which adorn her own speech, the counsel given her, and the sorrow of her disasters, we catch the accents of Castiglione's courtier as gardener. Hamlet himself warns her that "virtue cannot so inoculate our old stock but we shall relish of it." Yet the pales and forts of reason around a maiden's garden are necessarily less important to the Prince than the weeding of the royal garden of Denmark's Queen, the garden "that grows to seed" (I.ii.135–136). For this task he sorely needs to show understanding love, as the ghost of his father reminds him. Gertrude was by her dead husband's counsel re-

---

ure[s]" to talk less artfully of "the very cause" of Hamlet's madness, he still talks in the courtly phrases of a Sir Frederick at Urbino about

"*the cause* of this effect—
Or rather . . . *the cause* of this defect,
For this effect defective comes by *cause* [II.ii.101–103]."

Previously he has learned from Ophelia the "*time,* . . . *means,* and *place*" of Hamlet's solicitings (II.ii.127).

manded "to those thorns that in her bosom lodge / To *prick* and sting her" (I.v.87–88); in Hoby's words, "the woman must needs have always the remorse and *pricking* that is had of unlawful matters" (p. 239). By the same figure her son teaches her how the old courtier will resist sensual love, bids her "not spread the compost on the weeds / To make them ranker" (III.iv.151–152).

In its diction *Hamlet* is one long mixed metaphor, but the figures that emerge most consistently are those of the gardener and of the repair man, be he bonesetter, surgeon, or carpenter. These productive functions of the Prince of Denmark are strongly distinguished from the merely sensual preoccupations of the impatient Troilus, Prince of Troy. Also, Shakespeare's presentation of the diseases and corruptions of Trojan and Greek policy is distinct from his presentation of the culture of Denmark and the repair of the Danish state. Yet *Hamlet*, like *Troilus and Cressida*, reveals a wide familiarity with courtly procedures. The playwright's dramatic action is based squarely on the code of the courtier.

And in his aims, too, Shakespeare's Hamlet fully illustrates those furthest reaches of influential courtiership where the "goodly frames" with which artists and poets and princes of the Renaissance were so deeply concerned might be kept fair or made fair. In this view, the second quarto of *Hamlet* accomplishes what *Troilus and Cressida* could only predict. The familiar and signal passage from *The Courtier*, Book IV, may be quoted again here. Master Peter Bembo argues that "beauty is always good" and asks us to

> behold . . . this great Ingin of the world, . . . the heaven round beset with so many heavenly lights, . . . the earth environed with the elements, . . . the sun, . . . the moon, . . . the other five stars. . . . These things among themselves have such force by the knitting together of an order so necessarily framed, that with altering them any one jot, they should be all loosed, and the world would decay.

Courtly Code and Dramatic Action

... Think now of the shape of man ... necessarily framed by art and not by hap, and then the form altogether most beautiful. ... The like may be said of all other living creatures. ... Leave nature, and come to art. ... In conclusion this comely and holy beauty is a wondrous setting out of every thing.[17]

Few readers of both *The Courtier* and *Hamlet* would fail to associate this noble expression of a traditional theme with Hamlet's effort to lift himself above sensual preoccupation and thereby to cure himself of a distaste for earth, its "majestical roof fretted with golden fire," and for the men and women who inhabit it.

In short, within all his figures of speech, throughout all his dealing with himself, his friends, Ophelia, his mother, his time out of joint, Hamlet has sought to learn and to use Master Bembo's third kind of knowledge, "understanding, by the which man may be partner with Angels, [and] of which ariseth will"; and when at last his noble heart has cracked in the service of his invigorated will, his friend Horatio invokes "flights of angels" to sing him to his rest and carries the instructions of the Prince of Denmark to the Prince of Norway. Succeeding to Hamlet's principality, Fortinbras acknowledges the completion of the princely action (V.ii.406–409):

> Let four captains
> Bear Hamlet like a soldier to the stage;
> For he was likely, had he been put on,
> To have prov'd most royally.

[17] *The Courtier*, pp. 308–310. Cf. also Henderson's note on Castiglione and English literature.

CHAPTER VI

The Palace of Priam as a Bowre of Blisse

THAT *All's Well* and *The Merry Wives* had been before Shakespeare turned to the matter of Troy is a likely assumption. In scene they are provincial and in theme domestic. Neither concerns itself with well-known mythical or historical figures. Neither has demanded from the playwright careful treatment of a time-hallowed legend or examination of various possible sources and analogues. Neither has been grandly framed in reference to the weighty affairs of great states. *Troilus and Cressida*, on the other hand, would invite comparison with Chaucer's *Troilus and Criseyde* and other scarcely less familiar epic, dramatic, or romantic versions of the mighty Trojan War. Like *Hamlet*, with which also Shakespeare was challenging tradition, it required a powerful new synthesis of events, freshly accented, and, even more important, its agents must be conceived anew in a mode that would relate them to current problems in the contemporary world. All these difficulties of the playwright evoked the inmost energies of the artist. Here was a dramaturgic crisis comparable with the *agon* of antiquity.

Before we investigate the structure of *Troilus and Cressida* in the light of *The Faerie Queene*, we may briefly review the outline of its plot.

"In Troy there lies the scene." As if to match this unity of place in *Troilus and Cressida*, Shakespeare's plot is also unified. His Prologue tells us clearly that the Greeks have made a "vow . . . to ransack Troy"; and, when Hector falls under the strokes of the Myrmidons, Achilles cries out, "Now, Troy, sink down! / Here lies thy heart, thy sinews, and thy bone." Although we do not witness the final ruin of King Priam's "six-gated city," we share Agamemnon's belief that the death of Hector, allowed by the gods, indicates an action successfully concluded: "Great Troy is ours, and our sharp wars are ended." Moreover, in his prayer to these same gods Prince Troilus himself acknowledges Trojan defeat: "Smite all Troy . . . at once! / And linger not our sure destructions on!"

Since this outer action of *Troilus and Cressida* is explicit and vertebrate, disapproval of the play as confused or inconclusive [1] would seem to call in question Shakespeare's inner action, his management of the persons of the play. Is their behavior properly motivated, and is it justifiably and fruitfully rewarded or rebuked? "The rarer action," says Prospero, "is / In virtue than in vengeance." [2]

So elaborate a picture of treason and folly serves its action best when we are put in mind of high purposes misdirected and powerful energies misapplied. Therefore we must analyze the

---

[1] In his "Order out of Chaos in Shakespeare's *Troilus and Cressida*," *Tulane Studies in English*, IV (1954), 45–56, Professor George Wilbur Meyer particularizes such estimates of the play and argues that *"Troilus and Cressida*, as a whole and in its several parts, has unity and meaning that are nowhere more apparent than in its supposedly inconclusive ending. . . . Shakespeare presented to his audience certain lessons about war and sex, or sex and war, which, in the light of our own recent experience, might be said to have universal application."

[2] *The Tempest*, V.i.27–28.

ethical fabric out of which the play is fashioned to find its prevailing scheme of virtues and vices. To plot action as Shakespeare understood action when he was initiating his dramas of professional [3] crisis the playwright needed a contemporary pattern of responsible choices which, if they were to be approved or disapproved, must defer to or deviate from the accredited official or courtly code—even if not the actual behavior—of the sixteenth century. Just as the heroic incentives of Homer's agents were not in keeping with Chaucer's literary purposes for *Troilus and Criseyde*, so the Fate and Fortune of medieval chivalry would not suffice for Shakespeare's dramatization of the tale of Troy. Rather he must depend upon such rules of the dedicated life as poets of the Renaissance offered for the edification of its princes, warriors, and courtiers. In chief, he might avail himself of the "fierce warres and faithfull loues" of *The Faerie Queene*. This allegorical poem supplied not only a code but an ample, rich, and vivid iconograph for all likely dramatic persons in all likely dramatic situations.

In trying to substantiate this premise, we shall consider the "rarer," or ethical action of *Troilus and Cressida* to be an illustration of the ordeal and triumph of Gloriana's knight, Sir Guyon, in Spenser's Book of Temperance.[4] When separated

---

[3] As used here the adjective "professional" refers to the career of a responsible agent following a strict code toward a goal approved by his fellows and important for the common good. It betokens what C. S. Lewis calls "the Virgilian sense of Vocation" (*A Preface to "Paradise Lost"* [Oxford University Press, 1952], p. 35). It suggests the agent who is "a public man," as Una Ellis-Fermor terms him ("The Universe of *Troilus and Cressida*, *The Frontiers of Drama* [Oxford University Press, 1946], p. 14), or who understands and maintains the "Social Values" which W. B. Drayton Henderson considers imperiled in this play ("Shakespeare's *Troilus and Cressida* Yet Deeper in Its Tradition").

[4] Sir Guyon is prototype for Hamlet also, as illustrated in the following chapter. Watkins, in *Shakespeare and Spenser*, p. 20, associates Troilus and Cymochles; Whitaker, in *Shakespeare's Use of Learning*, p. 179, associates Troilus and Sir Guyon.

Palace of Priam as a Bowre of Blisse

from the Palmer Reason, Sir Guyon went astray with Phaedria on the Idle Lake, wandered into "Plutoes griesly raine" (2.7.21.4), where he was hard pressed by Mammon and his daughter Philotime (Love of Honor), and swooned on the brink of earth and air, between hell and heaven. Here, in deadly peril, he was rescued by the Palmer Reason at the behest of a flying pursuivant from God; and with this divine and rational help he made ready to overthrow the Bowre of Blisse.

If with Sir Guyon now in mind we review the ordeal of Prince Troilus, we find him also enticed from his martial duty, and by a Cressida very like Phaedria. He also emerges with difficulty, and with repeated mention of Pluto, from his hell in the shadows near the tent of the opportunist Calchas and his opportunist daughter. For the discovery at this point the dramatist again makes use of a situation he has already adapted—so scholars assume—from the Book of Temperance for *Much Ado*.[5] Spenser had placed his Phedon "in a secret corner" as "sad spectatour of [the alleged] Tragedie" (2.4.27.5–6), the infidelity of his lady. Shakespeare placed Claudio in a secret corner as spectator of Hero's alleged infidelity. There was still opportunity for dramatic effect in that device, and Shakespeare would now place Troilus in a secret corner as spectator of Cressida's infidelity. Phedon's "tormenting grief," the "wide" speaking of Claudio, and the "passion" of Troilus would be comparable; but Phedon's murderous rage and Claudio's injudicious cruelty might now be tempered into Troilus' hard-won "patience."

Especially pertinent for this new maker of an old plot was the way in which Sir Guyon had successfully concluded his ordeal, with the help of the Palmer Reason. Shakespeare in his turn would appoint the shrewd and rational Ulysses as mentor, not only for the Greek Achilles, but also for the Trojan Troilus.

---

[5] See Abbie F. Potts, "Spenserian Courtesy and Temperance in *Much Ado about Nothing*," pp. 103–111, 126–133, or Ch. II of this book.

During the "strange . . . fight . . . within [the] soul" of the disillusioned lover, it is Ulysses who recommends patience, bids the young Prince contain himself, and brings him "to the gates," comparable to "the gates of Pluto" (2.7.24.1) in the Spenserian allegory. And when finally Troilus as lover renounces Cressida, his "revolted fair," and dismisses Pandarus, his "broker lackey," he has accomplished a reversal in the manner of a Guyon, who learned to suspect and to resist the delightful but capricious Phaedria, was able to refuse the bribes of Mammon and Philotime, and disarmed "Pleasure's porter" at the ivory gate of Acrasia's garden. Finally, again like Sir Guyon, disciple of the valiant Prince Arthur, Troilus determines to rejoin the mighty Prince Hector on the field of battle. This dutiful change in his behavior after his personally bitter revelation is framed in quasi-Spenserian military ethic and enlivened by quasi-Spenserian martial imagery. For instance, as the deformed creatures taming "fiers Vulcans rage" (2.7.36.5) in the furnaces of Mammon had dismayed but did not daunt Sir Guyon, so Prince Troilus will not be daunted by Diomedes' helm (V.ii.170–171):

> Were it a casque compos'd by Vulcan's skill,
> My sword should bite it.

In *Troilus and Cressida* the Trojan Prince engages but does not defeat the Greek Diomedes; but that other less than temperate son of Priam, Hector, brings himself and Troy to grief when he is deflected from battle by his avaricious theft of "goodly armour." This incident reminds us of Mammon's offering to finance Guyon's "delight" in "faire shields, gay steedes, bright armes" (2.7.10.8). It would seem that the sons of Priam, Paris and Troilus and even the great Hector, have been initially and thoroughly seduced by the bribe of Philotime, Mammon's daughter, from whom alone "Honour and dignitie . . . / Deriued are" (2.7.48.7–8). Troilus echoes Mammon (II.ii.199):

Palace of Priam as a Bowre of Blisse

"[Helen] is a theme of honour and renown." Paris, describing Helen as her "whom . . . / The world's large spaces cannot parallel" (II.ii.162), echoes Mammon's praise of his daughter as "The fairest wight that wonneth vnder skye" (2.7.49.2). Moreover, the great Hector in yielding to his "sprightly brethren" in this same scene—

> For 't is a cause that hath no mean dependence
> Upon our joint and several dignities

—may be thinking of Philotime's "great gold chaine ylincked well" (2.7.46.2-9),

> Whose vpper end to highest heauen was knit,
> And lower part did reach to lowest Hell;
> . . . . .
> And euery lincke thereof a step of dignity.

The bribes of Mammon and his daughter Philotime would be no less effective in the dramatic economy of *Troilus and Cressida* than the stratagem of Philemon proved in *Much Ado*. Along Philotime's chain from heaven to hell Shakespeare reduces those Trojans for whom love of honor is the prime and ultimate theme. Obviously he intended the timocratic speeches in the second scene of his second act to suggest the deformity or flaw in Trojan polity. Above all, he would be encouraged to associate with his own study of intemperance that most hellish bribe in the Spenserian "Gardin of Proserpina," the "famous golden Apple" (2.7.55.4, 6-9)

> For which th' Idaean Ladies disagreed,
> Till partiall Paris dempt it Venus dew,
> And had of her, faire Helen for his meed,
> That many noble Greekes and Troians made to bleed.

Along with such general analogies in action we wish to furnish even more substantial evidence that Shakespeare designed not only a satire on the fashions of the day [6] or a challenging illustration of the code of the courtier [7] but primarily a dramatic equivalent for what in Book II of *The Faerie Queene* was a descriptive chart or map for temperate behavior and an album of temperate and intemperate characters. When thus tentatively invoked, Spenser's agents give authority and direction to Shakespeare's dramatis personae; they seem also to lend them doctrine and language and appearance. The hero and heroine of *Troilus and Cressida*, their associates in Priam's palace, and their foes outside the walls of Troy have absorbed many of the traits of Guyon and his abstractly virtuous allies and vicious enemies. Hector in his fair aspect would be a Prince Arthur defending the House of Alma. Paris and Troilus are comparable to Spenser's Pyrochles and Cymochles; they are seduced by two women, Helen and Cressida, comparable to Acrasia and Phaedria. As a result, the enemies of Troy gain a critical advantage. More vitally than in an allegorical poem—even *The Faerie Queene*—and more sensitively than in wormwood comedies such as Jonson's *Cynthia's Revels* and *Poetaster*, the author of *Troilus and Cressida* has related the follies, vices, and errors of lovers and warriors to the moral dignity and safety of the state itself.

Indeed, the timocracy preoccupied with keeping Helen in the Palace of Priam and the enfeebled and schismatic aristocracy led by Agamemnon on the windy plains of Troy are both akin to and might have been modeled after the brutalized, quarrelsome minions of Acrasia, those "seeming beasts" who met the "sad end . . . of life intemperate." Even when these were struck by the "vertuous staffe" of the Palmer Reason and "returned . . . vnto their former state, . . . / Yet being men they did vnmanly looke" (2.12.85.1, 6; 86.1–3). Witness likewise Shakespeare's

---

[6] See Oscar J. Campbell, *Comicall Satyre and Shakespeare's "Troilus and Cressida"* (San Marino, Calif., 1938) and Abbie F. Potts, "*Cynthia's Revels, Poetaster*, and *Troilus and Cressida*," pp. 297–302.

[7] See Ch. V of this book, pp. 84–105.

"bull," "ass," "ox," Menelaus; his "mongrel beef-witted lord" Ajax, "peacock," "cur," "ass," "camel," "draught-ox," "lion," "bear," "elephant"; Ulysses, the "dog-fox"; Achilles, the "lion," "camel," "elephant," and "whoreson dog"; Patroclus, the "brach," "finch egg," and "water fly"; that "Brabbler the hound" Diomed, leering as "a serpent hisses"; and that "porpentine," "raven," and "vile owl," Thersites. Witness also Paris and Troilus, in whom pleasure and revenge have "ears more deaf than adders"—Paris, a bear "besotted" on his "honey," and Troilus, who, like Spenser's Grill with "hoggish mind," wishes to "wallow in the lily beds." And, finally, witness the merrily singing "humblebee" Pandarus, for whom in Shakespeare's epilogue "sweet honey and sweet notes together fail."

Helen, Cressida, Paris, and Troilus are the Shakespearean agents whose personal traits and dramatic functions are most profitably studied in comparison with the languorous Acrasia and her servants and victims, the scintillating Phaedria—glamor girl to us—Pyrochles, symbol of firelike intemperance, and Cymochles, symbol of wavelike intemperance.

In Paris, most completely enslaved by Helen, we may discover traits of Spenser's Atin, with his device of "a flaming fire in midst of bloudy field"—"burnt I do burne"—and Furor, whose mother, Occasion, "brought to him a flaming fire brond" (2.5. 22.5–6). But the best Spenserian prototype for Paris is Pyrochles himself: "I burne, I burne, I burne. . . . / O how I burne with implacable fire" (2.6.44.1–2). These Pyrochlean traits of Paris are most clearly announced in the premonitory speech of his sister Cassandra (II.ii.110–112):

> Our firebrand brother Paris burns us all.
> Cry, Troyans, cry! A Helen and a woe!
> Cry, cry! Troy burns, or else let Helen go.

Consider also Paris' own declaration of the nature of love (III. i.139–142):

He eats nothing but doves, love, and that breeds hot blood, and hot blood begets hot thoughts, and hot thoughts beget hot deeds, and hot deeds is love.

Cymochles, so "Famous throughout the world for warlike prayse" (2.5.26.2) yet the victim of the "Enchaunteresse" Acrasia, is the prototype of Troilus, in the epithets of Ulysses a "true knight . . . matchless . . . firm . . . manly," yet by his own confession "weaker than a woman's tear." The "Arber greene" (2.5.28 ff.) in which Cymochles sojourned may be compared with the orchard (III.ii) where Troilus awaits Cressida. Its "gentle streame" anticipates both the Jonsonian "Fountayne of Self-love" in *Cynthia's Revels* and the "fountain of our love" in Shakespeare's *Troilus and Cressida;* in it are "more dregs than water." The "sweet bed of lillies" on which Cymochles was laid lends its deceptive beauty to Troilus' wish to "wallow in the lily beds / Propos'd for the deserver." And Spenser's Atin coming to arouse Cymochles with the taunt, "Up, up, thou womanish weake knight!" gives point to the passage in the first scene of the first act where Aeneas shames Troilus into an apology for his "woman's answer . . . / For womanish it is to be from thence." Above all, Cymochles (Greek κῦμα, wave) may have suggested to Shakespeare the marine metaphors that characterize Troilus' diction. Cymochles waded "in still waves of deepe delight, . . . dround" in "ioyes"; the hopes of Troilus lie "drown'd, . . . in . . . many fadoms deep . . . indrench'd." Furthermore, Troilus admits (I.i; II.ii) that he is separated from Cressida by "a wild and wand'ring flood"; his "eyes and ears" are

> Two traded pilots 'twixt the dangerous shores
> Of will and judgment.

Before his disillusionment he "stays for waftage" upon Stygian banks and begs for "swift transportance." But, once he knows the worst, he compares his sword, lifted for vengeance upon

Palace of Priam as a Bowre of Blisse 115

Diomedes, to "the dreadful spout / Which shipmen do the hurricano call." Finally, again in the field, he will "swim after" Diomedes even across the river Styx.[8] Indeed, water is the element of both Cymochles and Troilus, two ectypal agents in the same fluent archetypal pattern. We observe, however, that, whereas in the early scenes the hero "stays for waftage," in the end he makes ready to "swim."

Over the seas and shoals of passion Phaedria's little gondelay, "as swift as glaunce of eye" (2.6.2.5–6), is one likely original for the bark Troilus begs for conveyance to his "lily beds." Phaedria's task of going between and between is reserved for Pandarus; but Cressida herself, as we come to know her through the dialogue with Pandarus at her first appearance, is endowed with the "vaine iolliment," the "scoffing game," and the "fantasticke wit" of a Phaedria (2.6.3.9; 6.9; 7.2). In the orchard scene with Troilus (III.ii) she is less immodest than Phaedria; yet her repeated invitation to walk in, her provocations, blushes, enticements, her thoughts "like unbridled children," her seeming to beg a kiss, her confessed "craft," are qualified from the "light behaviour, and loose dalliaunce" of a Phaedria. "Prithee tarry. / You men will never tarry," begs Cressida when Troilus must leave her (IV.ii.15–16). When Sir Guyon resisted Phaedria's attempt to "withdraw [him] from thought of warlike enterprize," she "euer bad him stay." Troilus' anger on his way "to the port" where he must transfer Cressida to Diomedes, Cymochles marching "to the strond" where he raged to find Phaedria with Sir Guyon—both give us almost identical illustrations of the jealousy of knighthood. For Cressida's inconstancy in the scene witnessed by Troilus and Ulysses the fashion had been set by the mutable behavior, with Guyon and the Palmer Reason, of Phaedria, now attempting to allure them and

---

[8] Twice in the play Troilus imagines himself definitely in hell: here (V.iv.20–21) and earlier—and less resolutely—"upon the Stygian banks, / Staying for waftage" (III.ii.10–11).

finally disregarding them altogether. On their way to the Bowre of Blisse (2.12.20–22) Guyon and Reason proceeded over the quicksands to the Whirlpoole of decay, whose "surging waters like a mountaine rise," driven on by "wrathfull Neptune." The sword of the regenerate Troilus will be lifted over Diomedes' head like the "dreadful spout / Which shipmen do the hurricano call," and its descent likewise shall "dizzy . . . Neptune's ear" with clamor.

But it is the languorous Helen rather than the mutable Cressida who in Shakespeare's play most memorably bodies forth the enchanting, entangling, and enervating influence of wantons like Acrasia upon otherwise gallant warriors. Granted that Spenser's Bowre of Blisse and the Palace of Priam as Shakespeare represents it in *Troilus and Cressida* are only two out of numerous literary instances of a continuing archetypal situation, Helen's purlieus constitute no mere analogue of the Bowre of Blisse. All the particulars of her scene have a definite literary provenance, courtly or Jonsonian or Spenserian. When in Act III, scene i, the Servant admits Pandarus to the accompaniment of "good broken music," we are reminded of the Genius of the Bowre of Blisse, "deuizd to bee" Pleasure's porter (2.12.47 and 48); and the music itself echoes from Spenser's "musicke . . . consorted in one harmonee" (2.12.70.6–8). The song sung in the Bowre to urge the doctrine of *carpe diem*—"Gather the Rose of loue, whilest yet is time"—becomes Pandarus' song of "Love, love, nothing but love, still more." And when Paris confesses (III.i.148–150) that he "would fain have arm'd today, but my Nell would not have it so," he avows himself another like the victim of Acrasia (2.12.80), the knight whose

> warlike armes, the idle instruments
> Of sleeping praise, were hong vpon a tree,
> And his braue shield, full of old moniments,
> Was fowly ra'st, that none the signes might see;
> Ne for them, ne for honour cared hee,

Palace of Priam as a Bowre of Blisse

>Ne ought, that did to his aduancement tend,
>But in lewd loues, and wastfull luxuree,
>His dayes, his goods, his bodie he did spend:
>O horrible enchantment, that him so did blend.

Particular phrases in the amorous speeches of Pandarus and Helen sound like further echoes from the Bowre of Blisse. The "sweet words, dropping like honny dew" of the Bowre (2.5.33.4) can be heard again in Pandarus' "sweet queen, ... sweet queen, sweet queen! That's a sweet queen, i' faith! ... What says my sweet queen, my very very sweet queen? ... Now, sweet queen ... sweet queen ... Farewell, sweet queen. ... I will, sweet queen." This is the sweetness *ad nauseam* that underlines Shakespeare's satiric modifications of Spenserian—indeed of any typically romantic—beauty. And when Helen calls Pandarus "honey-sweet lord" and he calls her "honey-sweet queen," from Shakespeare's ridicule we gain an even greater respect for temperance than comes from Spenser's more alluring portraiture.

As with honied words, so with snaky glances. The Spenserian wanton as an "Adder, lurking in the weedes" of the Bowre of Blisse to feed "his fraile eye with spoyle of beautie" (2.5.34), is amplified by the Shakespearean Pandarus into a whole "generation of vipers." And yet, for all this ridicule of honey and venom—or possibly because of it—Paris and Helen are more salutary than are the Spenserian abstractions.

But Paris and Helen are themselves incurable; and Cressida, like Phaedria, chooses "present pleasures" (2.6.17.9). Shakespeare spends his redemptive skill rather on Prince Troilus, who is bidden to undergo an ordeal similar to that of Sir Guyon on his journey through the "desert wildernesse" to "Plutoes griesly raine." [9] The seventh canto of the Book of Temperance seems

---

[9] The *Concordance* indicates that more of Shakespeare's references to Pluto occur in *Troilus and Cressida* than in any other play. Plutonian associations are also suggested in II.i.36–37, when Thersites says to Ajax:

to be one possible source of the imagery of Act IV, scene iv, and Act V, scene ii, where the change in Troilus' fortune leads to the main discovery of the romantic action of the play. Throughout these two scenes the metaphors are Plutonian. Troilus, who had in the second scene of the third act represented himself to be "like a strange soul upon the Stygian banks," now describes his loss in terms reminiscent of the Cave of Mammon (IV.iv.41–45):

> We two that with so many thousand sighs
> Did *buy* each other, must poorly *sell* ourselves
> With the rude brevity and discharge of one.
> Injurious Time now *with a robber's haste*
> *Crams his rich thiev'ry up*, he knows not how.

And Diomedes, prospective guardian of Cressida, the treasure to be surrendered by Troilus at the port, is such a one as Spenser's Disdaine, "a sturdy villein, striding stiffe and bold" and threatening "batteill" to Sir Guyon at the "broad gate, all built of beaten gold" (2.7.40–52). In the "brave" of Diomedes, in Troilus' oath "by the dreadful Pluto" to cut Diomedes' throat if Cressida be ill used—indeed throughout the scenes where the lovers face separation—the hate, sorrow, and jealousy of the Trojan Prince, his lust for revenge and his fear of treachery, are human traits comparable to those Spenserian abstractions who lie "before the gates of Pluto": Payne, Strife, Reuenge, Despight, Treason, Hate, gnawing Gealosie, Feare, Sorrow, Shame, and Horror.

Now, there was "but a litle stride" between Hell-gate and the Cave of Mammon. Sir Guyon avoided Hell-gate, but once within the Cave he noticed several scenic details later to be appropriated by Shakespeare from Spenser or Spenser's Italian and

---

"Thou art as full of envy at [Achilles'] greatness as Cerberus is at Proserpina's beauty." And in III.iii.196–197 Ulysses tells Achilles: "The providence that's in a watchful state / Knows almost every grain of Pluto's gold."

Palace of Priam as a Bowre of Blisse

medieval sources for the setting, properties, and speeches of Act V, scene ii. First, there was the "cunning web," the "subtile net" of Arachne. Second, the "darkenesse" was "a faint shadow of vncertain light" (2.7.29.7–9):

> Such as a lamp, whose life does fade away:
> Or as the Moone cloathed with clowdy night,
> Does shew to him, that walkes in feare and sad affright.

Third, the chests and coffers were "all bard with double bends" and surrounded with "dead mens bones" and vile unburied "carcases." Fourth, and most characteristic of Spenser, Philotime, Mammon's daughter, held that "great gold chaine ylincked well," which we have already compared with the pattern of Hector's ambition. This was knit to heaven at its upper end, while its "lower part did reach to lowest Hell."

As if he might have remembered these properties and the lighting of this Plutonian scene, Shakespeare has placed Troilus and Ulysses—and Thersites, like Spenser's "vgly feend, more fowle then dismall day"—in the shadow near Calchas' tent (V. ii) "where the torch may not discover" them. Here they listen to Cressida as she forswears her lover "By all Diana's waiting women yond, / And by herself." Troilus, meanwhile, is swearing "By hell and all hell's torments"; and Thersites is swearing "by Pluto." And when Cressida, the treasure bought and sold, is discovered to be so easily transferable, Shakespeare's Troilus invokes not only Pluto but also Arachne; he is aware even of what Spenser had called the "litle stride" between Hell-gate and the Cave of Mammon. At the last he sees his beloved as if she were a thing tied up and then untied and fractioned; her love seems to him a matter of "orts . . . fragments, scraps, bits, and greasy relics / Of . . . o'ereaten faith." In Shakespeare's imagination Troilus has become another like Sir Guyon, bleakly surrounded by Mammon's coffers, dead men's bones, and unburied carcasses. Philotime, the woman with the chain linking heaven and earth, reappears in Cressida as a thing inseparate dividing wider than the sky and earth and yet not to be pierced by any subtlest wisp of Arachne's cobweb. All this takes place, not in a distant land of allegory and romance, but in the very soul of the disillusioned lover. The passage (V.ii.146–160) should be carefully reviewed:

> This is, and is not, Cressid!
> Within my soul there doth conduce a fight
> Of this strange nature, that *a thing inseparate*
> *Divides more wider than the sky and earth;*
> *And yet the spacious breadth of this division*
> *Admits no orifex for a point as subtle*
> *As Ariachne's broken woof to enter.*
> Instance, O instance! strong as *Pluto's gates:*
> Cressid is mine, *tied with the bonds* of heaven.
> Instance, O instance! strong as heaven itself:
> The bonds of heaven are slipp'd, dissolv'd, and loos'd;
> And with another knot, five-finger-tied,
> The fractions of her faith . . .
>
> . . . . .
>
> are given to Diomed.

Cressida will remain in the care of her father's ally, the disdainful Diomedes, as Philotime remained in the care of Disdaine. The opportunist Calchas, like the opportunist Mammon, remains in the Plutonian shadows. Troilus, "distracted" like Sir Guyon, whose "senses were with deadly fit opprest," will be led to "the gates" by the rational Ulysses, as the Palmer Reason rescued Guyon from his "swowne" at "the gates of Pluto." And on the morrow Troilus will regain his martial stance (V.v.39–42),

> Engaging and redeeming of himself
> With such a careless force and forceless care
> As if that luck, in very spite of cunning,
> Bade him win all.

Furthermore, as a formal likeness, the confusion of the battle scenes of Act V can be tentatively charged to the elaborate knightly encounters of the Book of Temperance. Arthur's mistaken offer of mercy to Pyrochles was less costly than is Hector's courtesy to Achilles. His encounter with both Pyrochles and Cymochles can be paralleled by Troilus' combat with both Ajax and Diomedes. And, most revealing of these analogies, when Cymochles "will reaue of armes" the senseless Guyon—"For why should a dead dog be deckt in armour bright?" (2.8. 15.7–9)—he anticipates a Hector who will slay the nameless Greek knight for his armor in a scene that has no excuse for being except to illustrate the intemperance of the great Trojan hero. This flaw in Hector's knighthood, the revelation of which directly precedes his slaughter by Achilles, is the efficient cause of the Trojan defeat, as Spenser's Palmer has warned us (2.8. 16.4–5):

> To spoile the dead of weed
> Is sacrilege, and doth all sinnes exceed.

The ethical standards from which Princes Troilus and Hector lapsed in their manhood and knighthood are rigorous enough to win for them at least as much understanding and compassion as we give to Sir Guyon. Hector goes blindly to his fate. His "day's work [is] done." His sword has had its "fill of blood and death." But Troilus is enlightened and invigorated. His final acceptance of his responsibility as a prince, tinged as it may be with personal rage, allies him with Hamlet, the Danish Prince.[10] The main accomplishment of the "rarer" or virtuous action of *Troilus and Cressida, Hamlet,* and the Book of Temperance is well-nigh the same. It calls for the destruction, by obedience to a princely code, of what is seemingly but falsely fair. In all three of these ordeals the hero, with the help of wise man or ghost or heavenly

---

[10] See Abbie F. Potts, "Hamlet and Gloriana's Knights," *Sh.Quart.,* VI (Winter, 1955), 31–43, reprinted as Ch. VII of this book.

pursuivant, must not only "contain" his personal appetites and passions but also "spur" himself to do his princely or, as we should say, professional duty. Troilus, on whose sword "the venom'd vengeance" rides, leaves "the hermit Pity" with his mother, Hecuba, when he attacks the "vile abominable tents . . . pight upon . . . Phrygian plains." Hamlet sets right the unjointed state and time of Denmark by deferring to the Ghost's "piteous action" where his mother, Gertrude, is concerned; but he, too, pursues his "stern effects" by driving the "unbated and envenomed" point of the poisoner Claudius to its "work" of just retribution. Both are allied with Sir Guyon, who "broke downe, with rigour pittilesse," the pleasant bowers and "Pallace braue" of the Bowre of Blisse.

When it is urged that the violence Troilus displays on the battlefield argues against the sincerity of his redemption, we may repeat that the Prince of Troy, like the Prince of Denmark, must be cured of intemperance on its defective side. Each has suffered from the lapse of his practical energies; both, when reinvigorated, exhibit courage like that of Sir Guyon, who performed his duty in "the tempest of his wrathfulnesse" (2.12. 83.4). Yet, as the reversal for Hamlet came too late to save the Prince of Denmark, even so the reversal in the action of the Prince of Troy comes too late to redeem the Palace of Priam.

Temperance is not speciously alluring; and when dramatized it is not likely to make a play popular, as the stage history of *Troilus and Cressida* would indicate. We who do read or watch, however, learn unforgettably that the timocratic Trojans are doomed to defeat by a Greek host finally obedient to the reasonable counsel of Ulysses. That the destruction of the

> proud towre of Troy, though richly guilt,
> From which young Hectors bloud by cruell Greekes was spilt,

comes little short of the tragic waste in *Hamlet* and hence dismays as well as grimly amuses us will indicate how powerfully

Shakespeare has vitalized persons who with Spenser had been chiefly romantic abstractions.

Now, however, and in conclusion, we may emphasize the likelihood of Shakespeare's debt to Spenser's Book of Temperance by pointing out the inadequacy of his other putative sources for supplying an ethical frame of reference to a work of dramatic art conceived in the decade of his greatest power and skill.

Avowedly Chaucer will tell not of how Troy came to destruction but of the joy and cold cares of Troilus; "Fortune" and "blinde lust" are his answers to the riddle of earthly love. This wretched world is "vanity" when viewed by the "playne felicite that is in hevene above." Indeed, he offers little rational comfort for human life: beyond this world is only heaven; beyond the faithless lover is only the "sothfast Crist"; beyond Criseyde, of whom no one writes "whether that she children hadde or non," who thanks God that she is not "religious," there stands only the faint, detached, and unattainable "mayde and moder . . . benigne." [11]

Shakespeare's familiarity with Lydgate's *Troy Book* is surely one of the important factors in the writing of *Troilus and Cressida*, as has been frequently pointed out. The informal, almost

[11] Chaucer's vocabulary in *Troilus and Criseyde* is impressive, and the native element (might, cunning, craft, wit, truth, goodness, worthiness, cowardice, dread, shame, thralldom, holiness, wisdom, fellowship) has been amplified to include substantive and adjectival references to the traditional virtues and deadly sins (pride, anger and wrath, envy, sloth, avarice, gluttony, lust, humble, covetous, mild, bounteous, charitable, voluptuous). Its Boethian elements and many Latinisms (pity, benignity, grace, perseverance, compassion, authority, mutability, prolixity, felicity, prosperity, discretion, vanity, abstinence, celestial, moral, eterne, vain, transitory, angelic) are echoed from medieval clerkly and churchly parlance; courtly distinctions based on the experiences of chivalry are numerous (service, mischance, beauty, noblesse, courage, despair, gentilesse, favour, sovereignty, jeopardy, largesse, secret, amorous); but the infrequent "reason" as ruling "love," "desire," "heat," delight," is the merest suggestion of an organic relationship.

folksy treatment of traditional persons and situations allies the medieval narrative with Shakespeare's play. But in no degree is Lydgate concerned with the analysis of conduct. Othea as goddess of prudence (Prol. 38) and Fortuna (1.776, 1506) are the main symbols of ethical opposition. Providence, discretion, patience, diligence, wisdom or prudent advertence, freedom, honor, and humanity are the unchallenged virtues. Doubleness, "newfangledness," inconstancy, flattery, mutability, treachery, "brotilnis," covetousness, and presumption are the unanalyzed vices.[12]

In *The Recuyell of the Historyes of Troye* Caxton reveals no articulate theory of conduct, personal, social, or civil. Throughout the Trojan deliberations cowardice is the chief sin, or possibly incontinence ("haste"). The shrewdness of the successful appears as "prudence" or "wisdom," but Helenus' warning against a revengeful spirit is easily discredited by the retort of Troilus—"coward priest." Caxton quotes Virgil's "non est misericordia in bello" as the right reason for Greek victory and Trojan defeat; likewise, from Breseyda's defection he takes only the bald Virgilian comfort "O how soon is the purpose of a woman changed and turned, certes more sooner than a man can say or think." He cannot, as does Shakespeare, relate the problem of the intemperate prince and the unjust state to an action wherein the prince must become, in Troilus' term, "patient," and the state must, as Nestor says, "draw together." [13]

[12] See the ed. by Henry Bergen for the Early English Text Society (London, 1906). Lydgate's Troilus remains in the medieval tradition. He was "a worthi knyghte, / Fresche and lusty" (II.282–283), "fers" (II. 4885), "in love trewe as any stele" (II.4874). Diomede was "impacient" (II.4615), "hasty, testif, to smyte rek[e]les" (II.461). Paris, "a ful manly knyghte" (II.63), "toke noon hede / Save un-to lust, & sette a-syde trouthe" (II.2831–2832). Helen, "aungillyk" and "femynyn," was "goodly on to se" (II.3651–3652), "hevenly faire" and "celestial" (II.3657); and Cressida was "symple and meke, and ful of sobirnes" (II.4657), "goodly of speche, fulfilde of pite, / Facundious, and there-to right tretable . . . / Of tendre herte and unstedfastness" (II.4758–4761).

[13] Caxton's Trojan ladies are right noble, fair, sage, and debonair; his

Henryson sets forth the "fatal destiny" of Cresseid, a matter with which Shakespeare is not primarily concerned. Not through any guilt of her own, says Henryson, has she been ruined. He blames "evil fate" for her plight and will himself defend her "wisdom, womanhood, and loveliness." Yet he warns women against "false deceit." Although Cresseid also blames Fortune's wheel, she too repents her fickle faith, her "unstableness . . . brittle as glass." It is not for infidelity, however, but for blasphemy that Cresseid is punished by the planetary gods.

The kinship of Henryson's "spittal house" and Shakespeare's Panders' Hall is undeniable; Henryson's device of a testament reappears in Pandarus' "will"; and the physical disfigurement of Cresseid is translated into Pandarus' "diseases." What Shakespeare has found most helpful in Henryson's poem is not the rudimentary judgments and the specious ethical assumptions but its lively portrayal of persons and situations. For instance, in Henryson's council of the seven deities who condemn Cresseid Shakespeare has before his eyes a painfully vivid design for Cressida's similar but more merciful ordeal in running the gauntlet of the Greek heroes. Henryson's Saturn, "with looks and mien of cold austerity," [14] becomes Shakespeare's Nestor, with

---

Trojan knights, great, strong, worthy, fair, true, right hardy and discreet, of great courage, valiant, "aspre." Helenus is of great science and knowledge in the liberal arts and Cassandra is learned with sciences; but their warnings against the peril of vengeance and the blindness and folly of the people amount to little more than the judgments of opportunists in a particular crisis. Dishonor and cowardice remain the chief sins; rage, hate, shame, and ire are the ruling passions. There is, however, a slight foreshadowing of the necessary triumph of the Greeks under a leader "wise and prudent and of good counsel," and Agamemnon exhorts his followers "to put away pride" and "use the right way of justice"; but Shakespeare would learn from Caxton no interpretation of either term, nor does he accept Caxton's delineation of the Greek generals (*The Recuyell of the Historyes of Troye*, ed. by H. Oskar Sommer [London, 1894], II, 557, 590, 604).

[14] Quoted from *A Modernization of Robert Henryson's 'Testament of Cresseid,'* by Marshall W. Stearns ("Indiana University Publications," 1945).

"winter [on his] lips"; Jupiter becomes Agamemnon; Mars, "like to a boar whetting his tusks keen," is paralleled by Diomedes; Phoebus, "lantern and lamp of light, . . . banisher of night," shines again in Achilles, who takes "the winter" from Cressida's lips after Nestor has kissed her; and Shakespeare's Ulysses judges Cressida "for Venus' sake" as harshly as Henryson's Mercury judged Cresseid. "All eloquent" was Mercury, "and full of rhetoric, / With book in hand," chosen unanimously to be "chief speaker in the parliament."

As Ulysses is surely in the line of Mercury, so Cressida, whom he calls one of the "daughters of the game," is an unforgettable illustration of her mother, Venus, as described by Henryson. The face of Henryson's goddess reveals "great variance" (lines 223–224, 230–231):

> Now perfect truth, and now inconstancy.
>   . . . . .
> Beware of her, from mood to mood she sweeps,
> With one eye laughs, and with the other weeps.

Just so Cressida acknowledges her own double vision (V.ii. 107–108):

> Troilus, farewell! One eye yet looks on thee,
> But with my heart the other eye doth see.

Shakespeare, however, spares his heroine the leprosy of Cresseid.[15] Cressida's doom is to be "kiss'd in general."

Shakespeare's might and skill in fusing these medieval sources is undeniable; but without the codes of such as Castiglione and Spenser his *Troilus and Cressida*, like his *Much Ado*, his *Hamlet*, and his *Measure for Measure*, would have lacked what now is seen to be their courtly significance and value. In spite of the

---

[15] And the image of the churl painted on the breast of Lady Cynthia, "bearing a bunch of thorns upon his back," would soon be apparent on another breast as "those thorns that . . . lodge in [the] bosom [of Hamlet's mother] to prick and sting her."

Palace of Priam as a Bowre of Blisse 127

large contribution of events, situations, persons, phrases, and images from medieval sources, neither *Troilus and Criseyde* nor *The Troy Book* nor *The Recuyell of the Historyes of Troye* nor *The Testament of Cresseid* can account for the ethical fabric or the dramatic action of *Troilus and Cressida*. For these we must look to the ethical prepossessions of the sixteenth century and chiefly to Edmund Spenser's allegorical poem setting forth the rigors and perils facing the knights of Gloriana.[16]

---

[16] Professor Robert K. Presson's able investigation of the sources of this play (*Shakespeare's 'Troilus and Cressida' and the Legends of Troy* [University of Wisconsin Press, 1953]) is fundamental for the study of its outer action. Moreover, his conclusion as to the unifying effect of the Homeric Passion-Judgment theme, which he believes came to Shakespeare through Chapman's *Iliades*, is helpfully in accord with my premise that Spenserian temperance directs and substantiates Shakespeare's inner action. Witness his remark (pp. 7–8): "The trials and harms dissension brings to a society, and the perturbations passion when unbridled by reason brings to the possessor and to his dependents are familiar humanistic ideas abundantly exemplified by the behaviour of the characters in play [*Troilus and Cressida*] and in poem [*Iliades*]." Professor Merritt C. Batchelder is still at work in the field of his dissertation, "The Elizabethan Elements in Shakespeare's 'Troilus and Cressida'" (University of Iowa).

CHAPTER VII

Hamlet and Gloriana's Knights

THE date and circumstances of composition of *Hamlet* are conjectural, as is the relation between its first quarto, 1603, and its second quarto, 1604. Nor do we know what version of the text is referred to in the Stationer's Register for July 26, 1602: "The Revenge of Hamlett Prince Denmarke as yt was latelie Acted by the Lord Chamberleyne his servants." We do know that the quarto of 1604 claims to have been "newly imprinted and enlarged to almost as much againe as it was, according to the true and perfect Coppie." While the relation of the quarto of 1603 to this "Coppie" is still debatable and while the "true and perfect Coppie" itself must remain unknown, it may be helpful to record analogies existing between Spenser's *Faerie Queene* and the quarto of 1604. Moreover, our assumption that both *Troilus and Cressida* and *Hamlet*, second quarto, drew largely upon the Legend of Sir Guyon to substantiate the struggle of their intemperate heroes toward the happy mean suggests that these plays were almost contemporary. Finally, and here we must be wary of an otherwise unsupported hypothesis, the passages of the second quarto not appearing in the first quarto and reminiscent of Spenserian images, phrases, and situations give to Prince Hamlet's courtly action an assurance and clarity lacking in the discovery and reversal of Prince Troilus. As a playwright Shakespeare seems to be operating with greater skill in the second quarto of *Hamlet*, 1604, than in *Troilus and Cressida*, 1602. Might this mean that *Troilus and Cressida* antedates the "true and perfect Coppie" of *Hamlet?*

Without asserting the indebtedness of *Hamlet* to *The Faerie Queene*, let us here [1] set forth passages in which the adventures of Prince Arthur, the Redcrosse Knight, Sirs Guyon and Artegall, and certain ladies of Gloriana's court supply a commentary on the ethical and dramatic cruces in the text of the second quarto of this widely debated Shakespearean play. Since Shakespeare's knowledge of Spenser's poem is granted by students of both, it may not be amiss to compare the tropes and phrases of the Danish Prince of "noble mind" and "noble heart" with those of "that most noble Briton Prince" and his compeers.

If we regard *Hamlet* as a conflict between the active political career of the hero and his contemplative nature, the play offers many fruitless paradoxes; if, however, Hamlet is found advancing in a fashion not more desultory than that of Gloriana's knights toward an understanding of temperance and justice and thereafter toward the deed it befits him to do, the drama is single and clear. The Redcrosse Knight, too, had been puzzled by a "fair-forged Sprite" and had given ear to the suicidal persuasions of Despaire (1.9.48.1). Sir Guyon, "slumbring fast / In senselesse dreame" (2.8.4.8–9), is the type of Hamlet, "laps'd in time and passion." Both Sir Guyon and Hamlet illustrate intemperance on its negative side; both are, as it were, defective; and to both heaven sends ghostly help. Even Artegall, for whom as for Hamlet "the world is runne quite out of square"

---

[1] Reprinted with occasional slight revision from *Sh.Quart.*, VI (Winter, 1955), 31–43.

(5.Prol.1.7), is endangered by the "faire visage" (5.5.12.4) of a woman, Radigund. Viewed against this concourse of chivalry, Hamlet's caution, delay, self-reproaches, and harshness to Ophelia can be better estimated. Temperance and justice are not easy virtues, particularly in a group which "calls virtue hypocrite," in pursy times when "virtue itself of vice must pardon beg." On this point Hamlet chimes with Spenser in a passage which Shakespeare may have read (5.Prol.4):

> For that which all men then did vertue call,
> Is now cald vice; and that which vice was hight,
> Is now hight vertue, and so vs'd of all:
> Right now is wrong, and wrong that was is *right*,
> As all things else in *time* are chaunged quight.
> Ne wonder; for the heauens reuolution
> Is wandred farre from where it first was pight,
> And so doe make contrarie constitution
> Of all this lower world, toward his dissolution.[2]

Many of Hamlet's reflections deal with the control of emotion by the reasoning man as distinguished from the beast that wants discourse of reason. He studies this problem within the diverse phenomena of grief, lust, and wrath; we approve his conclusions when they are applied to friendship and love and art; but we think too precisely on the event, i.e., the dramatic retribution, the killing of Claudius, when we shift our ground to rebuke him in his administration of justice for a thoughtful nature, which we mistakenly call his tragic flaw. To Sir Guyon the Palmer Reason was not a hindrance but a help.

The aim of Spenser's Book of Temperance, that "faire mirrhour" in which the "fairest Princesse vnder sky" would behold her face and her "owne realmes in lond of Faery," that "Image" of her great ancestry (2.Prol.4.6-9), may be compared with

[2] We need not cite Hamlet's variations on this theme, nor call attention to the rhyme, beyond reference to *Hamlet*, I.v.189-190 and II.ii.307-316. The "spite"-"right" rhyme occurs in both quartos.

Hamlet and Gloriana's Knights 131

Hamlet's end of playing, "to hold, as 'twere, the *mirror* up to nature; to show virtue her *own* feature, scorn her *own image*." Indeed, acting "overdone, or come tardy off" gives Hamlet his best opportunity for the discussion of temperance as a virtue. His praise of Horatio, the man "not passion's slave," "whose blood and judgment are . . . well commingled," his satirical rebuke of Laertes' mouthing and ranting at the grave of Ophelia, his mockery of the excessive speech of the "Bragart Gentleman" (Q_1), Osric (Q_2), are so many casual instances of his doctrine. But the most important dramatic portrayals of intemperance, which we may discuss in order, are the intemperate wrath of Pyrrhus against Priam and Hecuba, the drunkenness of Claudius, Hamlet's own defective and excessive passion at the end of the second act, his anger against his mother, rebuked by the Ghost in the Queen's closet, and his soliloquy beginning "Rightly to be great."

First, let us make a comparison of the Spenserian Pyrochles, "who rudely rag'd, and like a cruell Tygre far'd," with Shakespeare's "rugged Pyrrhus, like th' Hyrcanian beast." The one "round about him threw forth sparkling fire, / That seemd him to enflame on euery side." The other, "roasted in wrath and fire," is "o'ersized with coagulate gore." When Pyrochles was unhorsed, he was compelled "to matchen equall fight" (2.5.4.8); "Unequal match'd, / Pyrrhus at Priam drives." In the hands of Pyrochles, Arthur's sword Morddure proved rebellious (2.8.30.8–9); Pyrrhus' sword seems "i' th' air to stick." When Priam falls at the mere whiff and wind of the "fell" sword, we are reminded of the reeling of Prince Arthur and his horse at the "fell" blow of Pyrochles (2.8.31.1).

Intemperance in another aspect, the drunkenness of Claudius, provokes from Hamlet one of his most puzzling speeches. His words about the

> *o'ergrowth* of some complexion,
> Oft breaking down the pales and *forts of reason*,

remind us of Spenser's second Book, with its siege of the House of Alma by the legions of the five senses, and the assistance given to Sir Guyon by the Palmer Reason, whose sermon on the "affections" contains the same trope and similar phrases (2.4.34. 3–8):

> In their beginning they are weake and wan,
> But soone through suff'rance [*grow*] to fearefull end;
> Whiles they are weake betimes with them contend:
> For when they once to perfect strength do *grow*,
> Strong warres they make, and cruell battry bend
> Gainst *fort of Reason*, it to *ouer*throw.

Again, Hamlet's mention of the vicious mole of nature (i.e., nature as marred by vice) which the guiltless man inherits from nature at birth is illustrated by the bloody hands of the babe born of Mordant and Amavia, types of intemperance in love and woe. "Ah lucklesse babe, borne vnder cruell *starre*" (2.2.2.1), exclaimed Sir Guyon. Hamlet's reply would be (I.iv.30–38):

> These men,
> Carrying, I say, the stamp of one defect,
> Being nature's livery, or fortune's *star*,
> . . . . .
> Shall in the general censure take corruption
> From that particular fault. The [dram of eale]
> Doth all the noble substance [of a doubt]
> To his own scandal.

Here we are reminded of Scudamour's "dram of hony" in a similarly fluid metaphor (4.10.1.1–5):

> True he it said, what euer man it sayd,
> That loue with *gall* and hony doth abound,
> But if the one be with the other wayd,
> For euery *dram of* hony therein found,
> A pound *of gall doth ouer* it *redound*.

Hamlet and Gloriana's Knights   133

In suggesting "o'er-redound" as an emendation for "of a doubt" in the second quarto we should recall Milton's use of the word with a similar connotation (*P.L.*, VII.56–59):

> But the *evil* soon
> Driv'n back *redounded* as a flood on those
> From whom it sprung, impossible to mix
> With *Blessedness.*

Spenser speaks in the *Amoretti* (XVIII.3, and XLIII.4) of drops that "*oft*en doe *redound*," and of "ouerflowing gall." The prefix "o'er" is frequent in *Hamlet*.[3] Remembering that in the sentence under discussion Shakespeare uses a fluid image and that in the preceding lines occur the words "o'ergrowth" and "o'erleavens," we might then read:

> The dram of eale [? gall]
> Doth all the noble substance o'er-redound
> To his own scandal.

The heavy-headed revel of the drunkard Claudius soon gained its "swinish phrase";[4] the excessive boasting of Spenser's Bragadochio or the fantastic speech of Shakespeare's "Bragart Gentleman," Osric, could be clearly recognized. These are instances of excessive passion. When intemperance occurs in himself as a

[3] Young Laertes . . . *o'erbears* your officers; the potent poison quite *o'ercrows* my spirit; *o'erdoing* Termagant; this brave *o'erhanging* firmament; our *o'erhasty* marriage; *o'erhear* the speech; *o'ermaster't* as you may; certain players we *o'erraught* on the way; the pate of a politician, which this ass now *o'erreaches;* so you will not *o'errule* me to a peace; *o'ersized* with coagulate gore; *o'erstep* the modesty of nature; great command *o'ersways* the order; *o'ertook* in's rouse; all *o'erteemed* loins; noble mind . . . *o'erthrown;* to *o'ertop* old Pelion; the censure . . . must *o'erweigh;* though all the earth *o'erwhelm* them.

[4] Among the besiegers of Spenser's House of Alma were not only swine, but owls (cf. "the owl was a baker's daughter"), dogs ("the cat will mew and dog will have his day"), harts ("the hart ungalled play"), snakes ("the serpent that did sting thy father's life"), apes ("he keeps them, like an ape"), puttocks all in plumes arrayed ("I know a hawk from a handsaw" and "pajock"), and loathly toads ("a paddock").

defect of passion, memorably in his soliloquy at the end of Act II, Hamlet finds it harder to distinguish from prudence; only in the epithets uttered at the thought of Claudius is his passion excessive, and here most deftly rebuked, as Sir Guyon had rebuked the anger of Artegall against Braggadochio (5.3.36.6–9). Bitterly describing himself as one—a possible Braggadochio?—whose beard is shaven as a sign of infamy, Hamlet asks: "Who . . . plucks off my beard and blows it in my face?" Referring to one—like Sir Turpine—who "had no courage, or else had no gall" (6.3.36.5), Hamlet fears that he lacks "gall." He will not, like Spenser's Occasion, unpack his heart with words; so he helps himself out of his dull and muddy mettle, which is more than can be said for the Knight of Holiness. The cure for defective passion is not thoughtless action, but wiser thought—"About, my brain!" And for his delay he gives a reason not less specious than was given by Prince Arthur in his fight against Maleger to preserve the House of Alma (2.11.39.5–9):

> He doubted, least it were some magicall
> Illusion, that did beguile his sense,
> Or wandring ghost, that wanted funerall,
> Or aerie spirit vnder false pretence,
> Or hellish feend raysd vp through diuelish science.

Just as Artegall had been taught by Astraea (5.1.7.1–4)

> to weigh both right and wrong
> In equall ballance with due recompence,
> And equitie to measure out along,
> *According to the line of conscience,*

Hamlet will "catch the conscience of the King."

That done, setting aside the "bitter business" to which the time of night, the yawning churchyards, and the contagion of hell might have invited a hero of merely Senecan ancestry, he goes straightway to the task of catching the conscience of his mother. In his courtly action this move is rigorously economical;

Hamlet and Gloriana's Knights

to kill Claudius at prayer would be in life and in the drama an act not only offensive but stupid. It would not have been the Spenserian Astraea's "due recompence," as Hamlet says in grosser words. More important business awaits him; the purging of the Queen is necessary to the catharsis of the tragedy. Here the Ghost must help, although, unseen by Gertrude, he works through the reasoning power of Hamlet. He whets the almost blunted purpose of Hamlet as an avenger, essential in the old play; and more significantly in the second than in the first quarto he bids Hamlet step between his mother and "her fighting soul." The image is that of Spenser's House of Alma; and Hamlet's lapse and his achievement fall into the order of Sir Guyon's senseless slumber and Prince Arthur's brave battle with the legions of the five senses that assail the soul and with Maleger, Impotence, and Impatience. Like these knights, Hamlet frees Alma before he turns to the destruction of the Bowre of Blisse and the rebuke of Grill, Acrasia's man of "hoggish mind."

Furthermore, it may be said that the Ghost in Act III differs from the Ghost in Act I in a way suggesting that to his memory of Senecan ghosts Shakespeare adjusted Spenser's "flying Pursuiuant" (2.8.2.4). Both episodes open with an invocation and end with a reference to the pulse; and between the Spenserian "faire young man, / Of wondrous beautie" (2.8.5–6) and Hamlet's picture of his father in the second quarto there is an impressive likeness:

Spenser:
His snowy front curled with golden heares,
Like Phoebus face adornd with sunny rayes,
Diuinely shone, and two sharpe winged sheares,
Decked with diuerse plumes, like painted Iayes,
Were fixed at his backe, to cut his ayerie waves.

Like as Cupido on Idaean hill.
Shakespeare:
See what a grace was seated on this brow;

> Hyperion's curls; the front of Jove himself;
> An eye like Mars, to threaten and command;
> A station like the herald Mercury
> New lighted on a heaven-kissing hill.[5]

With Spenser's aid are we not in a position to understand the difference in quality between the earlier, Senecan appearance of the Ghost and this later entrance? And does the linking of Sir Guyon, his Palmer Reason, and the flying Pursuivant with Hamlet, his reason, and his ghostly father in an analogous situation not strengthen our argument that the action of *Hamlet* in Shakespeare's revision of an old play has become primarily ethical?

For the soliloquy in which Hamlet decides that, rightly to be great, he must follow the dictates of godlike reason, Sir Guyon's words in the last stanza of Spenser's Book of Temperance serve us well:

> See the mind of beastly man,
> That hath so soone forgot the excellence
> Of his creation, when he life began,
> That now he chooseth, with vile difference,
> To be a beast, and lacke intelligence.

If Grill's hoggish mind, subservient to Acrasia, was one hindrance in the exercise of reason, another was Braggadochio's craven scruple of thinking too precisely *on the event* (the vice of the man of mere action). "Ne thought of honour euer did assay / His baser brest" (2.3.4.3–4). Braggadochio's boastful question (2.3.16.6–7)—

> Is not enough foure quarters of a man,
> Withouten sword or shield, an host to quaile?—

would seem to Hamlet

---

[5] The traits of the god of war are retained as in the first quarto, where Mars stands as the figure of Hamlet senior and Vulcan of Claudius.

Hamlet and Gloriana's Knights

> A thought which, quarter'd, hath but one part wisdom
> And ever three parts coward.

Hamlet's must not be a mere excitement of the blood, but an excitement of "my reason and my blood"; from this time forth his *thoughts* will be "bloody." It is, then, to the establishment of his distinctive manly power that the triumph of his reason belongs.

This is even more clearly apparent if we read the soliloquy "Rightly to be great" bearing in mind the query of Artegall to the Gyant with the "huge great paire of ballance." Like Hamlet, Artegall and Talus had come to the shore of the sea. Like Hamlet, they saw before them (5.2.29.4–6)

> far as they could vew,
> Full many people gathered in a crew;
> Whose great assembly they did much admire.

His balance held on high [cf. Hamlet's "mass" and "charge"], the Gyant on the seashore weighed "idle toys" [cf. Hamlet's "straw" and "egg-shell"], boasting that he could also weigh earth [cf. Hamlet's "examples gross as earth"] against sea, fire against air, heaven against hell. He would reduce all things unto equality, thus repairing "realmes and nations run awry." Whereupon Artegall asked the simple question of right and wrong (5.2.44.5–6):

> Which is (sayd he) more heauy then in weight,
> The right or wrong?

But the Gyant was unable to counterpoise his scales; "right sate in the middest of the beame alone." Like Hamlet, Artegall concluded that "in the mind the doome of right must bee" (5.2.47.6). We may doubt whether there can be found in the literature read by Shakespeare any better gloss for Hamlet's somewhat confusing soliloquy as he meets the army of Fortinbras on his way to the Danish coast. In his mind the man of thought stands completely free from the defects of thinking hoggishly, of thinking falsely, and of thinking too precisely on the event.

Although Hamlet's prime concern be temperance and justice, secondarily and in a manner which brings him close to Ophelia and Polonius, Gertrude and Claudius, he must reconcile fleshly nature and ghostly loyalties. Here also the play may be read with advantage against a Spenserian background. The puzzles and frequent hardship of the lovers in *The Faerie Queene*, the rank natural fertility of the Garden of Adonis, and the romantic tradition typified in the Mask of Cupid and the Temple of Venus supply a perspective in which Hamlet and his group are at once representative and distinguished.

The two soliloquies on existence in the flesh and the speech of similar import to Rosencrantz and Guildenstern may first be considered. Nares has noted that the reduplication of the adverb in "too too solid flesh" of the second quarto occurs in Holinshed and Spenser.[6] The phrase is not uncommon; but the Spenserian parallel occurs in the similar warning against the love of woman given by Cymodoce to her son Marinell, "A lesson too too hard for liuing clay" (3.4.26.3). Better evidence connecting Spenser with the longer version of Hamlet's first soliloquy in the second quarto, especially with the "canon 'gainst self-slaughter," is the speech of the Knight of Holiness tempted by Despaire to suicide (1.9.41.2–3, 6–7):

> The terme of life is limited,
> Ne may a man prolong, nor shorten it;
> . . . . .
> Who life did limit *by almightie doome*,
> (Quoth he) knowes best the termes established.

Not in the first quarto but first in the second quarto we find Hamlet's image of the "unweeded garden / That grows to seed."

---
[6] Shakespeare Variorum, p. 41.

What this may owe to Spenser's Garden of Adonis and its "endlesse progenie / Of . . . weedes" (3.6.30.7–8) can only be hinted. Among the many metaphorical gardens at Shakespeare's disposal none seems more pertinent than this, which has no "Gardiner to set, or sow, / To plant or prune" (3.6.34.1–2). In both occur the word "euerlasting," the impossibility of dissolution, the hostility of time to goodly things, and the distinction between reasonable souls and beasts.[7]

Hamlet has first seen his world as an image of chaotic and

---

[7] "Infinite shapes of creatures there are bred,
And vncouth formes, which none yet euer knew,
. . . . .
Some fit for *reasonable soules* t'indew,
  [cf. discourse of reason]
Some made for *beasts*. [cf. a beast]
. . . . .
Daily they grow, and daily forth are sent
Into *the world*, it to replenish more;
  [cf. this world]
Yet is the stocke not lessened, nor spent,
But still remaines in *euerlasting* store,
  [cf. the Everlasting]
As it at first created was of yore.
For in the wide wombe of *the world* there lyes,
In hatefull darkenesse and in deepe horrore,
An huge eternall Chaos, which supplyes
  [cf. Chaos, in Q₁]
The substances of *natures fruitfull* progenyes.
  [cf. things rank and gross in nature]
. . . . .
Ne when the life decayes, and forme does fade,
Doth it consume, and *into nothing* go
  [cf. melt to nothing, in Q₁]
But chaunged is, and often altred to and fro.
. . . . .
Great enimy . . . [is] Time, who with his scyth addrest,
Does mow the flowring herbes and *goodly things*."
See also Spenser's Garden of Proserpina (2.7.51–55).

gross natural life, an unweeded garden. Next it takes on for him the aspect of the no longer goodly frames of cosmic life. Now Spenser's Castle Joyous was a "goodly frame" (3.1.31.1); but Britomart and the Redcrosse Knight were glad to leave it "ere the grosse Earthes gryesy shade [cf. "Examples gross as earth"] / Was all disperst out of the firmament" (3.1.67.7–8). Spenser's House of Pride was a "goodly heape for to behould" (1.4.5.1); but at its postern might be found a dunghill of dead carcasses. Spenser's House of Alma (2.11.15.5) and his Book of Temperance (2.12.1.1) were both "goodly frames"; and yet at the very height of his task Sir Guyon has Hamlet's experience (2.12.34.5–9),

> When suddeinly a grosse fog ouer spred
> [cf. things . . . gross in nature]
> With his dull vapour all that desert has,
> And heauens chearefull face enueloped,
> That all things one, and one as nothing was,
> And this great Vniuerse seemd one confused mas.

For Spenser the body, the House of Alma, is the subject of admiration and pity alike (2.9.1.1–4 and 21.7–9):

> Of all God's *workes, which do this world adorne,*
> There is no one more faire and excellent,
> Then is mans body both for powre and forme,
> Whiles it is kept in sober gouernment;
> . . . . .
> But O great pitty, that no lenger time
> So goodly workemanship should not endure:
> Soone it must turne to earth; no earthly thing is sure.

The mode of the dramatic imagination can scarcely be better observed than in a comparison of these lines with Hamlet's amplified exclamation for the bewilderment of Rosencrantz and Guildenstern (II.ii.316–322):

> What a piece of work is a man! how noble in reason! how infinite in faculties! in form and moving how express and admirable! in

Hamlet and Gloriana's Knights

action how like an angel! in apprehension how like a god! the beauty of the world, the paragon [8] of animals! And yet to me what is this quintessence of dust?

Hamlet's progress from physical distaste and a puzzled will to right princely action has two phases: not only must he as a playwright control his passion by his reason and as a detective catch the conscience of the King; as a thinker he will seek to understand the nature of conscience, which remits him to suffering in the mind rather than violence. For the soliloquy "To be or not to be" we should compare his words with the similar mixed metaphor in which the despairing Una shared her woes with Prince Arthur (1.7.39.1–7):

> What worlds delight, or ioy of liuing speach
> Can heart, so plung'd in *sea of sorrowes* deepe,
>   [cf. sea of troubles]
> And heaped with so huge *misfortunes*, reach?
> The carefull cold beginneth for to creepe,
> And *in my heart his yron arrow steepe*,
>   [cf. arrows of . . . fortune]
> Soone as I thinke vpon my *bitter bale*:
> *Such helplesse harmes yts better hidden keepe.*
>   [cf. in the mind to suffer]

Moreover, we should note that Spenser's Despaire matches Hamlet's list of good reasons for suicide, promising (1.9.40.8–9)

> Sleepe after toyle, port after stormie seas,
> Ease after warre, death after life.

And, finally, when Una's Redcrosse Knight was by Despaire offered "a dagger sharpe and keene,"

> troubled bloud through his pale face was seene
> To come, and goe with tydings from the hart;

---

[8] "Paragon" is a frequent Spenserian word. In the text of his plays Shakespeare had used it only twice before writing *Hamlet*.

and he, even the Redcrosse Knight, would have taken his own life but for Una's quick gesture and scornful rebuke (1.9.51–53). In Hamlet, too, "the native hue of resolution / Is sicklied o'er with the pale cast of thought"; fortunately he decides against self-murder; for heartache and natural shocks, the whips and scorns of time, the cure is not a quietus with a bare bodkin but conscience, thought, reason; and the suffering in the mind to which conscience remits Hamlet is in the Shakespearean as in the Spenserian ethic "nobler."

Ophelia herself has Spenserian traits. In her imprisonment she recalls Una; she reproaches Hamlet as Una reproached the false Redcrosse Knight (1.3.27.1–2):

> Ah my long lacked Lord,
> Where haue ye bene thus long out of my sight?

Again, her interest in the Mouse-trap bears comparison with that of Britomart in the Mask of Cupid, who "merueild" at the "strange intendiment" of the Prologue (3.12.5.1–2). Her madness resembles the feignedly strange demeanor of Britomart toward Amoret (4.1.7.4–9); she calls for her coach as did Lucifera (1.4.16.1–2); and for the description of her drowning, assumed to be a Shakespearean contribution to the old play, it is scarcely necessary to quote Spenser's description of the flower-garlanded, dew-trickling Medway at her bridal (4.11.46).

Yet the knights of Gloriana needed to be wary of women and shrewd old men. Duessa, masquerading as Una, and the false Florimell give ample excuse for Hamlet's suspicion of Ophelia; "as chaste as ice, as pure as snow," she would remind him of the false and "snowy Florimell" (4.4.8.1), whose body "Was purest snow in massie mould congeald" and whose face was mingled "with perfect vermily, / That like a liuely sanguine it seem'd to the eye" (3.8.6). Hamlet has heard of these paintings. The false Florimell could "hold a foole in vaine delight" (3.8.10.7); the characteristics of "the Monster" were set forth at length

Hamlet and Gloriana's Knights 143

(3.7.22.4; 23.6; 28.1; 30.7). In this fashion Hamlet pretends to conceive Ophelia as one to marry a fool and make monsters of wise men; and when over the grave of Ophelia, too late, Gertrude says, "I thought thy bride-bed to have deck'd, sweet maid," she reminds us of Cymodoce, Marinell's mother, when the true Florimell was released from the prison into which she had been locked by Old Proteus (cf. Polonius).

Polonius himself is in keeping with certain very shrewd old men in *The Faerie Queene*. Archimago's "artes" (2.1.1.7) and the "art" which Gertrude rebukes in Polonius are comparable. Polonius works by "encompassment and drift of question"; Archimago worked by "drift" to an "aymed end" (1.2.9.4 and 2.1.3.4–7). Indeed the amplified passages of the second quarto, where they concern the former Corambis, have frequent verbal associations with Archimago; witness (2.1.4):

> Still as he went, he craftie stales did lay,
> With cunning traines him to entrap vnwares,
> And priuie spials plast in all his way,
> To weete what course he takes, and how he fares;[9]
> To ketch him at a vantage in his snares.
>
> . . . . .
>
> [But] fish that once was caught, new bait will hardly bite.

If Spenser's Archimago was a fisherman, Spenser's Proteus was the chief of fishmongers. May Proteus have been in Shakespeare's mind when Hamlet scoffed at Polonius, for whom the clouds are so easily metamorphosed into camel, weasel, whale? Or had he been reading "words, words, words" about Ignaro the gaoler in Spenser's Book of Holiness (1.8.30.1–5; 31.3–7)?

> At last with *creeping crooked pace* forth came
> An old old man, with *beard as white as snow*,
> That on a staff his *feeble* steps did frame,

[9] Cf. the form of Polonius' instructions to Reynaldo.

> And guide his wearie gate both too and fro:
> For his *eye sight him failed* long ygo.
>
> . . . . .
>
> For as he forward moou'd his footing old,
> So backward still was turnd his *wrincled face*.
> Vnlike to men, who euer as they trace,
> Both feet and face one way are wont to lead.

The disloyalty of Claudius and Gertrude, however, most deeply preoccupies the mind of Hamlet. From this taint he cleans his thought only by the performance of his duty, the rebuke administered to Gertrude and the punishment of Claudius. The relation of these three characters in the court scene of Act I as it was printed in the second quarto bears so strong a resemblance to the theme of Concord and the two brothers, Love and Hate, of Spenser's Temple of Venus, that our understanding of Shakespeare's purpose may be assisted by quotation from the romance. Concord wore a crown "much like vnto a Danisk hood" (4.10.31.7; 32.1–5; 33.6–7):

> On either side of her, two young men stood,
> Both strongly arm'd, as fearing one another;
> Yet were they brethren both of halfe the blood,
>
> . . . . .
>
> Though of contrarie natures each to other:
>
> . . . . .
>
> Yet she was of such grace and vertuous might,
> That her commaundment he could not withstand.

Even though he hates Claudius, Hamlet dares not disobey his mother; in this he is again like Marinell, who attends his mother "in full seemly sort" and all the way mourns "inly . . . like one astray" (4.12.18.6–9). This inward grief, Hamlet's great distinction at his first appearance in the second quarto, is related to Spenser's Griefe of the Mask of Cupid (3.12.16.2–4, 8–9):

Hamlet and Gloriana's Knights 145

> Griefe *all in sable sorrowfully clad*,
> > [inky cloak . . . solemn black]
>
> *Downe hanging his dull head with heauy chere*,
> > [dejected haviour of the visage]
>
> Yet *inly being* more, then *seeming* sad:
> > [seems, madam? nay, it is;]
>
> . . . . .
>
> In *wilfull languor* and consuming smart,
> > [obstinate . . . stubbornness . . .
> > will most incorrect to Heaven]
>
> Dying each day with *inward* wounds of dolours dart.
> > [I have that within which passeth show.]

And when Hamlet must assume madness, it is in terms familiar to readers of the Mask of Cupid. Spenser's amorous Desyre, whose "Bonet sat awry" (3.12.9.6); his Doubt, who "lookt askew with his mistrustfull eyes" (3.12.10.5); his Daunger, "cloth'd in ragged weed," whose face was "dreadfull, ne did need / Straunge horrour, to deforme his griesly shade" (3.12.11.3-4)—all supply traits absent in Ophelia's account of Hamlet's madness in the first quarto but present in the second quarto.[10]

Now Cymodoce, mother of the lovesick Marinell (4.12.21.1-5; 19.1-2; 24.6-7),

---

[10] From the Mask of Cupid may come also the characteristics of Feare and Fancy: the former, for the description given of the Ghost; the latter, to adorn Hamlet's speeches before and after the so-called Mouse-trap (3.12.12.1, 6-7; 8.1-2, 8-9). Hamlet's delight over the success of the Mouse-trap need not suggest undue mental disturbance, nor does Horatio so take it: Spenser's Mask of Cupid is likewise attended by "Minstrals," "wanton Bardes," and "Rymers impudent" (3.12.5.4-5). The verse about Jove's successor, if read in connection with *F.Q.*, 3.11.30-35, suggests that the amorous Claudius has been outwitted by the fanciful Hamlet:

> "Whiles thus on earth great Ioue these pageaunts playd,
> The winged boy did thrust into his throne,
> And scoffing, thus vnto his mother sayd,
> Lo now the heauens obey to me alone,
> And take me for their Ioue, whiles Ioue to earth is gone."

> ne wist well what to weene,
> Ne could by search nor any meanes out find
> The secret cause and nature of his teene,
> Whereby she might apply some medicine.
>
> . . . . .
>
> Being returned to his mothers bowre,
> In solitary silence far from wight,
>
> . . . . .
>
> Vnto himselfe she came, and him besought,
> Now with faire speches, now with threatnings sterne.

In his answers to his mother Hamlet recalls Spenser's Reproach, "despightfull, carelesse, and vnkind." Reproach scolds and bears "sharpe stings" comparable with "those thorns" which the Ghost of the King predicts will lodge in Gertrude's bosom "to prick and sting her." The Spenserian Shame held burning brand irons in her hand; she was "most ill fauoured, bestiall, and blind." In both quartos Hamlet calls Gertrude blind, but in the second quarto he names her more explicitly "Shame": "Shame, where is thy blush?"

Gertrude is closest allied to Spenser's Lady of Delight (3.1. 50–56):

> *Nought so of loue* this looser Dame did skill,
> But as a coale to kindle fleshly *flame,*
> Giuing the bridle to her wanton *will.*
>
> . . . . .
>
> Such loue is hate, and such desire is *shame.*
>
> . . . . .
>
> And *through her bones* the false instilled *fire*
> Did spred *it selfe*, and *venime* close *inspire.*

"You cannot call it love," says Hamlet to Gertrude (III.iv.82–88, 148–149):

> Rebellious hell,
> If thou canst mutine in a matron's *bones,*

Hamlet and Gloriana's Knights

> To *flaming* youth let virtue be as wax
> And melt in her own *fire*. Proclaim no *shame*
> When the compulsive ardour *gives the charge*,
> Since frost *itself* as actively doth burn,
> And reason panders *will*.
>
> . . . . .
>
> Whiles *rank corruption*, mining all within,
> Infects unseen.

The frustrations of the Prince of Denmark in the tasks laid upon him should also be compared with those of Marinell, Scudamour, and Prince Arthur. Marinell was full of self-reproaches (4.12.16.1–5):

> At last when as no meanes he could inuent,
> Back to him selfe he gan return the blame,
>
> . . . .
>
> And with vile curses, and reprochfull shame
> To damne him selfe by euery euill name.

When Scudamour entered the Temple of Venus, Delay (4.10.14.5–6)

> in close awaite
> Caught hold on me, and thought my steps to stay,
> Feigning full many a fond excuse to prate.

Finally, in his suspicions of Rosencrantz and Guildenstern Shakespeare's Hamlet may have remembered Spenser's two knights whose assistance Turpine tried to gain against the "gentle Prince not farre away"; they attacked him (6.7.9.1–2)

> As when a cast of Faulcons make their flight
> At an Herneshaw, that lyes aloft on wing.

The simile is not unusual, but the situation, two younger knights in the guileful service of a villain, seems strikingly comparable with the services rendered to Claudius by Rosencrantz and Guildenstern. But Hamlet knows "a hawk from a handsaw."

Of the passages for which we have offered Spenserian parallels, the greater number appear in the second quarto. Such are the expansion of the second scene of the first act, especially the influence of the Queen on the two hostile men and the remarks of Hamlet about grief; in Hamlet's first soliloquy the figure of the unweeded garden; Hamlet's speech on "the pales and forts of reason" and "the dram of eale"; Polonius' crafty scene with Reynaldo; Ophelia's account of Hamlet's madness; the new importance given to the search for the cause of Hamlet's madness by Polonius, the King, and the Queen; the expansion of Hamlet's speech, "I have of late . . . lost all my mirth" and the figure of hawk and handsaw; additional Spenserian traits in the speech of the first player concerning Pyrrhus and Priam; the elaboration of the soliloquy at the end of the second act; the revision of "To be, or not to be" and of Hamlet's instructions to the players; Hamlet's praise of the temperance of Horatio; the second of Hamlet's jingling verses after the Mouse-trap and the reference to his forest of feathers; the major part of Hamlet's scene with the Queen; the new conception of the Ghost at his last appearance; the soliloquy uttered on the plain in Denmark as Hamlet makes his way to the coast with Rosencrantz and Guildenstern. What Spenserian echoes are evident in the first quarto occur in the earlier rather than the later portions of the text.

May the Spenserian Books of Chastity and Friendship, containing the romantic tradition of the Garden of Adonis, the Mask of Cupid, and the Temple of Venus, be contributive to the second quarto? Furthermore, is it not possible that the ordeals toward holiness, temperance, and justice of Prince Arthur, the Redcrosse Knight, Sir Guyon, and Sir Artegall may have encouraged in Shakespeare's final revision of his play that reflective quality which is its chief distinction? Due allowance being made for coincidence, common figures and phrases, situations alike in both drama and romance, there remains a substantial kinship between this great English tragedy and the greatest ethical poem in English.[11]

[11] In "Hamlet as Minister and Scourge," *PMLA*, LXX (September, 1955), 740–749, Professor Fredson T. Bowers gives the argument for Hamlet's intemperance at the excessive extreme and considers his delay submissive to heaven rather than defective. The "tragic fact" demanding repentance from the hero and his punishment was the rash murder of Polonius mistaken for Claudius, an instance of private revenge rather than public justice.

CHAPTER VIII

Measure for Measure and the Book of Justice

NO play of Shakespeare is more timely for us than *Measure for Measure*, with justice as its theme and the testing or weighing of civil officers as its main action; but none of his plays needs more careful study of doctrines and procedures unfamiliar to our less courtly day. As in his two earlier dramas of professional crisis, *Troilus and Cressida* and *Hamlet*, here, too, the dramatist has enriched an old story with those ethical discoveries and reversals which alone transmute ruinous life into properly dramatic form. Prince Troilus, Prince Hamlet, Angelo the civil judge, and, in a play soon to be composed, Othello the general —all are led to recognize their flaws and then are permitted a conscious share in their own professional doom. All four go through an ordeal devised by the dramatist less for their personal salvation or destruction than to redeem them from their official excesses and defects into that admirable mean which allows them to perform, however briefly and finally, their duty to the state.

This chapter, then, deals with an ethical constituent of Shake-

The Book of Justice

speare's dramatic art not yet evident when he wrote the ordeals in court of the pathetic Richard II and the unregenerate Shylock. Here in the judicial discipline of Vincentio's deputy, Angelo, we find illustrated both the circumstances of civil wrongdoing and the method of civil redemption. To make this clear, Shakespeare adopts as the initial trope of his play the assaying, minting, and counterfeiting of the coinage.[1] His first scene, in which the "metal" of Angelo is to be put to the "test" and "stamped," would at once remind his auditors of the angels jingling in their purses.[2] Moreover, even as Vincentio's deputy exhibits in himself the struggle between false coinage and true value, he also foreshadows the dramatic action, the restoration in Vienna of the Duke (cf. ducat) and of that civil honesty or validity without which theories of government, in Vienna or in Shakespeare's "Angle-land," are of little worth.

The second trope in the play, the balancing of the scales,[3] with the difficulty of arriving at an exact poise, furnishes the title; it also represents the nature of justice to be no mere legalis-

[1] My evidence to follow was set down before I had read the article by Professor Wylie Sypher, "Shakespeare a Casuist: *Measure for Measure*," *Sew.Rev.*, LVIII (1950), 262–280. There he, too, and most appropriately, has referred to "the image of counterfeiting and weighing." Since my interpretation of these images in the light of Spenser's Book of Justice differs somewhat from his, I have let my evidence stand as I first arranged it.

[2] The angelot of the reign of Henry VI, 1427, was an Anglo-Gallic gold coin bearing the figure of the Archangel Michael slaying the dragon. The angel was an English gold coin in circulation 1470–1634. Lawrence (in *Shakespeare's Problem Comedies*, p. 89) derives the name Angelo from Giraldi Cinthio's play, *Epitia*, where "the sorella di Juriste is named Angela." The feminine of Angelo, Angela, is the name given by Spenser to the queen of the Angles (*F.Q.*, 3.3.56); is Angelo, then, the Englishman? Will Shakespeare's readers think of Gregory's pun?

[3] In Whetstone's play the figure of the balance occurs several times. See the text as given by James O. Halliwell, *The Works of William Shakespeare* (London, 1854), III, 244 ("justice with pitee payse, / Which two, in equall ballance waide . . .") and 290 ("measure grace with justice evermore").

tic act of summary reward or punishment but rather the condition of balance or imbalance, health or malady, in all the affairs of all men and women, among all citizens. Forewarned, we must not expect the agents to be whitely good or blackly evil, nor shall we be puzzled by a doom held in abeyance or by compromises which defeat our expectations. Shakespeare is balancing the too-much and too-little of the institutions and functionaries of his age. He places on the one scale the defect of appetence in the nunnery and on the other lust in the stews, fruitful love being, as it were, the happy mean—witness Julietta's pregnancy and Mariana's unflagging devotion. Again, disavowal or independence of contract on the one scale (Angelo with Mariana, Claudio with Julietta) attempts to balance on the other the rigors of what Claudio terms "the demigod Authority," [4] the desirable mean being the Duke's freedom of device and action or Mariana's freedom of passion and affiance. In the difficult Platonic art of minding one's own business, the Aristotelian duty of performing one's own function, other instances of the unfortunate extreme are the "insensible" and "stubborn" Barnardine versus the flighty and compliant Lucio; the inept Escalus versus Pompey, "yare" for his new task of executioner; Isabella's contentious arguments with circumstance versus Julietta's well-nigh mute surrender to destiny.

That Shakespeare was reworking his material in the mode of defect and excess is also indicated by the strongly adversative structure of many of the significant speeches. Witness Escalus (II.i.297–299):

> Mercy is not itself that oft looks so.
> Pardon is still the nurse of second woe.
> But yet—poor Claudio!

"But yet" is the dialectical pattern of *Measure for Measure*. Those who are tempted to underestimate Angelo's difficulties and overestimate Isabella's righteousness should review the play

---

[4] *Measure for Measure*, I.ii.124.

The Book of Justice

as an ethical action for the weighing of either agent against the other in a kind of balance, *quid pro quo*. Over their canceling flaws, right will be found, as Spenser tells us, sitting "in the middest of the beame alone" (5.2.48.9).

Let us, then, assume Shakespeare's familiarity, not only with *Promos and Cassandra*, Whetstone's play and narrative, and the story and play of Giraldi Cinthio about Juriste and Epitia, but with Spenser's great poem on justice, Book V of *The Faerie Queene*.[5] Such a "treatise"—Spenser's own word (5.3.3.7-9)—clarifies the action of *Measure for Measure* (its Aristotelian *praxis*) and illuminates the choices and thoughts of the agents (its Aristotelian *ethos* and *dianoia*). Also it furnishes—at least it, too, exhibits—the leading metaphorical images, counterfeit coin and tottering balance, upon which Shakespeare conducts his action. This imagery and metaphor we might call the Aristotelian *opsis* and *lexis* of both the Spenserian poem and the Shakespearean play. Even in a cursory reading of the Book of Justice we notice a literary kinship between Spenser's Artegall and Shakespeare's Duke Vincentio where both are admirable and between Artegall and Angelo where both are flawed.[6] The

---

[5] In *Shakespeare's 'Measure for Measure'* (London, 1953), Mary Lascelles reviews exhaustively the evidence on literary sources for this play and interprets it anew. She does not refer to Spenser's Book of Justice. Other important studies, following which this of mine takes its new direction, are—besides that of Professor Sypher—Elizabeth Marie Pope, "The Renaissance Background of *Measure for Measure*," *Shakespeare Survey*, II (1949), 66–82; Robert M. Smith, "Interpretations of *Measure for Measure*," *Sh.Quart.*, I (October, 1950), 208–218; Clifford Leech, "The 'Meaning' of *Measure for Measure*," *Sh.Surv.*, III (1950), 66–73; Doran, *Endeavors of Art*, pp. 385–389.

[6] Lucio's account of Angelo's ancestry (III.ii.115-117)—"Some report a sea-maid spawn'd him; some, that he was begot between two stock fishes"—recalls the Spenserian passage dealing with the origin of Artegall, who (3.3.26.3-9, Spenser's italics):

> "wonneth in the land of *Fayeree*,
> Yet is no *Fary* borne, ne sib at all
> To Elfes, but sprong of seed terrestriall,
> And whilome by false *Faries* stolne away,

Amazonians Radigund and Britomart help us to understand the extreme of initial severity, the mounting self-righteousness, and the final deference of Isabella. Spenser's Talus, the Iron Man, has served Artegall much as the Provost of the prison in Vienna serves Duke Vincentio (IV.2.89–90)—

> This is a gentle provost. Seldom when
> The steeled jailer is the friend of men

—the victims Sir Terpine and Claudio, under sentence of death, have somewhat in common; and the rascal Braggadochio has bequeathed himself to the rascal Lucio. Above all, the Temple of Isis and the Court of Mercilla have set the stage for Judgment Day in Vienna.

The testing of Spenser's allegorical abstractions in the various tourneys of justice from the Castle of Radigund to the Court of Mercilla is simpler and surer than the discipline given Angelo, Isabella, Claudio, and Lucio. Shakespeare must exercise his total ingenuity to bring to full dramatic life those wooden proxies of *Promos and Cassandra* which he was rearranging upon the framework of Spenserian ethical ideas. Now the traditional liability in any story or play about justice is the danger of unfair advantage or disadvantage to plaintiff or to defendant in the pronouncement of award or penalty. This being the case, a skillful artist is at some pains to maintain the personal validity of his agents, their human truth; and Shakespeare might well note with approval that Spenser had driven his action through equity to mercy. What better could he himself do than subject to compassionate scrutiny precisely those instances of defective and excessive feeling that his predecessor had only schematized? His Angelo and Isabella, therefore, would be bred to suspect and restrict feeling; Claudio and Lucio would be inclined to trust and exaggerate it. Among them the Duke must represent the happy

> Whiles yet in infant cradle he did crall;
> Ne other to himselfe is knowne this day,
> But that he by an Elfe was gotten of a *Fay*."

The Book of Justice

mean.⁷ The long and heated discussion as to the real nature of the agents in this central group bears sufficient witness to Shakespeare's skill in fusing an old story with a renascent ethics.⁸

How has this been accomplished in an action so impersonal as that of *Measure for Measure?* Where Spenser's similes are explicit, Shakespeare's metaphors are for the most part implicit. Spenser's persons illustrate or talk about justice and injustice; Shakespeare's agents, talking, are just and unjust. Like most men and women who serve as coinage in human transactions, the subjects of Vincentio are not very wise about themselves as money or about the ways in which they are spent in exchange. Only the Duke has become aware of the doctrines upon which both Spenser and Shakespeare depend; and even he must redeem his bad debts under the pressure of Angelo's bungling and Lucio's slander before he fully understands the cost of justice and his own responsibility for mercy. Yet the identity of doctrine in Book V of *The Faerie Queene* and in *Measure for Measure* is so easily demonstrable that a comparative study of the texts will go far to annotate the problems and solutions of the dramatic poet.

Artegall and Angelo; Terpine and Claudio

With the pun Angelo-angel, Shakespeare begins the assaying of the Viennese deputy. "What figure of us think you he will bear?" asks the Duke. And Escalus—like Spenser's Aegyptian wisards old, / Which in Star-read were wont haue best insight" (5.Prol.8.1–2)—reassures him (I.i.23–25):

---

⁷ On this point Miss Lascelles says (p. 148): "What [Shakespeare] fails to communicate is feeling: the impression that [the Duke] is deeply engaged." She refers to the world of *Measure for Measure* as "this strangely *un-familied* world" (her italics on p. 149).

⁸ See Hardin Craig, "Morality Plays and Elizabethan Drama," *Sh. Quart.*, I (April, 1950), 71: "It is part of Shakespeare's greatness that practically all of his characters have a definite pattern of aberration like that of the full-scope morality."

> If any in Vienna be of worth
> To undergo such ample grace and honour,
> It is Lord Angelo.

In adopting the Duke's metaphor, Angelo recognizes the nature of his ordeal (I.i.48–51):

> Now, good my lord,
> Let there be some more test made of my metal
> Before so noble and so great a figure
> Be stamp'd upon it.

Later, when fully deputized and himself proceeding to exercise justice, he applies the same metaphor to Claudio, the counterfeiter whose illegal paternity has debased the human currency (II.iv.42–46):

> It were as good
> To pardon him that hath from nature stol'n
> A man already made, as to remit
> Their saucy sweetness that do coin heaven's image
> In stamps that are forbid. 'T is all as easy
> Falsely to take away a life true made
> As to put metal in restrained means
> To make a false one.

Claudio, in his turn, begs Lucio to bid Isabella "assay" the deputy (I.ii.186); with a difference, Lucio says to her, "Assay the pow'r you have" (I.iv.76). Obediently she offers to "bribe" Angelo for her brother's life (II.ii.149–151)

> Not with fond sicles [shekels] of the tested gold,
> Or stones whose rates are either rich or poor
> As fancy values them; but with true prayers.

And, lastly, to further his stratagem the disguised Duke pretends to believe that "Angelo had never the purpose to corrupt [Isabella]; only he hath made an assay of her virtue to practise his judgment with the disposition of natures" (III.i.162–165).

The Book of Justice

With this revelatory end in view the Duke assays the virtues and vices of his subjects, and Shakespeare assays the ethical mean or extreme of his persons.

Kindred phrases extending the reference to coinage occur when the Duke holds "in idle price" the assemblies where young people display and amuse themselves (I.iii.9–10); Lucio slanders him as one who steals "from the state and usurp[s] the beggary he was never born to" (III.ii.99); Claudio and Julietta have postponed the outward ceremony of their "true contract" for the sake of "a dow'r . . . in the coffer of her friends" (I.ii.149–159), and for this Claudio must "pay down for [their] offence by weight" (I.ii.124–125). Elbow refers to buying and selling men and women like beasts, and Pompey answers, "'T was never merry world since, of two usuries, the merriest was put down and the worser allow'd by order of law a furr'd gown to keep him warm" (III.ii.1–9); but the diseases "purchas'd" in the bawdyhouse of Mistress Overdone are spoken of as "three thousand dolours" plus "a French crown" (I.ii.50–52). Meanwhile "strong statutes / Stand like the forfeits in a barber's shop" (V.i.322–323), and Angelo tells Isabella that, if he were to remit Claudio's penalty, "Mine were the very cipher of a function" (II.ii.39). When the deputy has decided to act, Escalus the legalist corroborates him: "You have paid the heavens your function and the prisoner the very debt of your calling" (III.ii.263 ff.). "Recompense" is the word used by the Duke in prophesying the amends to be made by Angelo to Mariana for his broken contract (III.i.263); Isabella, on the other hand, will not accept "redemption of the devil" (V.i.29).

Most significant for the dramatic assaying of his human coinage is the Duke's criterion of fruitfulness or increment, set forth at the very beginning of the play when he refers to Nature as "a creditor" thriftily lending out the "smallest scruple of her excellence," for which she demands "Both thanks and use [interest]." Hitherto Angelo with all his virtues has not been a good investment; his "proper . . . belongings" and he are confined to and wasted on each other; can he, if invested anew, really produce? Will his virtues "go forth of [him]"? Since the delegation of power is the distinctive function of Jacobean government—indeed of all civil government—the decision to put an Angelo to "use" instead of hiding his talent in the earth would at every turn clarify the play for its auditors; it would justify the Duke's procedure and help to win understanding and compassion for the deputy in his two bungling efforts to go forth of himself, potently toward Isabella and authoritatively toward Claudio. His liabilities are well-nigh tragic. That the action ends with a slight per centum for all the persons of the play—even Kate Keepdown, who gets a husband in the transaction—may be credited to the Duke's skillful brokerage.

This not very deeply hidden metaphor shows the dramatist concerned with what lies below the surface of judicial procedure, a theory of value. The "Great heapes of gold" in the Spenserian Cave of Mammon (2.7.5.8–9) were mostly

> stampt, and in their metall bare
> The antique shapes of kings and kesars straunge and rare;

but in *Measure for Measure* Shakespeare is not studying disproportionate monetary wealth or intemperate ways of hoarding or spending it. Under the figure of a sound currency he will rather accredit or discredit human worth or worthlessness. Vienna may be redeemed if its angels and ducats are found on testing to be true to their face value (I.iii.53–54):

> hence shall we see,
> If power change purpose, what our seemers be.

For his metaphor of a counterfeit coinage Shakespeare was of course not dependent solely on a literary source; but it strengthens our argument to recall that Artegall's first tourney in the Book of Justice had been won in disguise, that it had brought to light the infamy of Braggadochio, and that it had ended with

The Book of Justice

an analogy between bad pennies and knavish knights as follows (5.3.39.1–5):

> Now when these *counterfeits* were thus vncased
> Out of the foreside of their *forgerie*,
> And in the sight of all men cleane disgraced,
> All gan to iest and gibe full merilie
> At the remembrance of their knauerie.

When he probed below the surface of this figure of speech for concepts of civil honesty and knavery, Shakespeare would find helpful also Spenser's lines on the "antique vse" in the golden age (5.Prol.3.5–7),

> When good was onely for it selfe desyred,
> And all men sought their owne, and none no more.

He would represent Duke Vincentio as a student of the Socratic γνῶθι σεαυτόν; "one that," in the words of Escalus, "above all other strifes, contended especially to know himself" (III.ii.245–247). And, indeed, self-knowledge with its corollary, minding one's own business, is the main discovery of the plot in regard to all its redeemable agents.

Again, Spenser's prologue had derived injustice from change in the upper world, appearing in the lower world as "dissolution" (4.9). And the Spenserian picture of the zodiac amiss may well have suggested Claudio's bitter account of his sad predicament as a result of error on the part of his higher-ups (I.ii.162–175):

> Whether it be the fault or glimpse of newness,
> . . . . .
> Whether the tyranny be in his place
> Or in his eminence that fills it up,
> I stagger in—but this new governor
> Awakes me all the enrolled penalties
> Which have, like unscour'd armour, hung by th' wall
> So long that nineteen zodiacs have gone round

And none of them been worn; and for a name
Now puts the drowsy and neglected act
Freshly on me.

Comically stated by Mistress Overdone on hearing that all bawdyhouses in the suburbs must be pulled down, the doctrine reads (I.ii.107–108): "Why, here's a change indeed in the commonwealth! What shall become of me?" She, too, is minding her own business. And, as if Shakespeare would leave us in no doubt of the main cause of injustice, the disguised Duke "late come from the See / In special business from his Holiness," answers the query of Escalus—"What news abroad i' th' world?" —with an explicit diagnosis of the world's real trouble (III.ii. 232–245):

Novelty is only in request. . . . There is scarce truth enough alive to make societies secure. . . . This news is old enough, yet it is every day's news.

The transition in Vienna from Duke Vincentio, who has contended to know himself, to Lord Angelo, who knows himself not at all, thus runs parallel to Spenser's "golden age" transformed into "a stonie one." And from Spenser's metallic frame of reference Shakespeare might furnish his own prevailing figures in *Measure for Measure*. From the Book of Justice he would learn that Artegall's sword, Chrysaor, with which Jove had quelled the Titans, was made "of most perfect metall, . . . / Tempred with Adamant" (5.1.8–10) and that the "character" of Britomart (5.6.2.6–9)

> in th' Adamantine mould
> Of [Artegall's] true hart so firmly was engraued,
> That no new loues impression euer could
> Bereaue it thence.

In spite of his fidelity to Britomart, however, Artegall met a perilous challenge from an equally, if less admirably, resolute

The Book of Justice

woman, Radigund. In her attack upon him Spenser had compared her with (5.5.7.6–9)

> a Smith that to his cunning feat
> The stubborne mettall seeketh to subdew[;]
> Soone as he feeles it mollifide with heat,
> With his great yron sledge doth strongly on it beat.

Alas! the adamantine Artegall, having promised that if he were defeated he would serve his victorious opponent, discovered Radigund to be a woman, was mollified by her beauty, threw away his sword, Chrysaor, and was then by her compelled to deliver up his shield (5.5.12–17).[9]

> No hand so cruell, nor no hart so hard,
> But ruth of beautie will it mollifie.
>
> . . . . .
>
> Yet was he iustly damned by the doome
> Of his owne mouth, that spake so warelesse word,
> To be her thrall, and seruice her afford.

This is the very process of personal shock and resulting judicial folly that Shakespeare sets forth in his overconfident Angelo, suddenly smitten by the beauty of Isabella, thereupon renouncing the sword of justice, damned by the doom of his own mouth, and finally made thrall to Mariana. Also in this connection we may compare the "secret liking" of the man-hating Amazonian Radigund for Artegall in his woman's weeds at his womanish task of spinning with the secret lust for Isabella suffered by Angelo, formerly "A man of stricture and firm abstinence" (I.iii.12). Then Britomart's liberation of Artegall from his thralldom to Radigund would parallel Mariana's redemption of Angelo from his irrational passion for Isabella.

[9] We may still quote Spenser in apology for Angelo as well as for Artegall (5.6.1.8–9):

> "For neuer yet was wight so well aware,
> But he at first or last was trapt in womens snare."

What might seem to us an arbitrary device in the plot of *Measure for Measure* would not dismay readers of Spenser's deft allegorical changes of fortune. Beneath both lay the sound theories of human behavior induced from careful observation of human beings by two masters of the science of ethics and the art of conduct.

In that other fallible agent, society itself, the dangers of disintegration concern all who study justice and injustice. To Radigund's Amazonian "troupe of women warlike dight" (5.4. 21.8) Radigund herself proved faithless, and to Radigund her "trustie Mayd" Clarinda was disloyal. Is there a kind of injustice, a fruitless character, in the antisocial segregation of women from men, rendering women too mannish and men too womanish? This is the obvious conclusion of Spenser's allegory, as it was almost three centuries later of Tennyson's romance, *The Princess*. If Britomart was wise in repealing the "long vsurpt . . . liberty of women" in the Amazonian Castle of Radigund, we may infer that in the minds of Shakespeare and his lay auditors it would not seem unfitting for Isabella to abandon her career in the nunnery of St. Clare (Radigund's deputy in the Book of Justice was *Clarinda*) and become Duchess of Vienna. Isabella's defection must not be—indeed it was not—made an issue; but who could object to the heroine's change from a self-righteous novice whose best hope was for "a more strict restraint / Upon the sisterhood" of St. Clare (I.iv.4–5) into a gentler Isabella, refined by human sorrow and peril and at last to be stamped in the image of the Duke himself, his strength, prudence, justice, and mercy? Thus love had softened Britomart toward Artegall.

The loving but heedless fornication of the uxorious Claudio with Julietta is injustice at its other extreme. When Angelo accuses Claudio of being thief and counterfeiter, one who has "put metal in restrained [forbidden] means / To make a false [coin]" (II.iv.48–49), he is preparing for a denouement in which the

The Book of Justice 163

metaphor of coinage will still prevail. Angelo and Claudio as extremes—the one too brittle, the other too malleable—weaken the Court of Vienna in contrary ways; yet when they are weighed in the scales of justice—"An Angelo for a Claudio! death for death!" (V.i.414–416)—they are both found susceptible of reminting.

Now the reminting of Claudio, who has for that purpose been withdrawn from circulation (I.ii.128–132)—"So every scope by the immoderate use / Turns to restraint"—may be better understood when we compare it with the less successful ordeal of Spenser's imprudent Sir Terpine, another thrall of the ruthless Radigund. The point at issue in the bitter struggle between Radigund and Terpine is honor versus shame, not true justice; and this is the very theme dramatized in the debate between Claudio and his self-righteous sister. Except for the intervention of the Duke, Claudio would perish at the word of Isabella as surely as Sir Terpine, despite his temporary reprieve by Artegall, had been hanged by the decree of Radigund.

Artegall had come upon Sir Terpine (5.4.22, 25)

> With both his hands behinde him pinnoed hard,
> And round about his necke an halter tight,
> As ready for the gallow tree prepard:
> His face was couered, and his head was *bar'd*,
> That who he was, vneath was to descry.
>
> . . . . .
>
> Him Talus tooke out of perplexitie,
> And horrour of fowle death for Knight vnfit,
> Who more than losse of life ydreaded it;
> And him restoring vnto liuing light,
> So brought vnto his Lord, where he did sit.

The image of Sir Terpine's "bared head" reappears in the directions given by the Duke to his Provost (IV.ii.187–189): "Shave the head and trim the beard [of Barnardine as if he were

Claudio], and say it was the desire of the penitent to be so *bar'd* before his death"; and Sir Terpine's "couered" face is the prototype of Claudio, muffled, led before Vincentio by the Provost for judgment.[10]

[10] There is more than a similarity in appearance between the victimized Sir Terpine and Claudio; and they have even more in common than their preoccupation with honor and shame. "More then losse of life" Sir Terpine dreaded the "horrour of fowle death for Knight vnfit"; and Claudio complains to Isabella, "Death is a fearful thing. . . . 'T is too horrible." Artegall had lectured Sir Terpine in a series of interrogations (5.4.26–28):

> "Sir Terpine, haplesse man, what make you here?
> Or haue you lost your selfe, and your discretion,
> That euer in this wretched case ye were?
> Or haue ye yeelded you to proude oppression
> Of womens powre, that boast of mens subiection?
> Or else what other deadly dismall day
> Is falne on you, by heauens hard direction,
> That ye were runne so fondly far astray,
> As for to lead your selfe vnto your owne decay?"

The Duke, on the other hand, in a speech about value which gives to *Measure for Measure* much the same kind of help that Ulysses' speech on "degree" gives to *Troilus and Cressida*, attempts to redeem Claudio from his fear of death (III.i.5–43).

The argument that "death" makes both life and death "sweeter" is not quite in the line of medieval homily, still less in the sex jargon of Jacobean England. The Duke seems rather to have in mind a spiritual essence which improves or validates a physical thing. Claudio's weakness has been the substitution of earthly satisfaction for spiritual dignity. Analogized, the riddle might read somewhat as follows: Physical life is to spiritual life as a coin is to the value we spend it for. "If I do lose thee, I do lose a thing / That none but fools would keep." Physical life, like a coin or other such mere token, is "servile to . . . skyey influences"; it is ignoble—"For all th' accommodations that thou bear'st / Are nurs'd by baseness." The origin of physical life is base: "Thou art not thyself; / For thou exist'st on many a thousand grains / That issue out of dust." Physical life is "not certain; / For thy complexion shifts to strange effects, / After the moon." And—here again like the currency—physical life resembles "an ass whose back with ingots bows . . . / And death [cf. expenditure] unloads thee." Physical life is the fool of value. Laboring to shun questions of value, we still must confront them. In

The Book of Justice

Braggadochio and Lucio are both irredeemable, bad pennies both. In the nature of their badness, however, they suggest unanimity on the part of their creators, Spenser and Shakespeare. Spenser (2.3.4.1–7) had described his "losell" as

> One that to bountie neuer cast his mind,
> Ne thought of honour euer did assay
> His baser brest, but in his kestrell kind
> A pleasing vaine of glory vaine did find,
> To which his flowing toung, and troublous spright
> Gaue him great ayd, and made him more inclind.

Lucio's vainglory and flowing tongue relate him to the tradition of the boaster bequeathed by the Latin comic writers to the sixteenth century; but Lucio is no mere Ralph Roister Doister. In his comradeship with Pompey he recalls the association of Braggadochio and Trompart, and in his juxtaposition with Isabella he is another Braggadochio insolent in the presence of Belphoebe. His gratuitous slanders and his abandonment of his cronies are all of a piece with the behavior of the classical boaster; but no reader of the Spenserian passage in which Braggadochio aroused the ire of Artegall and was handed over to Talus for punishment would fail to recognize the similar irritation of Duke Vincentio because of the slanders and impertinence of Lucio, whom he hands over to the Provost for punishment—marrying a punk in lieu of whipping and hanging.

---

physical existence resides neither valor nor happiness nor friendship nor progeny nor comfort. Life, it would seem, is something to be spent; and death is the value purchased. In this view we can better understand the Duke's text: "Be absolute for death."

And Claudio replies in the same veiled language: "To sue to live, I find I seek to die; / And seeking death, find life. Let it come on." When the Duke overhears him weakening, in his request that Isabella win life for him at the cost of her honor, again he intervenes: "Do not satisfy your resolution with hopes that are fallible." At this reminder Claudio asks his sister's pardon, and the Duke approves: "Hold you there. Farewell." Claudio's sense of value has been set right.

Spenser left the knights and ladies who had witnessed the uncasing of Braggadochio (5.3.40.1–3)

> in pleasure and repast,
> Spending their ioyous dayes and gladfull nights,
> And taking vsurie of time forepast.

This is, in his phrase, the end of one fair furrow; the problem of "licentious lust" must still be solved by Artegall, who henceforth would deal with the equity of human claims and judicial awards.

Amidas-Bracidas-Lucy and Angelo-Mariana

Henceforth we, too, in our study of the metaphorical fabric of *Measure for Measure*, must come to the scales of justice as the dominant figure of Spenserian "treatise" and Shakespearean drama alike.

Did Shakespeare know Spenser's solution in equity for the contention of the two brothers Bracidas and Amidas, owners of two islands (5.4.8.1–4)? Said Bracidas:

> But tract of time, that all things doth decay,
> And this deuouring Sea, that naught doth spare,
> The most part of my land hath washt away,
> And throwne it vp vnto my brothers share.

As a result, the well-dowered Philtera, betrothed of Bracidas, jilted him for his lucky brother Amidas, who then jilted "Lucy bright, / To whom but little dowre allotted was." Lucy threw herself into the sea where, "the billowes beating of her . . . / She chaunst vnwares to light vppon" a sea-beaten chest; on this she floated to the diminished island of Bracidas. Philtera claimed that the treasure in the chest was *her* dowry, lost by "cruell shipwracke." The brothers submitted their strife to Artegall, who adjudged the coffer to Bracidas and Lucy, as a gift from the sea to recompense them for the land given by the sea to Amidas

The Book of Justice

and Philtera. "For equall right in equall things doth stand" (5.4.19.1–9).

The old sea-beaten chest has indeed suffered a literary sea change in *Measure for Measure*. May we imagine that it comes into the plot as Mariana's dowry, lost in the shipwreck of her brother Frederick? The diminished island on which Lucy found asylum would then become Mariana's moated grange. Of Mariana herself, dowerless, Bracidas' remark about Lucy is true: "Her vertue was the dowre, that did delight." But Shakespeare's judge, Vincentio, is allowed greater discretion than Spenser's judge, Artegall. Where Artegall substituted one good for another merely, the Duke makes spiritual restitution. Mariana is restored to Angelo, who has jilted her, and Claudio is sent back to Julietta, whom he has demeaned. Each reprobate is firmly held to his contract.

In the opinion of the Provost, who serves *Measure for Measure* as a kind of Talus, obedient Iron Man, the hangman Abhorson and the bawd Pompey "weigh equally; a feather will turn the scale" (IV.ii.31–32). In the same trope Angelo encourages Isabella to agree to his price for Claudio's life (II.iv.67–68):

> Pleas'd you to do't at peril of your soul,
> Were equal poise of sin and charity.

He threatens her repeatedly with perverse reference to the scales of justice (II.iv.156–159, 170):

> My place i' th' state
> Will so your accusation overweigh
> That you shall stifle in your own report
> And smell of calumny.
>
> . . . . .
>
> Say what you can; my false o'erweighs your true.

At the crises of the play, however, both Isabella and the Duke are quick to remind us of the value which cannot be determined by balancing *quid pro quo:*

Isabella: [II.ii.126] We cannot weigh our
brother with ourself. [II.iv.185] More
than our brother is our chastity.
Duke: [III.ii.275–280]
He who the sword of heaven [11] will bear
Should be as holy as severe;

. . . . .

More nor less to others paying
Than by self-offences weighing.
Duke: [V.i.110–112]
If he had so offended,
He would have weigh'd thy brother by himself
And not have cut him off.

Yet, as the Duke has prophesied to Isabella, Angelo is in equity "compel[led] to [Mariana's] recompense" and "the corrupt deputy [is] scaled" (III.i.262–265). "Like doth quit like, and Measure still for Measure" (V.i.416).

All other judicial skirmishes of *Measure for Measure* are subordinate to the ordeal of the Duke of Vienna. Like Artegall, who learned from Astraea (5.1.7.1–4)

to weigh both right and wrong
In equall ballance with due recompence,
And equitie to measure out along,
According to the line of conscience

but who later came to suspect the "mighty Gyant . . . holding forth on hie / An huge great paire of ballance in his hand" (5.2.30.1–3), the Duke, too, finds that there are things which cannot be reduced "vnto equality." "By no meanes," said Artegall, "the false will with the truth be wayd. . . . All the wrongs [can] not a little right downe way." Spenser's Gyant was drowned in the sea by Talus, and all his rout was scattered (5.2.49.9; 54.1–2)

[11] Cf. the Spenserian Chrysaor.

The Book of Justice

> As when a Faulcon hath with nimble flyght
> Flowne at a flush of Ducks.

Does Isabella recall Spenser's images when, in conversation with her brother, she uses these same two similes within ten lines of each other (III.i.81, 89-92)? "As when a giant dies . . . as falcon doth the fowl." Right cannot be weighed with wrong; Isabella's projected dishonor cannot be weighed against Claudio's threatened life.

Statutes are ineffective; courts of law are inadequate. What, then, is the proper procedure in matters supervening equity? Artegall had rebuked the Gyant, enraged with his failure to "poise" his balances (5.2.47.4-6):

> Be not vpon thy balance wroken:
> For they doe nought but right or wrong betoken;
> But in the mind the doome of right must bee.

He declared that when "heauenly justice" prevails, "euery one doe know their certaine bound." Such a general revelation stars the final scene of *Measure for Measure*, with the added assurance of the Duke to Isabella, "What's mine is yours, and what is yours is mine." Thus love transcends justice. And thus we may consider the temporary retreat of the Duke from his studies in Vienna not as a surrender but as an interlude in his official education, an opportunity Shakespeare would later give to another scholarly protagonist, Prospero, Duke of Milan. Both are remitted to the practice of their theories. Moreover, Vincentio, who has believed at the start of the action that no dart of love could "pierce [his] complete bosom" (I.iii.3), must at the end, like Angelo, "find an apt remission in [himself]" (V.i.503).

And that brings us to the place of mercy in the administration of justice.

Spenser had dealt with equity and judicial mercy in his myth of Isis, wife of Osyris. At the Temple of Isis the crocodile sleeps under the feet of Isis (5.7.22.7-9)

> To shew that clemence oft in things amis,
> Restraines those sterne behests, and cruell doomes of his
>   [Osyris].

If we compare Angelo with Osyris and Isabella with Isis—"For that they both like race in equall iustice runne" (5.7.4.7–9)—we can the better understand Isabella's bitter retort, "By *course* of justice," to Angelo's excuse for Claudio's conviction "by *course* of justice." As contrasted with the stern Angelo, therefore, Vincentio would seem to be a priest of Isis rather than the crocodile under her feet. Although at first the Duke apologizes for his failure to enforce the laws (I.iii.21–23),

> Which for this fourteen years we have let sleep,
> Even like an o'ergrown lion [12] in a cave,
> That goes not out to prey,

he soon comes to believe rather in "correction and instruction" (III.ii.33). Restoration, pardon, forgiveness, are the magic words at the end of *Measure for Measure*.

Such a scene Spenser had outlined at the Court of Mercilla, and he had prepared for it, not only by the disguises of Artegall (5.3.20; 5.8.25) and Britomart (3.3.51.9; 5.7.21.4–5), but by the helpful pretense of one of Mercilla's maidens to "weepe and wayle" (5.9.9.9). The efforts of the Spenserian Litae, who (5.9.31.5–9) calm Jove's anger, "cruell vengeance stay," should also be considered when we look upon the stage picture of Mariana and Isabella on their knees before the Duke to plead for the life of Angelo.

Now whereas disguise pays "with falsehood false exacting"

---

[12] Here in the stock allusion the playwright may have been glancing also at the Spenserian passage (3.3.30.1–5):

> "Like as a Lyon, that in drowsie caue
> Hath long time slept, himselfe so shall he shake,
> And comming forth, shall spred his banner braue
> Ouer the troubled South, that it shall make
> The warlike Mertians for feare to quake."

The Book of Justice

and thus performs "an old contracting," the final aim and mode of justice is truth. Artegall "Did cast about by sleight the truth thereout to straine" (5.1.24.9). Not until the truth be known can grace avail. This Angelo has paid heavily to learn; the Duke's qualified sentence follows upon his deputy's full confession (V.i.372–379):

> I should be guiltier than my guiltiness
> To think I can be undiscernible
> When I perceive your Grace, like pow'r divine,
> Hath look'd upon my passes! Then, good prince,
> No longer session hold upon my shame,
> But let my trial be mine own confession.
> Immediate sentence then, and sequent death,
> Is all the grace I beg.

"Like pow'r divine." This is the prototype for the earthly judge, as Spenser had made clear in the Prologue to Book V (10.6–9):

> That powre [God] also doth to Princes lend,
> And makes them like himselfe in glorious sight,
> To sit in his owne seate, his cause to end,
> And rule his people right, as he doth recommend.

Such delegation of power Spenser traces with summary skill (5.4.1.1–9):

> Who so vpon him selfe will take the skill
> True Iustice vnto people to diuide,
> Had neede haue mightie hands, for to fulfill
> That, which he doth with righteous doome decide,
> And for to maister wrong and puissant pride.
> For vaine it is to deeme of things aright,
> And makes wrong doers iustice to deride,
> Vnlesse it be perform'd with dreadlesse might,
> For powre is the right hand of Iustice truely hight.

The circumstances of mercy he sets forth in a passage (5.9.20–37) too long to quote here but rich with such judicial circumstances as Shakespeare put to use in his last scene. Moreover, the dramatist appears to have ended his action in full agreement with Spenser's doctrine as to the grounds of mercy (5.10.2.1–9):

> For if that Vertue be of so great might,
> Which from iust verdict will for nothing start,
> But to preserue inuiolated right,
> Oft spilles the principall, to save the part;
> So much more then is that of powre and art,
> That seekes to saue the subiect of her skill,
> Yet neuer doth from doome of right depart:
> As it is greater prayse to saue, then spill,
> And better to reforme, then to cut off the ill.

"[Mercie is] pour'd down on men, by influence of grace" (5.10.1.9). Shakespeare's Duke of Vienna needs no further apology. The accident of Ragozine's death, which allows him to solve his problem successfully, he acknowledges as "an accident that heaven provides" (IV.iii.81). Those who remember that the disguised Duke comes back to Vienna on "special business from his Holiness" (III.ii.233) will not refuse to look still further, beyond the papal See, for the source of that Justice who is, in Spenser's phrase (5.Prol.10.1–2),

> Most sacred vertue she of all the rest,
> Resembling God in his imperiall might.

And all of us who try to interpret *Measure for Measure* can in one particular at least agree with Shakespeare's clownish Lucio: "Grace is grace, despite of all controversy" (I.ii.25–26).

In this chapter two poems of the same era on the same theme and of comparable length and intricacy have been set side by side for the better understanding of ethical action in narrative and drama. Surely it is a primary obligation of scholarship to explain the import of a drama in terms familiar to the dramatist himself; and when Spenser's Book of Justice is used as com-

The Book of Justice

mentary upon *Measure for Measure*, the critic need no longer invoke later systems of ethic and poetic to answer riddles of characterization and thought. As a result, Shakespeare's gift to the tradition of masterpieces on the theme of justice can be seen more clearly in its sober outlines of an equity tempered by compassion, a compassion deriving from grace. That Shakespeare —possibly with Spenser's help—has consciously trained himself to deal with justice the virtue rather than justice the vengeance augurs well for the series of tragedies we must next consider.[13]

[13] I append certain of Professor Sypher's remarks from his article cited above: "Vienna's darkest problems are darkly answered" (p. 262). "The balance in Vienna between mercy and justice is thematic, a dramatic abstraction of the problem of equity to which Shakespeare gives an ambiguously hilarious answer" (p. 268). "This kind of fissure between 'comedy' and 'morality' does not open in the earlier and later plays. Here the issues are all held in the loose of question" (p. 271). "The counterpositions are schematic, though the effects are indeterminate" (p. 274). "Already, in *Measure for Measure*, Shakespeare may—unguardedly and dimly—have had the intimation of [the] larger justice [in Cymbeline]" (p. 279). His evidence and mine are frequently in accord; what he calls the "indeterminate effect" may, however, be a result of the similarly unconcluded ordeal of the Spenserian Artegall.

Watkins (*Shakespeare and Spenser*) associates the decadent society of *Measure for Measure* with Spenser's Castle Joyous (p. 49), Isabella with Belphoebe (p. 50), Mariana with Amoret and Claudio with Timias (p. 51), Angelo with Artegall (p. 54), Lucio with Braggadochio, and Vincentio with Mercilla (p. 57).

CHAPTER IX

The Book of Holiness as a Design for Tragedy

THE experience of feeling whole or asunder, hale or ill, which underlies the belief in unity as the condition of organic life, also furnishes the central archetype in poetry, especially in drama. The archetype itself is variously sophisticated in the form of a dilemma: holiness versus unholiness in religious and ecclesiastical practices and institutions; unity or disunity in the state; wholesome as against corrupt social habits; integrity or disintegration in personal conduct; and mental and physical health or disease. The record of corruption, disintegration, and disease in the literature of our own time demands rather less of the poet than did older, more energetic, and more carefully articulate actions; but even amid our manifold literary qualms and pangs we go on assuming the desirability of what in Old English would be called *hāl* or *hālig*, that is, whole or holy. Like Macbeth before he met the witches, we are ambitious, but in our hearts we do not approve the "illness" attending ambition; what we would "highly," that would we "holily."

This archetypal dilemma constitutes the frame of choice

The Book of Holiness

within which literary actions acquire human significance. Probably the most elaborate statement of the dilemma in English literature is Spenser's Book of Holiness; surely Shakespearean tragedy is its supreme illustration. Have these aught in common? Might our hypothesis that Shakespeare studied Spenserian temperance and courtesy, chastity and justice, be extended to assume that he was familiar also with the Book of Holiness? Would this Book shed light on the action of the great tragedies?

In order to motivate the ethical action and then, mimetically, the literary action of the first and fundamental Book of his *Faerie Queene*, Spenser regards holiness, the end in view, as imperiled by diverse kinds of disintegrative evil. Becoming holy, therefore, must be made to appear as difficult in literature as it is in life, with hazards not less great than the stakes are high; threats from the outside and flaws within will be combined to burden and heighten the task of the hero. Now, since no threat concerns us more nearly than the threat to our whole-ness and no flaw sickens us more woefully than ill-ness of the self, the poet best serves us when through his fictitious agents he makes us, too, aware of the nature of whole-ness and ill-ness and the cost of healing. Understanding alone, however, does not assure health or holiness. If the action is to succeed, the hero and we who share his adventure must be willing candidates for the right spiritual or imaginative therapy. Literary devices to bring this about are the stock in trade of narrative and dramatic poetry. How did Spenser refine them? And how would Shakespeare intensify them for tragic effect?

The malignant or unholy agents in the Book of Holiness are Archimago and Duessa; their evil character is duplicity, their aim is to divide, and their agency is deception. All this would encourage a dramatist reading Spenser's allegory to conceive his tragedies on the intellectual plane, not as mere exhibitions of passion or vice with agents merely brutal or bestial. The initial flaw of credulity, however complicated later with violent emotions, would thus distinguish the properly tragic hero; deception as a means toward a questionable or even a speciously desirable end might then be more and more finely represented as self-deception; witness Othello, Lear, and Macbeth.

Spenser calls his benign agent, Una or Truth, a "type." Such a typical heroine Shakespeare places at the center of his later tragedies and romances, to be villainously maligned and as a result to be deserted by the easily credulous and hence unfaithful hero. The action, therefore, is at the outset an intellectual process leading to the discovery of the heroine's truth, but then, and most urgently, it is an ethical ordeal for the healing of the hero. Such a pattern had already been attempted in *Much Ado* (where Hero is slandered), in *Twelfth Night* (where Viola in disguise is threatened by Orsino), in *All's Well* (where Helena is first repudiated by and later, when disguised, is got with child by the willful Bertram), in *The Merry Wives* (where Anne Page must deceive her parents), in *Troilus and Cressida* and the second quarto of *Hamlet* (where Cressida and Gertrude, seeming fair, are really false), and in *Measure for Measure* (where the spotless Isabella, like Ophelia in *Hamlet*, is arbitrarily entangled in evil). But whatever justification of or judgment on the heroine takes place in these ironic comedies and near tragedies is not accompanied by a satisfactory discipline of the erring Claudio, Orsino, Bertram, Mistress and Master Page, Troilus, Claudius, or Angelo. Only in the case of Hamlet, the least iniquitous of these heroes, do we feel that the ethical action has been justifiably concluded.

When, in later plays, truth as troth becomes the role of Desdemona and Cordelia, of Imogen and Hermione, or when a discredited country or city is to be saved from villainy or reunited—Malcolm's Scotland or the Rome of Coriolanus and Octavius—the gravity of the situation demands a proper reversal. Before the blindly or willfully schismatic hero can repair what has been impaired, he must learn to recognize and to know himself, and—the main characteristic of Shakespeare's mature tragic

The Book of Holiness

art—he must be significantly healed, be made whole or holy again in such a way that he heals us, too. To this end, his spiritual ordeal may take the form of an extended discipline like that of the Redcrosse Knight in the House of Holiness under the tutelage of Dame Caelia: witness Lear's contemplations on the heath, Posthumus in manacles, and Leontes' sixteen years under the rod of Paulina. Or the ordeal may be intensified into a fatal agony like that of Othello goaded by Iago, Macbeth tormented by the riddling witches, Coriolanus at banishment, or Antony in the uneasy enslavement of his self-imposed exile.

These mythic resemblances are not yet close poetic analogies; but they lead us to consider more strictly the relation between successive stages in Spenser's Book of Holiness and Shakespeare's succession of five mighty tragedies: *Othello, King Lear, Macbeth, Coriolanus,* and *Antony and Cleopatra.*

Othello

Othello is the first of the tragedies of which it may be said that duplicity innervates the action. Deceits and disguises abound in earlier Shakespearean plays, as in all plays; but Portia pretending to be a lawyer, Rosalind pretending to be a forester, Viola pretending to be a page, even Hamlet pretending to be a madman and Vincentio pretending to be a friar, are for the most part benign. In *Othello,* however, when good is misrepresented as evil, the worth of human life is cloven throughout. Othello, uxoriously prepossessed with the true seeming or false seeming of a woman on the insinuation of a guileful villain, invites comparison with the Redcrosse Knight, deceived by Archimago into thinking Una a wanton. The mythic pattern is identical. Furthermore, Spenser's myth or "legend" is just what a dramatist needs to invigorate the story of the Moor and Disdemona in the *Hecatommithi* of Giraldi Cinthio. Cinthio's unnamed ensign might even be endowed with the lesser half of Arch*imago*'s name, be called "Iago" for short.

Whether or not the name Iago is suggested by the name

Arch*im*a*go*, Iago himself is an opportunist in the tradition of the Spenserian archplotter. He is not merely the evil turn of events; with the unvarying persistence of his allegorical prototype he uses every occasion to deceive and divide. His victim, Othello, like the Redcrosse Knight, has been sent on an errand of vital importance to the state. This time it is the rescue of Venice and Cyprus from the threat of invasion by the Turks—those same Turks who, as the Paynims Sansfoi, Sansloi, and Sansjoi, thwarted the endeavors of the Redcrosse Knight. In Othello's company, also, travels "a louely Ladie."

After a "blustring storme" and their wanderings "too and fro in wayes vnknowne" and after the hero's victory over Errour in the first canto of the Book of Holiness, Una wished for him many such victories: "And henceforth euer [I] wish that like succeed it may!" After a similarly "desperate tempest," perilous wandering over the sea, and an earlier rescue from the erroneous allegations of witchcraft made against Othello by Brabantio, Desdemona and Othello are reunited in what seems to be permanent happiness. Othello's soul

> hath her content so absolute
> That not another comfort like to this
> Succeeds in unknown fate.

Desdemona calls on the heavens to

> forbid
> But that our loves and comforts should increase
> Even as our days do grow!

Alas for both Una and Desdemona!

Right here, however, allegory will not serve the needs of tragedy. Unlike Una, Desdemona is not flawless; she has deceived her father. Upon this flaw will be based and validated Iago's plot against the "supersubtle" heroine and the knightly but "perplex'd" hero. The false vision of Una's wanton behavior which deceived the credulous Redcrosse Knight becomes credi-

The Book of Holiness   *179*

ble for Othello. The Turkish wars against Cyprus may be "done"; but "Great Jove, Othello guard!" Meanwhile, Othello has no suspicions of himself. For him, too, "Our wars are done; the Turks are drown'd." At this point, Iago, who swears he is no "slanderer"—"or else I am a Turk"—activates his plot; and during the ensuing brawl Othello ironically foreshadows his own part in the action:

> Are we turn'd Turks, and to ourselves do that
> Which heaven hath forbid the Ottomites?

The answer is yes. Once Othello's trust in Desdemona has been shaken, the three sins—lack of faith, lack of control, lack of joy—which as Sansfoi, Sansloi, and Sansjoi had been combated by the Knight of Holiness (and Satyrane), are now given free rein to work their divisive mischief upon the island of Cyprus. The faithless Othello, the ill-governed Michael Cassio (notably in his lewd behavior toward Bianca as well as in his drunkenness), and the grumpy Roderigo are manipulated by the deceitful Iago to thwart the good faith, mutual respect, and happiness of the hero and heroine. But Shakespeare's master stroke, highly characteristic of his tragic art, is the transformation of such abstractions as Spenser named Sansfoi, Sansloi, and Sansjoi into faithlessness, lawlessness, and joylessness on the inner stage of Othello's soul. The "rage dispiteous" of Sansfoi, "the fowle reproches and disdaineful spight" of Sansloi, the fury of Sansjoi who "seemd in hart to harbour thoughts vnkind, / And nourish bloudy vengeaunce in his bitter mind" (1.4.38.8) are now seen to be the latent flaws of the Moor. Desdemona's prayers to him in the crisis of his ill government avail as little as the prayers of Una to Sansloi.

In *Othello* there is no Satyrane to save Desdemona, no Prince Arthur to save Othello. And when finally Othello learns the truth about Desdemona and about himself he is not permitted the services of Dame Caelia's leech, Patience, for his "disease of grieued conscience." The Redcrosse Knight had been subjected to "bitter Penance, with an yron whip . . . And sharp Remorse . . . And sad Repentance." These brought him "to torment . . . so great" (1.10.28.2–3)

> That like a Lyon he would cry and rore,
> And rend his flesh, and his owne synewes eat;

and this was only the first stage in his disciplinary ordeal. Shakespeare allows his remorseful hero a triple roar; then Othello the military governor of Cyprus must execute judgment on Othello the Turk (V.ii.352–356):

> And say besides that in Aleppo once,
> Where a malignant and a turban'd Turk
> Beat a Venetian and traduc'd the state,
> I took by th' throat the circumcised dog
> And smote him—thus.

The Venetian Othello slays the Turkish Othello as Gloriana's Knight of the Red Crosse slew the Turk Sansfoi.[1]

King Lear

But when Spenser ended his Book of Holiness, Sansloi, son of "old Aveugle," was still at large. Did Shakespeare have him in mind when he created the bastard Edmund, son of the blindly lawless Gloucester? "Fine word—'legitimate'!" Surely Duessa has bequeathed to Goneril her characteristic hypocrisy. When she deserted the Redcrosse Knight for Sansjoi and, at the end of the Book of Holiness, sent a desperate letter by Archimago to thwart the alliance of the Redcrosse Knight and Una, she possibly suggested to Shakespeare an end for *King Lear*. Witness the letter Goneril sends by Oswald to urge upon Edmund the murder of Albany on the eve of his alliance with the friends

---

[1] In their respective natures and situations, Watkins (*Shakespeare and Spenser*, p. 212) associates Amoret and Scudamour with Desdemona and Othello; he notices the similarity between Archimago and Iago (p. 63).

The Book of Holiness

of Cordelia. Both intrigues fail; and the final encounter between the power of good, championed by Albany and Edgar, and the power of evil, championed by Goneril and Edmund, bastard, has certain echoes of the battle between the Redcrosse Knight and Sansjoi in the lists of Lucifera at the House of Pride. In the latter episode the throwing of gauntlets and the "shrilling trompett" may have helped to furnish the last scene of *King Lear* with its "pledge" and "exchange" and its triply sounded trumpet.

The most arresting similarity between the Book of Holiness and *King Lear* will be indicated in a review of Spenser's House of Pride, Cave of Despaire, and House of Holiness (cantos 4–5, 9, and 10). As the Redcrosse Knight departed from the first, escaped from the second, and climbed the utmost reaches of the third, we shall see the allegorical design behind the ordeal of Lear and Gloucester.

In the House of Pride, whither Duessa had enticed the Redcrosse Knight, reigned Lucifera; these two unpleasant ladies parallel and in some part may account for the "large speeches," "deprav'd quality," and "plighted cunning" of King Lear's elder daughters. Especially does the disdainful usurper Lucifera (Pride) spell out a formula for the usurper Goneril. The six other deadly sins are referred to or illustrated in their Spenserian imagery now by one, now by another of Shakespeare's agents.

1) Lucifera herself, with the "dreadfull Dragon . . . vnderneath her scornefull feete" and the "mirrhour bright" in her hand and her "Husher, Vanitie by name," come to mind when Goneril subjugates her father ("the dragon and his wrath"). Oswald is a "glass-gazing . . . rogue"; and does he not take "Vanity the puppet's part against the royalty of [Goneril's] father"? The Fool cries out, "There was never yet fair woman but she made mouths in a glass." We might even wonder whether it is Lucifera-Goneril's mirror that Lear borrows to determine the breathing life or the breathless death of Cordelia,

a gesture which furnishes the supreme irony of the play. Some truths are invisible in the glass of pride.

2) When Lucifera called for her coach, the first of her beastly company in harness was "sluggish Idlenesse . . . / Vpon a slouthfull Asse," leading his life "in lawlesse riotise." Lear's knights, says Goneril, "grow riotous"; again and again Goneril and Regan speak of them as "riotous": their "not-to-be-endured riots," their behavior characteristic of a "riotous inn," "the riots of your followers." Lear himself is an "idle old man." And Idlenesse's Asse? Thus the Fool describes Lear's retinue: "Thy asses are gone [to make ready thy horses]. . . . May not an ass know when the cart draws the horse?"

3-4) Third in Lucifera's equipage came "loathsome Gluttony . . . on a filthie swyne" and fourth, "lustfull Lechery, / Vpon a bearded Goate." The association of these vices with these animals is of course traditional; we note, however, that Edgar —pretending to be "one that slept in the contriving of lust, and wak'd to do it"—places early in his list of self-imputed vices lechery and sloth. He is "hog in sloth, fox in stealth, wolf in greediness, dog in madness, lion in prey [? pride]." It is unimportant that poor Tom keep these allegorical emblems straight; and the imagination of the mad Lear amplifies the list of lechers beyond the traditional fauna into wren and fly, fitchew and horse; but Edmund properly associates lechery with a "goatish disposition."

5-6) Spenserian "Greedy Auarice . . . / Vpon a Camell loaden all with gold" is glanced at in Edmund's attempt to steal Edgar's inheritance and in Lear's demand that pomp "shake the superflux" to wretchedness. Spenserian "Enuie . . . / Vpon a rauenous wolfe" may be detected upon Goneril's "wolfish visage." In Envy's bosom is "an hatefull snake," this usual association accounting for several of Lear's references: the "serpent's tooth," the "tongue most serpent-like." Albany calls Goneril "this gilded serpent."

7) If Goneril, like Lucifera, be proud and envious, Lear is an

The Book of Holiness

illustration of Spenserian Wrath, "reuenging Wrath / Vpon a Lion, . . . Trembling through hasty rage, when choler in him sweld." Lear is not "ague-proof"; in him, too, the "mother," the "hysterica passio, . . . swells up toward [the] heart." Again, witness the followers of Spenser's Wrath (1.4.35.7–9):

> The swelling Splene, and Frenzy raging rife,
> The shaking Palsey, and Saint Fraunces fire:
> Such one was Wrath.

On the heath under "the wrathful skies" Lear is described as if Shakespeare has remembered the vivid picture of the "ruffin raiment . . . / . . . all to rags yrent" of Spenser's Wrath in his furious fit "Through vnaduized rashnesse woxen wood." Running "unbonnetted" on a night when the cub-drawn bear, the lion, and the belly-pinched wolf keep their fur dry, the mad old King is brought to understand and share the misery of "loop'd and window'd raggedness."

The Redcrosse Knight and his Dwarf, escaping from Lucifera and Duessa of the House of Pride, prefigure Lear and the Fool, emerging from the clutches of Goneril and Regan. If Shakespeare needed aught to strengthen his representation of vice and deadly sin, he would find it in Spenser's fourth canto. Nevertheless, on that very heath where the terrible Lear and the pitiable Gloucester become fellows in the wrack of the elements begins the healing discipline which will wring from the one the last bit of his willfulness and from the other every remnant of his disregard for the moral law. With Spenser's help we can recognize in the text of the tragedy not merely certain of its structural metaphors or its profound if ambiguous ethical system or its ironic presentation of human destiny, but also a possible origin for its tragic action. The carcasses at the postern of the House of Pride are not the answer to the seven deadly sins. Something must be done; and the tragic poet proceeds to his task in full view of Spenserian allegory.

For the woeful story of the disaster in the life of the Earl of Gloucester Shakespeare was indebted in part to Sir Philip Sidney's *Arcadia* (II, 10) and, hypothetically, also to Edmund Spenser's Cave of Despaire. Readers of the ninth canto of the Book of Holiness and Despaire's arguments for suicide, which have been earlier cross-referred to Hamlet's soliloquy on suicide, will recognize in Gloucester's persistent efforts to make way with himself the weakness of a man "credulous" and unholy. As was true of Sansloi's father, Aveugle, Gloucester's vision is flawed. The father cannot see the general in the particular or the real behind the accidental; and this makes him fair game for his shrewd but lawless son. He has opposed and opposes the "great opposeless wills" of the gods. When he has been enlightened, he must still be "saved from despair." This is a task for his legitimate son, Edgar, who henceforth becomes another Knight of the Red Crosse, dealing with despair in his father after he has dealt with it in himself.

Surrounding the Cave of Despaire on the unholy side of Spenser's Faeryland (1.9.34.1–3)

> old stockes and stubs of trees,
> Whereon nor fruit, nor leafe was euer seene,
> Did hang vpon the ragged rocky knees.

"For many miles about" the Castle of Gloucester, too, "there's scarce a bush." Shakespeare has sketched the scene of Edgar's hovel in comparably bleak and desperate terms. Within the Cave was one (1.9.35)

> low sitting on the ground,
> Musing full sadly in his sullein mind;
> His griesie lockes, long growen, and vnbound,
> Disordred hong about his shoulders round,
> And hid his face; through which his hollow eyne
> Lookt deadly dull, and stared as astound;
> His raw-bone cheekes through *penurie* and pine,
> Were shronke into his iawes, as he did neuer dine.

> His garment nought but many ragged clouts,
> With thornes together pind and patched was,
> The which his *naked* sides he wrapt abouts.

As just such a one Edgar has disguised himself, taking (II.iii. 7–12)

> the basest and most poorest shape
> That every *penury*, in contempt of man,
> Brought near to beast. My face I'll grime with filth,
> Blanket my loins, elf all my hair in knots,
> And with presented *nakedness* outface
> The winds and persecutions of the sky.

Obviously, then, Edgar's "foul fiend" in *King Lear* is kin to Spenser's Despaire; and the reference to this fiend "that hath laid knives under [poor Tom's] pillow and halters in his pew" may derive originally from Despaire's offer of a "rope" to Sir Trevisan and a "rustie knife" to Sir Terwin—although Shakespeare would also find the rope and knife associated in Harsnet's *Declaration* (1603), from which he drew other phrases for Edgar as poor Tom.[2]

Sir Trevisan, barely escaping from Despaire's "hollow caue, / Farre vnderneath a craggie clift ypight," helps us to imagine Edgar, almost hopeless, emerging from his hovel with the cry "Away! the foul fiend follows me! . . . Take heed o' th' foul fiend." He is also the allegorical type for Gloucester saved from despair after throwing himself, as he supposes, from the crown of the cliff of Dover. Moreover, except that Shakespeare would conceivably remember Despaire's ceaseless and unavailing attempts at suicide, and all the circumstances of the Spenserian episode, Shakespeare's Edgar might not have hit upon a practical device for proving to his unholy old father that "the clearest gods . . . have preserv'd [him]." Thus the Redcrosse Knight, attempting suicide, was lessoned by Una: "In heauenly mercies

---

[2] *King Lear*, ed. by George Lyman Kittredge (Boston, 1940), p. 184.

hast thou not a part?" With such doctrine "the foul fiend" is exorcised and disappears from the "crown o' th' cliff." "Henceforth," says Gloucester (IV.vi.75–77),

> I'll bear
> Affliction till it do cry out itself
> 'Enough, enough,' and die.

In the crisis of Britain's woes he holds true Edgar's reminder that "men must endure / Their going hence, even as their coming hither." And at the last, when Gloucester has been made whole again, in his recognition of Edgar his "flaw'd heart . . . [bursts] smilingly." As a Knight of Holiness Edgar has succeeded where the Redcrosse Knight almost failed—except for Una.

Similarly, in the image of her prototype, Una, Lear's Cordelia shakes "the holy water from her heavenly eyes" and serves the misweening mad old King as Una and Mercie served the Redcrosse Knight. In this she has the help of a doctor not unlike Spenser's leech, Patience. Lear has promised to be "the pattern of all patience"; and when Cordelia says (IV.vii.26–29),

> O my dear father, restoration hang
> Thy medicine on my lips, and let this kiss
> Repair those violent harms that my two sisters
> Have in thy reverence made,

she echoes the "med'cines" given to the Redcrosse Knight while "bitter Penaunce" with "yron whip," "sharpe Remorse," and "sad Repentance" were also doing their best. Cured in conscience, Spenser's hero had also been reunited with his beloved Una, who (1.10.29.4–6)

> Him dearely kist, and fairely eke besought
> Himselfe to chearish, and consuming thought
> To put away out of his carefull breast.

The Knight of the Red Crosse had been led "by a narrow way / Scattred with bushy thornes, and ragged breares . . .

The Book of Holiness

vnto an holy Hospitall" and to the Hermitage of Contemplation (1.10.35–46). King Lear (IV.iv.3–6),

> Crown'd with rank fumiter and furrow weeds,
> With hardocks, hemlock, nettles, cuckoo flow'rs,
> Darnel, and all the idle weeds that grow
> In our sustaining corn,

also ends his ordeal on the contemplative level within his "wall'd prison." In appearance he resembles Contemplation: his "white flakes" may be compared with the "snowy lockes" like "hoarie frost with spangles" on "an Oke halfe ded" of Spenser's old man; and the disregard of physical comfort or discomfort in both is comparably related to "the tempest in [the] mind" of Lear and Contemplation's "mind . . . full of spirituall repast," while his flesh was "pyn'd . . . to keepe his body low and chast."

And, finally, the unforgettable phrases in which Shakespeare's Lear and Cordelia take upon themselves "the mystery of things" as if they were "God's spies"[3] to wear out those "that ebb and flow by th' moon"—although Lear's "eyes are not o' th' best"—should be cross-referred to the imaginative insight of Contemplation, who often saw "God . . . from heauens hight" (1.10.47),

> All were his earthly eyen both blunt and bad,
> And through great age had lost their kindly sight,
> Yet wondrous quick and persant was his spright,
> As Eagles eye, that can behold the Sunne.

Under the influence of Contemplation and from the "sacred chappell" and "little Hermitage" the Redcrosse Knight was at last able to see

> The new Hierusalem, that God has built
> For those to dwell in that are chosen his.

[3] See "The Gods and God in *King Lear*," by Alwin Thaler, in *Renaissance Papers* (University of South Carolina and Duke University, 1955), pp. 32–39.

Less glorious is the scene allowed Lear and Cordelia from their "wall'd prison," "gilded butterflies and . . . poor rogues" talking of court news instead of allegorical "blessed Angels." But if our comparisons be appropriate, two centuries before Blake imagined Jerusalem in England's pleasant land Spenser at Cleopolis and Shakespeare in London had sketched in their own characteristic ways a right goodly city for a regenerated British hero in the legendary tradition of St. George.

Macbeth

Meanwhile, in circumstances amounting to a royal command, Shakespeare must supply the court of James Stuart with a royal play.[4] This time the fate of Scotland would be put in question. For a third instance of Spenserian holiness as a design for tragic action, the tyrannical Giant Orgoglio, that "monster mercilesse," should be compared with Shakespeare's Macbeth; and "fowle wel favoured" witch Duessa will be heard again in the evil counsel of Lady Macbeth. These two villains are as successful in making away with Duncan and Banquo and usurping the throne of Malcolm as were their allegorical prototypes in capturing the Redcrosse Knight. Spenser's phrases—"griesly Night . . . in a foule blacke pitchie mantle," "mirkesome aire," "ghastly Owle," "dreadfull Furies," and "damned sprights sent forth to make ill men aghast"—echo in Shakespeare's lines. Most significant, the initial duplicity of the Book of Holiness serves to introduce a drama where once more "fair is foul and foul is fair."

Therefore, from the start we shall consider the action of *Macbeth* to be, not primarily personal or domestic, not even in the limited sense dynastic or civic, but in the highest sense holy. Scotland must be healed, made whole again; and thereby human nature must be cured of something essentially and profoundly evil, both "false" and "disjoint." Malcolm (like the

---

[4] These circumstances are set forth by Henry N. Paul in *The Royal Play of 'Macbeth'* (New York, 1950).

The Book of Holiness

Redcrosse Knight) and Macduff (like Prince Arthur) are the restorative agents of the play; and Macbeth and his Lady, the tyrant and the witch in the semblance of Spenser's Orgoglio and Duessa—however generously Shakespeare may have humanized them—at every point thwart the proper action.

Previous to the defeat and capture of the Redcrosse Knight by the Giant Orgoglio (cf. Duncan and his sons overcome by Macbeth; or cf. the Scottish hero Macbeth delivered into the hands of the tyrant Macbeth), Duessa had secured the help of Grandmother Night and her "coleblacke steedes yborne of hellish brood" to carry the wounded Sansjoi to the leech Aesculapius in hell (cf. Lady Macbeth's appeal to "thick night" and "murth'ring ministers" for help in her "fell purpose" of making a man of the "brainsickly" Macbeth; cf. also the Aesculapian doctor who fails both Lady Macbeth and Macbeth in that he cannot "minister to a mind diseas'd"). On her return from hell, Duessa learned that the Knight had escaped from the House of Pride (cf. the escape of Malcolm and, later, of Fleance). She hurried after him and in his moment of weakness seduced him, thus permitting his capture by the Giant Orgoglio (cf. Macbeth, the quondam Scottish hero, as Glamis and Cawdor, seduced by his false-appearing and false-hearted Lady into the hands of his evil self, the usurping and tyrannical Macbeth, King of Scotland). Meanwhile Una, deserted and dismayed (cf. Lady Macduff), obtained the services of Prince Arthur and his Dwarfe, who challenged the Castle of Orgoglio (cf. Macduff and Lennox knocking at the gate of Macbeth's castle in Inverness). After combat Arthur cut off Orgoglio's head (cf. Macduff with the head of Macbeth). Duessa was stripped "of roiall robes, and purple pall" and sent to wander "wayes vnknowne" (cf. Lady Macbeth in her nightgown, lacking sanity, wandering in mind). Finally, the Redcrosse Knight was set free, saved from despair, and restored to his knightly task (cf. Malcolm's self-recriminations and, later, his coronation).

Shorn of the tragic irony, the pitiable and terrible revelations of evil in Shakespeare's play, such a forthright analysis of action brings it close to the Spenserian episode. The events and persons of *Macbeth* come out of Holinshed's *Chronicle;* its theories of kingliness and witchcraft are doubtless indebted to the writings of King James; but its dramaturgy rests on the two archetypal situations supporting Spenser's allegory in cantos 5, 7, and 8, the appeal of the "fowle" witch to the forces of darkness and the capture of a hero by a giant who is later beheaded by a princely deliverer.

In chief, we must note the possible derivation of Act II of *Macbeth* from the scene at Orgoglio's castle. Recalling those ruthless murders committed by giant and witch, who are interrupted by the "shrilling sound" of the "horne of bugle" blown by Arthur's Squire so

> That all the castle quaked from the ground,
> And euery dore of freewill open flew,

recalling also the dismay of "the Gyaunt selfe,"

> rushing forth from inner bowre,
> With staring countenance sterne . . .
> And staggering steps
> . . . . .
> And after him the proud Duessa, . . .
> High mounted on her manyheaded beast,

we are in a position to understand the ethical plight of Macbeth and Lady Macbeth when Macduff and Lennox knock at their gates. Shakespeare's Porter is a far cry from Spenser's Ignaro, the porter of Orgoglio, with his bunch of rusty keys and the refrain "he could not tell . . . he could not tell"; but the effect upon our nerves and hearts of the bugle call in Spenser's poem and the repetitious knocking in Shakespeare's play is identical. The "filthy" floor of the Castle of Orgoglio and the "filthy wit-

The Book of Holiness 191

ness" on Macbeth's hand are the same kind of filth. The loud braying "with beastly yelling sound" of the wounded Orgoglio may be compared to the "lamentings heard i' th' air, strange screams of death," which are mentioned in Lennox's description of the unruly night about Inverness. And in one speech made by Lady Macbeth a curious oversight points most tellingly to Spenser's canto as one origin of Shakespeare's second act. After the alarm bell is rung at Macduff's order (II.iii) Lady Macbeth enters asking,

> What's the business,
> That such a hideous *trumpet* calls to parley
> The sleepers of the house?

This "trumpet" is no "alarum bell," no mere "knocking"; this is the Spenserian "bugle" of canto 8 of the Book of Holiness (1.8.4.5–6).

> No false enchauntment, nor deceiptfull traine
> Might once abide the terror of that blast;

Lady Macbeth faints.

Nor should we neglect to mention Shakespeare's reference to the giant at the end of *Macbeth*. Spenser had said (1.8.24.6–9):

> But soone as breath out of his breast did pas,
> That huge great body, which the Gyaunt bore,
> Was vanisht quite; and of that monstrous mas
> Was nothing left, but like an emptie bladder was.

In this same figure of deflation Angus speaks of the diminished tyrant of Act V of *Macbeth*:

> Now does he feel his title
> Hang loose about him, like a giant's robe
> Upon a dwarfish thief.

Giant and dwarf? Orgoglio and Arthur's Dwarfe have possibly helped to supply this powerful simile.

Orgoglio had given Duessa (1.7.16.3–5)

> gold and purple pall to weare,
> And triple crowne set on her head full hye,
> And her endowd with royall maiestye.

To no avail. Similarly, Shakespeare's dramatic action has not only thwarted the usurpers and restored Scotland; it has also compelled King Macbeth to recognize that "juggling fiends" have paltered with him in a "double sense" and Macbeth's Queen to acknowledge that "Hell is murky." The "sencelesse speach, and doted ignorance" of Ignaro, jailer of Orgoglio's castle—"he could not tell . . . he could not tell . . . he could not tell . . . he could not tell"—seem to prefigure Macbeth's most pitiful apology: Life is

> a tale
> Told by an idiot, full of sound and fury,
> Signifying nothing.

Coriolanus

In the dungeons of Lucifera's House of Pride, as the Redcrosse Knight learned only just in time, lay (1.5.47–49) "that great proud king of Babylon" (Nebuchadnezzar), Croesus, Antiochus, Nimrod, Ninus, Ammon's son; and

> in another corner wide were strowne
> The antique ruines of the Romaines fall:
> . . . .
>
> Proud Tarquin, and too lordly Lentulus,
> Stout Scipio, and stubborne Hanniball,
> Ambitious Sylla, and sterne Marius,
> High Caesar, great Pompey, and fierce Antonius.

"Amongst these mighty men were wemen mixt": Semiramis, Sthenoboea, and "high minded Cleopatra." Reading of these proud men and women, a dramatist familiar with Plutarch's *Lives* might wish to add to the victims of Lucifera, not only Antony and Cleopatra, but also Volumnia and her son, the opponent of Tarquin. The Roman ladies in *Coriolanus*, Volumnia, Virgilia, Valeria, who play with a grace not derivable from Plutarch interpretative parts around the proud and ruthless Roman general, are grouped in three as if the dramatist might have remembered Spenser's diversification of his triads, in chief, Elissa, Medina, Perissa, the haughty, the temperate, the "loosely light." And Volumnia has certain traits in common with Lucifera: "earth she did disdayne," "lowly she did hate." Of the six deadly sins drawing the couch of proud Lucifera, Wrath, riding upon a lion, is the prototype of Coriolanus the general, as earlier of Lear the king.

The dramatic action of *Coriolanus* is the preservation of Rome. In Plutarch's Life of Coriolanus as Englished by Sir Thomas North Shakespeare found his necessary materials, the historical events and persons; but for the pattern which was to turn biography into tragedy he depended on the old myth of a monster to be slain by a hero. At the very center of Rome there is monstrous mischief. The plebeians are called "Hydra" (III.i.93), the "beast with many heads" (IV.i.1–2) and "multitudinous tongue" (III.i.156); and the leader of the patricians, Caius Marcius, at first honored by Rome with the name Coriolanus, later at his banishment describes himself as (IV.i.30–31)

>Like to a lonely dragon, that his fen
>Makes fear'd and talk'd of more than seen.

Tullus Aufidius, too, says that Coriolanus "fights dragon-like" (IV.vii.23); and Menenius, the authoritative person of the play, points out, "This Marcius is grown from man to dragon. He has wings; he's more than a creeping thing" (V.iv.13–14).

Who, then, is the monster-slaying hero of *Coriolanus?* The Coriolanus who has defeated the Volscians at Corioles? The Coriolanus who flouts the plebeian Hydra at Rome and is butted out of the city by the many-headed beast? Or the Coriolanus who, having vowed to destroy Rome, struggles with the traitorous dragon in his own soul and spares the city at the cost of his own life?

This triple combat, which gives form to Shakespeare's tragedy, parallels the three-day combat of the Redcrosse Knight with the Dragon in the eleventh canto of Spenser's Book of Holiness. On the first day of that encounter, forth from the Dragon flowed fresh "a gushing riuer of blacke goarie blood" and from its maw a "scorching flame"; the hero was "with durty bloud distaynd"; his face was "sore swinged" and "all his bodie seard." Comparably, we notice the unusual repetition in *Coriolanus* of the words, *blood, bloody, bleed, bled:* "His bloody brow"—"his bloody brow? O Jupiter no blood!" prays Virgilia; but Volumnia considers "Hector's forehead" lovely "when it spit forth blood." Meanwhile Caius Marcius comes bleeding out of Corioles, re-enters it bleeding:

> Worthy sir, thou bleeds't.
> —The blood I drop is rather physical
> Than dangerous to me.

"Who's yonder / That does appear as he were flay'd?" asks Cominius, as Caius Marcius rushes to his rescue. Is he "mantled" in "the blood of others" or in his own? "By th' blood we have shed together" Caius Marcius begs of his general the chance to oppose Tullus Aufidius, arouses all who "love this painting / Wherein you see me smear'd," boasts to Aufidius, " 'Tis not my blood / Wherein thou seest me mask'd," and puts the Antiates to rout. "From face to foot," says Cominius, recommending him for the consulship, "he was a thing of blood." Later in the play, after his banishment from Rome and traitorous league with Aufidius, he still boasts of "the drops of blood / Shed for [his] thankless country" and the "tuns of blood" he has drawn out of the breast of the Volscian state. Like the Knight of the Red Crosse, the "bloudie Crosse" (2.1.18.9), Caius Marcius is signed in red. Moreover, the signification by Shake-

The Book of Holiness

speare of his hero's "large cicatrices," those "wounds" of which the candidate for Roman consulship makes light—"unaching scars," "scratches with briers"—again furnishes Coriolanus with a mythic equivalent for the red cross of St. George.

At the end of that first day of bloody combat Spenser's hero was "Faint, wearie, sore, emboyled, grieued, brent" (I.11.28.1); may it be with this in mind that Shakespeare permits Coriolanus a brief moment of weakness? "I am weary; yea, my memory is tir'd" (I.ix.90). Curiously, too, as the Knight of the Red Crosse fell backward into a convenient "well of life," which could restore the dead and the "guilt of sinfull crimes cleane wash away," Coriolanus needs a bath after his bloody encounter. Earlier he has disregarded Cominius' wish that he be "conducted to a gentle bath / And balms applied." Now, although he deprecates "acclamations hyperbolical, ... For that I have not wash'd my nose that bled," he obeys (I.ix.67–69).

> I will go wash;
> And when my face is fair, you shall perceive
> Whether I blush or no.

In these references there is more than a hint to ally Spenserian and Shakespearean heroes in their need for lustration after blood guiltiness.

The ordeals of Spenser's Redcrosse Knight are Herculean (I.11.27):

> Not that great Champion of the antique world,
> Whom famous Poetes verse so much doth vaunt,
> And hath for twelue huge labours high extold,
> So many furies and sharpe fits did haunt,
> When him the poysoned garment did enchaunt
> . . . . .
> As did this knight twelue thousand dolours daunt.

"The shirt of Nessus" will later appear on the Herculean Antony enraged with Cleopatra (*Antony and Cleopatra*,

IV.xii.43); here also in *Coriolanus* echoes of the myth of a Hercules support the myth of a St. George. The "gown of humility" that Coriolanus is reluctant to wear in seeking the consulship is a garment out of which he is impatient to change; and his lungs shall "Coin words . . . against those measles, / Which we disdain shall tetter us." At his banishment he exhorts Volumnia as if she were "the wife of Hercules" (IV.i.17–19); and after his banishment Cominius and Menenius warn (IV.vi. 98–100):

>—He will shake
>Your Rome about your ears.
>   —As Hercules
>Did shake down mellow fruit.

But the exasperation of the hero in the second episode of the play is no mere shirt of Nessus clinging to the outside of him. Deep within him lurks the dragon that will sting him on to his immoderate rage. This is foreshadowed when the Roman tribune Sicinius asks (III.i.263–264, 286–287):

>   Where is this viper
>That would depopulate the city and
>Be every man himself?
>
>   . . . . .
>
>For we are peremptory to dispatch
>This viperous traitor.

We are never allowed to forget the older myth of the monster to be slain.

On the second day of combat the Redcrosse Knight wounded the Dragon on the skull. This time the monster tossed aloft his "stretched traine" and the "sting" from his "angry needle" pierced the shield of the hero, who must hew off "fiue ioints" of the "huge taile." The grip of the "cruell claw" upon the shield, the severed "paw," are further indications of bitter struggle in the allegorical body politic. Shakespeare in his turn will

The Book of Holiness

respond with notable instances of wounds to the patrician head, perils to the patrician shield, and severe reprisals on the plebeian "great toe" of the Roman state. Again and again either faction is bitten, curbed, pricked, poisoned, gored, pecked, licked, butted, clawed, pierced, stung ("teeth," "curb," "cockle," "poison," "horn[?]" and noise o' th' monster's," "peck," "tongue," "goat," "hands off," "lay hold," "lay hands upon him," "tent"). Finally, the dragonish Coriolanus will be sheared from the consulship and severed from the city—"He's a disease that must be cut away" (III.ii.295).

All such clawing and stinging took place in Spenser's narrative to the accompaniment of the "burning Aetna" of "flames," "rockes," "clouds," "smoke," "stench," and "heate." Shakespeare's Coriolanus likewise cries out: "The fires i' t' lowest hell fold-in the people!" And the people respond by shouting "To th' Rock, to th' Rock with him." Now this "steep Tarpeian death" barely avoided by Coriolanus, the "lonely dragon," reminds us that the allegorical dragon slain by Spenser's allegorical hero on the third day of their encounter was not so fortunate (1.11.54):

> So downe he fell, and forth his life did breath,
> That vanisht into smoke and cloudes swift;
> So downe he fell, that th' earth him vnderneath
> Did grone, as feeble so great load to lift;
> So downe he fell, as an huge rockie clift,
> Whose false foundation waues haue washt away,
> With dreadfull poyse is from the mayneland rift,
> And rolling downe, great Neptune doth dismay;
> So downe he fell, and like an heaped mountaine lay.

Coriolanus is not thrown down from "ten hills [piled] on the Tarpeian Rock"; and thanks to the intercession of Volumnia, his mother, Rome will be spared. But, instead of any "trickling streame of Balme" flowing from such a goodly "tree of life" as healed the wounds of the Redcrosse Knight after his second day of fighting, Coriolanus treacherously seeks asylum at the house of Tullus Aufidius, enemy of Rome. There, to match the restorative "fruit and apples rosie red" of Spenser's version of the myth, Shakespeare's Roman rebel finds "wine, wine, wine," and a "feast [smelling] well"; and there, now an exile, he is set at the "upper end o' th' table" among the enemies of Rome.

Although the third day of combat between the Redcrosse Knight and the Dragon of the Book of Holiness saw the monster vanquished, Shakespeare's final action in preserving Rome from the attack of her traitorous exile begins where Spenser's third day ended. The "rages" and "revenges" of the "unholy" Coriolanus must still be allayed in a conflict whose marginal agony is beyond Spenser's power or ken (V.iii.185–189):

> O my mother, mother! O!
> You have won a happy victory to Rome;
> But for your son—believe it, O believe it!—
> Most dangerously you have with him prevail'd,
> If not most mortal to him.

The victory made possible by the heroic arguments of Volumnia is indeed mortal for her son, the "lonely dragon." Meanwhile, the "laurell boughes" thrown at the feet of the victorious Redcrosse Knight have become the "flowers" strewn before Volumnia, Virgilia, and Valeria, returning to Rome from their successful but costly errand.

We cannot think of Caius Marcius, victim of Volscian swords, as a thoroughgoing St. George. Nor can we, in view of his surrender to Volumnia, call him a complete monster. Yet in Shakespeare's version of the monster-slaying hero what was monstrous has been overthrown as surely as in the Book of Holiness; "Dead was it sure, as sure as death in deed" (1.11.12.3).

Finally, we may note in *Coriolanus*, as earlier in *King Lear*, Shakespeare's skill in apportioning a Spenserian version of the deadly sins among the patricians and plebeians of that other

The Book of Holiness

House of Pride, the Eternal City, Rome; here again, the fourth canto of the initial Book of *The Faerie Queene* seems likely to have furnished distinct and identifiable images. The play opens with an accusation of gluttony against the patricians: "What authority surfeits on would relieve us" (I.i.16–17). Menenius suggests that the beards of the dilatory tribunes be entombed in an ass's pack saddle, which we assume will be placed on such an "Asse" as was ridden by Spenser's Sloth; and Brutus, the tribune, complains (II.i.265–269) that the avaricious patricians hold the plebeians,

> In human action and capacity,
> Of no more soul nor fitness for the world
> Than camels in the war, who have their provand
> Only for bearing burthens

—a probable reminiscence of Spenser's Avarice on a camel. Coriolanus calls the tribune Sicinius "old goat!" (III.i.177). Coriolanus himself is not covetous, says Cominius; but throughout the text there are frequent references to his "wrath," his "anger," his "rage," his "choler," and—with emphasis—his "tiger-footed rage" (III.i.312). The recurrent epithet hurled upon him is "proud"; five times in the first scene and again and again in later scenes Shakespeare's agents refer to this trait. He is not only the son of a Volumnia very like Spenser's Lucifera; he is himself a veritable Lucifer. Only by a kind of self-defeat does he complete his dramatic task of saving his city.

Antony and Cleopatra

The references to witchcraft and magic in *Antony and Cleopatra* suggest that Shakespeare would crown his tragic series with a dramatic version of the Duessalike Cleopatra to balance the Archimagolike Iago with which, we have assumed, he began it in *Othello*. Here at last deception and division are more than artifices; they are the wayward tendencies in all humanity. Holiness is still the desideratum; Octavius Caesar is looking for a "hoop" to hold the world "staunch"; but his sister Octavia will prove less strong "to join . . . kingdoms and . . . hearts" than Cleopatra is to divide them. We are never allowed to forget the opposition of these two tragic women in a conflict as thoroughgoing as that between the two allegorical ladies of the Book of Holiness. Octavia, with her "holy, cold, and still conversation," deserted by Antony for the "infinite variety" of Cleopatra, bears more than an accidental likeness to holy Una, deserted by the Redcrosse Knight for the variously deceptive Duessa.

What kind of holiness is possible, then, for this hero and this heroine? What is the action of *Antony and Cleopatra?* Not, as in *Othello,* the protection of Cyprus and Venice against the Turks; not, as in *King Lear,* the regeneration of a king of Britain. Neither is it, as in *Macbeth,* the deliverance of Scotland from the usurper and tyrant; nor, as in *Coriolanus,* the costly redemption of Rome. This supreme effort toward holiness will probe through imperial, royal, noble, and gentle circumstances to the very center of the manly and womanly nature—the action of *Antony and Cleopatra* is conjugal. Antony's debt to the Empire will be paid by a sword thrust, and he will become a "bridegroom in [his] death"; and Cleopatra's triumph over her wavering and hypocritical self is fully expressed in her words, "Husband, I come!"

Let us, then, consider this mightily expansive play as a record of pomp and circumstance surrounding what will turn out to be a betrothal, such banns as were celebrated in the last canto of the Book of Holiness for Una and the Knight of the Red Crosse. Would Spenser's hymeneal myth yield anything to help the tragic poet see within the disasters of Antony and Cleopatra as set forth by Plutarch somewhat more than another *casus illustrium?* How might Shakespeare give proper tragic effect to the incidents as he found them in Sir Thomas North's translation of the Life of Marcus Antonius?

The Book of Holiness

Only in an occasional image does the tragedy reflect the elaborate pictures of Spenser's allegory. Deceit and credulity have been relegated to a subordinate place in the final change of fortune, when Cleopatra sends Antony a false account of her death and Caesar and Cleopatra beguile each the other with hypocritical offers of kindness and deference. Yet the seduction by the gypsy Cleopatra of a doting and idle Antony has clearly enough repeated the seduction by the witch Duessa of a Redcrosse Knight enfeebled by his drink from the "dull and slow" waters of the enervating fountain (1.7.5–7) and

> Pourd out in loosnesse on the grassy grownd,
> Both carelesse of his health, and of his fame.

This trope prefigures the "Lethe'd dulness" of Shakespeare's Antony, who must from his "enchanting queen break off."

Again, we must confess that Duessa does little more than lend implications to Shakespeare's Cleopatra. "Great maistresse of her art" was that false Duessa; and no less can be said for the Queen who, in Antony's words, "Pack'd cards with Caesar and false-play'd [his, Antony's] glory," who "robb'd [him] of [his] sword." "Let witchcraft join with beauty, lust with both!" (II.i.22). Such is Pompey's wish for the hero and heroine; and it is likely to be granted except for a certain conviction learned, it may be, by Shakespeare from the ethical art of Spenser. This gives the lovers a fighting chance even while, or just because, their mistakes grow monstrous upon them.

As the "noble ruin of [Cleopatra's] magic" (III.x) the hero is not more reprehensible than was the Redcrosse Knight; and Shakespeare not less explicitly than Spenser leaves us in no doubt about what he intends (I.i.57–59). His Antony

> when he is not Antony
> . . . comes too short of that great property
> Which still should go with Antony.

In this regard, the action must restore for us the proper self of the Roman, not alone in his self-inflicted penalty, but supremely in the "dream" of Cleopatra, where he takes on the glorious attributes of St. George as loved by Una or Prince Arthur as the Knight of the Faery Queen. Antony a kind of Prince Arthur? Cleopatra a Faery Queen?

Those who are willing at this point to reread the North translation of Plutarch's Life of Marcus Antonius will be impressed by what of it Shakespeare disregards: the indescribable cruelty, treachery, baseness, of both hero and heroine; the massive record of military and political concern—witness the Parthian campaign—which far overbalances the conjugal entanglements of the hero; his leaden or brutal years spent with one or the other or a third lady; the ugly forms of self-abuse; and the progeny, willful or pitiful. Here is no great lover. Yet Cleopatra must love him.

Even before Antony's death Shakespeare would seem to depend on Arthurian traits and associations for help toward the tragic reversal. In appearance Arthur and Antony are matched. Arthur's "bauldrick" with its "pretious stone . . . / Shapt like a Ladies head" and thus denoting the Prince's complete fidelity to the Faery Queen, comes to mind when Cleopatra buckles Antony into his armor. She is "the armourer of [his] heart," he says, and the acts of those who helped him defend Alexandria will be commended to her as to a "great fairy," Queen of Egypt (IV.viii.12–16).

> O thou day o' th' world,
> Chain mine arm'd neck! Leap thou, attire and all,
> Through proof of harness to my heart, and there
> Ride on the pants triumphing.

Nevertheless Antony has no Arthur's shield "of Diamond perfect pure and cleane" with which to daunt the "unequall armes of his foes." The victory on land to which his "great fairy" sends

The Book of Holiness

him will be followed by the betrayal and defeat at sea for which he blames her. Therefore the Arthurian baldric embossed by the queenly head becomes again a Herculean "shirt of Nessus" (IV.xii.43); and his "great fairy" can pacify him only with a false account of her death, which provokes his suicide.

When Cleopatra and her maids heave Antony's dying body up to the monument, we are again reminded of a scene from *The Faerie Queene*. With Una to applaud, "After long paines and labours manifold," Arthur "found the meanes . . . vp to reare" the "pined corse" of the chastened Redcrosse Knight from the Dongeon of Orgoglio (1.8.40.5–9)—"A ruefull spectacle of death and ghastly drere." Cleopatra's words (IV.xv.62–68)—

> O, see, my women,
> The crown o' th' earth doth melt. My lord!
> O, *wither'd* is the garland of the war,
> The soldier's pole is fall'n! Young boys and girls
> Are level now with men. The odds is gone,
> And there is nothing left remarkable
> Beneath the visiting moon—

indicate that she sees him as Una saw the Redcrosse Knight (1.8.41–42):

> His rawbone armes, whose mighty brawned bowrs
> Were wont to riue steele plates, and helmets hew,
> Were cleane consum'd; and all his vitall powres
> Decayd, and all his flesh shronk vp like *withered* flowres.
> . . . . .
> Ah dearest Lord, what euill starre
> On you hath frownd, and pourd his influence bad,
> That of your selfe ye thus berobbed arre,
> And this misseeming hew your manly looks doth marre?

Withered . . . garland, withered flowers; visiting moon, evil star. This is a richly proportionate analogy.

It is in Cleopatra's dream of Antony, as reported to Dolabella

(V.ii.82–92), that the would-be Roman Emperor vies in magnificence with the allegorical Knight and Prince. Compare his "dolphin-like" delights, which "show'd his back above / The element they liv'd in," with the "deare delights" of St. George, "swimming in that sea of blisfull joy" at his betrothal to Una; or, for pictorial quality, compare this description with that of the dragon-crested helmet of Arthur, whose "scaly tayle was stretcht adowne his backe full low" when first he appeared to Una (1.7.31–32):

> Vpon the top of all his loftie crest,
> A bunch of haires discolourd diuersly,
> With sprincled pearle, and gold full richly drest,
> Did shake, and seem'd to daunce for iollity,
> Like to an Almond tree ymounted hye
> On top of greene Selinis all alone,
> With blossomes braue bedecked daintily;
> Whose tender locks do tremble euery one
> At euery little breath, that vnder heauen is blowne.

May it not be that the Spenserian almond tree is the original happy image for the Shakespearean damaged pine tree whence Antony sees the betrayal of his fleet and in terms of which he, the pine "that overtopped" his competitors, had been "bark'd"? This detail does not appear in the account of Sir Thomas North.

The nobility that a hero of romance, like Arthur, would lend, justifiably or not, to Antony's Roman rehabilitation as a bridegroom, the romantic lady, typified by Una, contributes to Cleopatra's transformation into an admirable Roman bride in her hours of penitence. The Queen, when upon the Cydnus, surrounded by her gentlewomen "like the Nereides, / So many mermaids," shares with Spenser's Acrasia, surrounded by the mermaids and damsels of the last canto of the Book of Temperance, a splendor more splendid than that of the account both authors knew in the words of Plutarch or Amyot or Sir Thomas North; and the tone of the Bowre of Blisse, with its memories of

The Book of Holiness

Ariosto, had prepared Shakespeare's sophisticated auditors for a highly intensified heroine. But the Queen whose "desolation" has begun "to make a better life" may receive from Una those modifications which entitle her to her final beauty and, it may be, her tragic stature. Una cried out at Fortune, as does Cleopatra; both heroines wish the sun darkened; both swoon. Recovering from her third swoon, Una bade, "Tell on . . . the wofull Tragedie." Cleopatra's nature does not permit the happy ending granted to Una; yet, when the doting captain and the false witch, the "right gypsy," are brought into the kind of marriage possible to them under the terms of their choice, all takes place "after the high Roman fashion" (IV.xv.87)—we might even say in Spenserian phrases, "By dew desert of noble cheualree" (1.12.20.8).

Throughout Acts IV and V of *Antony and Cleopatra* Shakespeare uses the gay ceremonies of a betrothal with deeply ironic intent. Antony's "bounteous . . . meal," his "torches," his urgent command to "drown consideration," his effort to bring tears to his servitors and the "onion-eyed" Enobarbus—all such details portraying sentimental collapse—seem to parallel the circumstances of the "bains" of the Redcrosse Knight and Una. Witness the "meates and drinkes of euery kinde" with which "their feruent appetites they quenched had," "the bushy Teade" (torch), the "salt teares" of those who listened to the "lucklesse" adventures of the Knight. The legend of "marvelous sweete harmonie" which Plutarch records Shakespeare would find again in the "heauenly noise" at the end of Spenser's twelfth canto: "Yet wist no creature, whence that heauenly sweet / Proceeded." Caesar, asserting that "The time of universal peace is near," lends to the end of the tragedy the deceptive comfort given to the allegory by Una's father, who "Proclaymed ioy and peace through all his state." Una, arrayed in "lilly white, withoutten spot, or pride," seems to provoke Shakespeare to outdo North in his last tremendous passage, where Charmian and Iris dress Cleopatra in her "best attires . . . her crown and all." For a climax, Una's laments on receiving the news of the overthrow of the Redcrosse Knight (1.7.20–27) and her sorrow when "left to mourne" his return to the Court of his Faery Queene (1.12.41) point the way to Cleopatra's grief; yet they are a pale harbinger of the "fire and air," the "immortal longings" and the "noble act" of the "lass unparalleled."

The machinations of Octavius Caesar and his messengers give to the last scenes of the tragedy the suspense made possible in the allegory by the guileful attempts of Archimago and Duessa to thwart the banns of the Redcrosse Knight and Una. Within the events set forth in Plutarch's account of the disaster there has come into view, it may be thanks to Spenser, a strict pattern of conjugal loyalty. Thanks to Shakespeare, Antony and Cleopatra have earned at terrific cost the title to the relationship they craved.

That Shakespeare has seen the truth in Cleopatra, the possible Una in the actual Duessa, the possible holiness or magnificence in the actually faithless Antony, gives him complete control of his ethical action. Otherwise he might not have discovered for his hero and heroine the "new heaven, new earth" which Antony has prophesied. Moreover, he has achieved the miracle in an ordeal and discipline appropriate for all Herculean and Arthurian heroes and for all bewitching heroines. To imagine an Antony and a Cleopatra were "nature's piece 'gainst fancy [or allegory], / Condemning shadows quite." Or, as Octavius Caesar spells out the artistic principle earlier in the play (I.iv.41–42):

> It hath been taught us from the primal state
> That he which is was wish'd until he were.

The literary artist, in chief the dramatic poet, is more interested in kind than in accident. He will himself write still another work within the genus. He avoids literary sports. His problem is recreative, such growth from the has-been to the might-be as will not deprive his labor of its inherited value. May these functional analogies of the Book of Holiness with Shakespearean tragedy not help to explain the speed with which *Othello, King Lear, Macbeth, Coriolanus,* and *Antony and Cleopatra* were actually set down? The ethical pattern for their respective actions was already established in Shakespeare's scholarly mind; and in his rapidly maturing art, right at hand, were the necessary ethical devices—those codes, choices, and ordeals many times practiced in the precedent ironic comedies but now more profoundly, if less demonstrably, related to *The Faerie Queene.*

Looking at these five tragedies on a common background, we arrive at a conclusion helpful in our interpretation of Shakespeare's tragic art. Although the origin of his tragic plots in biography and chronicle is undeniable and although we may not question his own power unassisted to evolve spiritual issues from actual situations, yet his literary ideas as distinguished from outlines of story, character, doctrine, bear a close resemblance to the literary ideas of his great predecessor. Call these ideas "legends," "myths," "archetypes," or "devices," without them narrative or dramatic poetry would lack literary form. They owe their effect not so much to observed fact as to inherited feeling. However disguised in pictorial splendor, as by Spenser, or in dramatic action, as by Shakespeare, they are simple. They concern themselves with right and wrong, yes; but even more, they are remnant convictions from our ageless experience that when we are hale or holy we are fully alive and from our equally ageless correspondent fear that when we come apart, asunder—or are unholy—we are about to die.

CHAPTER X

Tutorial Action in the Late Plays

WHEN Prince Arthur enters the Book of Holiness as the pattern of knighthood, the redeemer of the Redcrosse Knight, the lover of the Faery Queen, and the type of Magnificence, we foresee an expanded action which in literary fact Spenser never accomplished. We are therefore left to surmise the further deeds of a hero "perfected in the twelue priuate morall vertues" and, if his story were "well accepted," destined "after that hee came to be king" to serve as frame for the "polliticke vertues." What is most pertinent for our investigation at this point, Arthur had been "throughly instructed" by Timon.[1] Twice in the letter to Sir Walter Raleigh Spenser offers this information; and Arthur in his own person tells us that as an infant he had been brought "vnto old Timon," expert in warlike feats and "wisest now on earth" (1.9.4):

[1] I can find no ancestry or provenience for Arthur's Timon; but, like Shakespeare, Spenser would learn of Timon of Athens through Plutarch or Lucian. He refers to him in his poem *Daphnaida* (1591), lines 248–249.

> His dwelling is low in a valley greene,
> Vnder the foot of Rauran mossy hore,
> From whence the riuer Dee[,] as siluer cleene[,]
> His tombling billowes rolls with gentle rore:
> There all my dayes he traind me vp in vertuous lore.

Like Spenser's Arthur, Plutarch's Antony was an illustration of magnificence ("liberality" is Sir Thomas North's word); and in Cleopatra's dream of an "Emperor Antony" Shakespeare has allowed him to be Magnificence indeed. With power like Antony's and a destiny so clear, a heroic King of Faeryland without Antony's flaws would satisfy even a Faery Queen. That the Shakespearean "triple pillar of the world" could neither establish nor maintain such an imperial court marks the ironic quality, not only of this one hero, but of the heroic life itself. Proficient as was Shakespeare in the control of tragic action, there could be no more such tragedies. The depths of tragic possibility had been plumbed.

How then might the energies of the playwright be spiraled upward again to represent the contemplative life without which no court of any queen could long survive?

In Antony's critical hours after Actium he had withdrawn like a misanthrope, not to study, but to sulk (his "Timonion"). Reading North's translation of the Life of Marcus Antonius, or the Life of Alcibiades, Shakespeare would learn the outlines of Timon's story; here was a tragic grotesque comparable with the comic burlesque in which he had made his farewell to such as Sir John Falstaff. If, further, with the Plutarchian Timon, whose example tempted Antony to withdraw from manly action and provoked Alcibiades to attack his native Athens, he associated the Timon and Arthur of romance, these Timons in their tutorial responsibility for these magnificent young men would furnish him with still another dramatic irony and a heightened sense of dramatic urgency. He would—as he did—proceed from the misanthropic Timon to certain more philanthropic agents. He would compose a series of tutorial actions in which the younger generation, although not spared the scars of circumstance, might be saved, in their turn to save the state.

Timon of Athens

Timon of Athens is a "Life," derived in large part from Plutarch and from Lucian's dialogue, *Timon the Misanthrope*. There is evident also some help in plotting from an anonymous play of *c.* 1600, where first we hear of the banquet of stones painted to resemble artichokes. Shakespeare did not complete the text; but, in spite of interpolations, there remains enough of what is with good reason assumed to be his [2] to establish his belief that the state cannot be saved by its rich men, its poets, its painters, its jewelers, its merchants, its usurers and courtesans, its sycophants and misanthropes, or even by its captains or its senators or its gold. By whom, then? And by what?

The classical Timon's change of fortune from wealth to penury invites dramatic treatment. If its lesson could be rightly understood by the pauperized rich man himself, it might furnish a proper ethical action. In this action Timon's doctrinal flaw would be followed by the realization of his mistake, the acknowledgment of his own share in his downfall, and his effort to teach to others, however rigorously, the right doctrine of justice and value. When we probe into the fourth and fifth acts of this so-called "Life"—those acts least challenged by scholars —we detect the outlines of an old myth familiar in western didactic literature from Boethius and Chaucer to Spenser, the myth of the golden age.

This myth is set forth notably in the Prologue to the Book of Justice, where Spenser suggests the reason for and outlines of an ethical action:

[2] Consult Ernest Hunter Wright, *The Authorship of 'Timon of Athens'* ("Columbia University Studies in English"; New York, 1910).

Tutorial Action in the Late Plays 211

> For from the golden age, that first was named,
> It's now at earst become a stonie one.

Men themselves "Are now transformed into hardest stone." On this mythic assumption, Timon with his banquet of stones instead of his gifts of gold represents the modern man learning in the hard way what value is. That Shakespeare has in mind the myth of the golden age, whether or not in Spenser's version, is indicated by his change in the purpose of Timon's digging. Ernest Hunter Wright (pp.19–20) observed that, whereas in the anonymous play he seemed to dig for no special purpose and in Lucian's version he hired out to dig for sixpence a day, in the Shakespearean play "Timon is digging for roots." May we add that in Act IV he emphatically allies himself—"O, a root! Dear thanks!"—with the Spenserian "discipline / Of vertue"? As a contingent tutor he will not form his life "to the common line / Of present dayes, . . . / But to the antique vse" (5.Prol.2–3, 9),

> When good was onely for it selfe desyred,
> And all men sought their owne, and none no more.
>
> . . . . .
>
> Peace vniversall rayn'd mongst men and beasts,
> And all things freely grew out of the ground.

Digging for roots, Timon found gold also. The finding of gold comes from Lucian, but the roots do not; nor, of course, does the highly revealing speech to the banditti (IV.iii.420–424):

> Why should you want? Behold, the earth hath roots;
> Within this mile break forth a hundred springs;
> The oaks bear mast, the briers scarlet heps;
> The bounteous housewife Nature on each bush
> Lays her full mess before you. Want? Why want?

Timon at least, but only Timon, remains true to the roots and springs and mast and hips, to "Nature's" bounty. And this is as much of a discovery and reversal as we have a right to expect, granted the relevance of the myth itself.[3]

Now when the Spenserian Astraea, setting an example for misanthropic behavior, was provoked by human wickedness to betake herself to heaven, on earth she

> left her groome
> An yron man, which did on her attend
> Alwayes, to execute her stedfast doome.

Talus with his iron flail may be considered a prototype for the later Timon, Timon as scourge; and Artegall, whom Talus accompanied and who had been taught "all the discipline of iustice" by Astraea in a cave "from companie exilde" also would lend dignity to the Shakespearean Timon as self-exile. Together Artegall and Talus destroyed Lady Munera and her "mucky pelfe," and then advanced to the shore of the sea to deal with the monstrous "Gyant" holding on high his "huge great paire of ballance." In the erroneous doctrine of this Gyant with the Scales, who "stroue extremities to way" (5.2.49.3), we see prefigured that mistaken Lord Timon of the early scenes who has believed that he could "counterpoise" the poor groom and the rich bride with gifts of gold (I.i.139–140) and "weigh [his] friend's affection with [his] own" (I.ii.222). He has much to learn about "confounding contraries" (IV.i.20–21). Unlike the Gyant, however, Lord Timon survives his particular doctrinal error; and like Talus he begins to use his flailing tongue upon a rapacious society.

In various minor ways, too, the allegory helps to define the agents of the play. Spenser's Gyant had been much admired of "fooles." Learning that he could reduce all things "vnto equality" (5.2.30–33),

---

[3] R. P. Draper has described Timon "as a would-be Saturnian figure, living in an imaginary Golden Age, who is unaware of the nature of the fallen world in which he actually exists" (*Sh.Quart.*, VIII [Spring, 1957], 196).

Tutorial Action in the Late Plays 213

> Therefore the vulgar did about him flocke . . .
> Like foolish flies about an hony crocke,
> In hope by him great benefite to gaine,
> And vncontrolled freedome to obtaine.

Lucian's Gnathonides with his new song and the Hermogenes of the anonymous play are not the only ancestors of Timon's sycophantic poet; Spenser had described one such in the Bonfont-Malfont of Mercilla's Court of Justice. And by this same Court Duessa had been doomed in words which antedate the rebuke given to Timandra and Phrynia on Timon's judgment day at his cave by the shore of the sea. Finally, Apemantus, only sketched in the classical sources, has taken on the bestial attributes of the hideous monster under the golden idol in the country of Belge (5.11), whose dog's body, lion's claws, dragon's tail, and eagle's wings may be in Shakespeare's mind when he engages Timon and Apemantus in a discussion of assorted beastliness (IV.iii.320–371):

—What wouldst thou do with the world, Apemantus, if it lay in thy power?
—Give it to the beasts, to be rid of the men.
—Wouldst thou have thyself fall in the confusion of men, and remain a beast with the beasts?
—Ay, Timon.
—A beastly ambition, which the gods grant thee t'attain to! If thou wert the lion, the fox would beguile thee, . . . [the lamb, the fox, the ass, the wolf, the unicorn, the horse, the leopard]. What beast couldst thou be that were not subject to a beast? And what beast art thou already, that seest not thy loss in transformation! . . . Away, thou issue of a mangy dog!

Timon routs Apemantus with his words as Prince Arthur destroyed the monster lurking under the golden idol to whom Belge's many sons had been sacrificed.

Compared with the myths of justice in Spenser's allegory, Timon's accomplishment seems true to mythic form. The discovery of his mistake has made possible his return to that other golden age when each man dug his own roots and there were no metals to raise conflict or balances to impose artificial value. Most important in his change of fortune, he has accepted the tutorial responsibility. Athens can be saved only if her young leaders are rightly taught.

Since these young men have hitherto been bred awry, led into a mistaken assumption as to the nature of wealth and the duty of citizens, the tutor must begin their new course of study by questioning the doctrinal basis of Athenian society, and in words of the utmost vigor. This is the matter of the authentic Acts IV and V of the Shakespearean play. Once the tutorial relationship has been established with Alcibiades and the politicians, artists, and cynics of his city-state, once the right doctrine has been set forth, the relentless schoolmaster will go on to give his pupils their major examination, in this case the bribe of gold. If they do not "pass," then, with his tongue like the flail of the Spenserian Talus, he will be justified in upbraiding them. What rudimentary action there is in *Timon of Athens* would thus appear concerned less with the military than the pedagogical crisis in the destiny of Athens. Yet we may be sure that Shakespeare was not finally satisfied with the imprecations and hopeless ranting of Timon at his cave by the sea—so much like the dwelling of that other and wiser Timon in the green valley by the "tombling billowes" of the river Dee. He would soon turn from a didactic Timon to a dramatic Prospero, from his ironic parable to an apocalyptic action of the teacher and the taught.

Tutorial Agency in the Earlier Plays

To elucidate this matter we may swiftly reconsider the instances of tutorial action and agents in the plays which antedate both *Timon of Athens* and the five mighty tragedies dealing with the disciplinary or regenerative principle.

Pinch, the schoolmaster of *The Comedy of Errors*, and Holofernes of *Love's Labour's Lost* are caricatures, and the Academe of Navarre is considered ridiculous. In *The Two Gentlemen of Verona* Proteus woefully exhibits the lack of good teaching, away from "studious universities" and the "royal court" where his friend Valentine hears "sweet discourse" and "converse[s] with noblemen" or is taught love by Silvia under the figure of pupil and tutor (I.iii; II.i). For the most part the early plays are content to accept "Time [as] the nurse and breeder of all good" (III.i.243). Corrections from Puck and the fairies in *A Midsummer Night's Dream*, from the courts in *The Merchant of Venice*, or from such persistently masterful individuals as Petruchio taming his shrew are not in the tradition of the liberal arts. The Friars of *Romeo and Juliet* help too little and too late, as does the Soothsayer in *Julius Caesar;* Parson Hugh Evans of *The Merry Wives of Windsor* is no better a schoolmaster than was Holofernes. Richard II and Prince Hal listen to uncles, fathers, and dignitaries of the state with inattentive ears; Richard does little studying until he finds himself in Pomfret Castle; and Hal owes his reform to "Consideration like an angel": "Never was such a sudden scholar made."

In the joyous comedies, which still permit the ill-taught or uncourtly to bicker and struggle into happiness, and in the ironic comedies, the playwright more frequently acknowledges poor teaching to be the root of awkward, credulous, or irrational conduct. Orlando is the most outspoken about lack of breeding (*As You Like It*, I.i):

His horses are bred better; for, besides that they are fair with their feeding, they are taught their manage, and to that end riders dearly hir'd.

The Clown of *Twelfth Night*, foreshadowing the Fool in *King Lear*, is a sagacious person who subtly puts things in order. He fetches "light and paper and ink" to the thoroughly disciplined

Malvolio and seems pleased when "the whirligig of time brings in his revenges." Sebastian, too, makes the most of his sojourn in Illyria (III.iii.19, 22–24):

> Shall we go see the relics of this town?
>
> . . . . .
>
> I pray you, let us satisfy our eyes
> With the memorials and the things of fame
> That do renown this city.

Neither in *As You Like It*, however, nor in *Twelfth Night* does the pastoral story of Thomas Lodge or the Latin- or Italian-originated history of Barnabe Riche allow more than traditional references to the schoolmaster as responsible for courtly or uncourtly behavior. Nor in *Much Ado about Nothing*, where Spenser's thought echoes clearest, does Shakespeare intend a tutorial action. Dogberry and Friar Francis emerge from the Constabulary and the Church as skeptical and intelligent agents without whom no action may be significantly concluded; but they are not in any sense liberal artists. Only with Helena in *All's Well That Ends Well* may be felt the stirring in Shakespeare's drama of a new regulatory principle. Between Helena and her gifted father the relationship has been tutorial; and between Helena and the Countess the association is not that of woman with woman alone, nor is it primarily maternal or filial; we might rather say that through Helena the Countess will teach manners to her unmannerly son. From the beginning she has "those hopes of [Helena's] good that her education promises" (I.i.45–46). Something good does come of Helena's education, but the treatment is not too skillfully administered by either Helena or Shakespeare.

In *Troilus and Cressida* and *Hamlet* the need for indoctrination and discipline is frankly acknowledged; what the Palmer Reason did for Guyon, Ulysses tries to do for Achilles and Troilus, and Hector, quoting Aristotle's *Ethics*, tries to do for the sons of Priam. Thersites jeers at Patroclus: "Heaven bless thee from a tutor, and discipline come not near thee." And in *Measure for Measure* it is Vincentio the teaching friar rather than Vincentio the duke who, surrendering the rudder of government for the winged words of a counselor, sets things somewhat shakily in order. The first and last of these three plays are so overburdened with traditional situations as to risk their comic effect; and Hamlet's relatively minor flaw of intemperance at its defective extreme, when compared with the dire perfidy of Claudius, seems to deprive him of full tragic quality. Nevertheless, here, too, as earlier in *Much Ado, Twelfth Night,* and *All's Well,* the ethical premises of Spenserian allegory are by Shakespeare put to work on the dramatic task of redemption; and here explicitly he asks help from the schools. Hamlet comes from Wittenberg to set right the unjointed "time" in Denmark. He and his friend Horatio are scholars. Isabella brings from the nunnery of St. Clare sound, if somewhat dogmatic, instruction for her heedless and restive brother. Priam's sons are exposed to Aristotelian ethics, although they overbear the interpreter, Hector; and Achilles and Troilus must listen to the remarks of Ulysses about Neoplatonic theories of beauty, love, and time or Stoic doctrines of patience—to little avail.

Brabantio fails his daughter Desdemona as surely as Shylock has failed Jessica; and the prophetic warnings of Macbeth's witches have no touch of compassion. It is the Fool in *King Lear,* with his axioms at the center of the tragic action, who first speaks with full authority. Following him, ineffective as they are with Caius Marcius and Marcus Antonius, Menenius and Enobarbus play their parts as befits the cautious pedagogue, but they speak with assurance. Both are tutorial agencies or functionaries; both were newly created from the persons as mentioned by Plutarch.

Meanwhile, the "brave new world" was in the making. Although the disciplinary constituent in the tragedies had called for the ordeals of generals of Venice and Rome, kings of Britain and Scotland, and a would-be emperor "of the world," little by little Shakespeare clarified his dramatic procedure until he felt able to reveal the full power of the studious life in that series of so-called romances which never leave us in doubt as to what he considered the major action of life and the major "action" in dramatic poetry. Whether or not they are dependent on Spenser's hopeful premise in *The Faerie Queene*, they supply us with frequent overt and hidden reference to the teacher or tutor in a kind of fairyland: on the ship of a Tyrian Prince, at the cave in Wales of a spirited British exile, at the Court of a Sicilian Queen, and on an uninhabited Mediterranean island. Finally, in each of these four authentic dramas the action concerns the younger generation; and that indeed would have been, must have been, the final "polliticke" concern of the magnificent Arthur at the court of his resplendent Faery Queen.

Pericles, Prince of Tyre

The earliest of these four romances, *Pericles, Prince of Tyre*, is thought to be Shakespeare's only in part. The first act and most of the second are as ethically insignificant as the comparable passages in John Gower's *Confessio Amantis* (VIII.271–2008),[4] and not so swift or delightful. Only with the scenes at Pentapolis, which drive Shakespeare's plot through its last three acts to its denouement, do we come upon a properly gerundive action. It is a tutorial action. It adds to the adventures of the Shakespearean Pericles, Thaisa, and their daughter Marina, born at sea, the cogency lacking in the adventures of Apollonius, his unnamed wife, and their daughter Thaisa. Marina's education is not merely an adornment; it is the consciously redemptive cause of her own and her parents' escape from the terrifying flux of circumstance. For his "absolute Marina" the dramatist exploits

---

[4] *The English Works of John Gower*, ed. by G. C. Macaulay ("Early English Text Society," extra ser. no. LXXXII [Oxford, 1901]).

to the full such an ordeal as he had formerly shaped for Isabella, Desdemona, and Cordelia in the tradition of Una. The lady from the sea, educated by Cleon, envied by Dionyza and Philoten, threatened by them and the murderous Leontine when her nurse Lychorida is dead, captured by pirates and sold to bawds, will now be sent to the very core of that monstrous blight on human worth, the brothels of Mitylene.

Gower's Apollonius, the prototype of Pericles, was a well-educated man, to be sure (VIII.390–393):

> Of every naturel science,
> Which eny clerk him couthe teche,
> He couthe ynowh, and in his speche
> Of wordes he was eloquent.

Although he bade the Burgess of Tharsus, one Strangulio, set his daughter "to bokes lore" (1300), he had himself no part in her education; it was Strangulio who arranged the musical training she would later use to good purpose (1328–1333):

> Sche was wel tawht, sche was wel boked,
> So wel sche spedde hir in hir youthe,
> That sche of every wisdom couthe,
> That forto seche in every lond
> So wys an other no man fond,
> Ne so wel tawht at mannes yhe.

In her peril she besought the bordeller's "oghne man" to let her become a schoolmistress (1462–1465)

> Of such a schole that is trewe,
> I shal hire teche of thinges newe,
> Which as non other womman can
> In al this lond.

According to Gower, it was "a grace God hir sent" (1428) that spared her "eny vileinie" from any of a dozen young men in the brothel. None of these, we observe, is a person of note like Shakespeare's Lysimachus, who can recognize the breeding of Marina, take upon himself the unraveling of the plot, and—however sudden his reformation—henceforth appear as the good pupil of an able schoolmistress. Lysimachus, it may be, owes his more influential role to Spenser's Satyrane in the sixth canto of the Book of Holiness. This canto begins in a way to associate itself with adventure at sea (1.6.1):

> As when a ship, that flyes faire vnder saile,
> An hidden rocke escaped hath vnwares,
> That lay in waite her wrack for to bewaile,
> The Marriner yet halfe amazed stares
> At perill past, and yet in doubt ne dares
> To ioy at his foole-happie ouersight.

With this "Marriner" escaping shipwreck Spenser had compared the Redcrosse Knight escaping from the House of Pride somewhat as Pericles escapes from the plots of Antiochus. Still more to our purpose is the remainder of the canto, which shows Una surprised and carried off by the satyrs, envied by the malicious Naiades, then saved from disaster, first because old Sylvanus took her to be Diana, but mainly because she used her lore to teach the animalish creatures who would otherwise abuse her (1.6.9.6–9).[5]

> All stand amazed at so vncouth sight,
> And gin to pittie her vnhappie state,
> All stand astonied at her beautie bright,
> In their rude eyes vnworthie of so wofull plight.

During one of these tutorial classes Satyrane came upon Una as later Lysimachus was to come upon Marina (1.6.30.7–9),

> Straunge Lady, in so straunge habiliment,
> Teaching the Satyres, which her sat around,
> Trew sacred lore, which from her sweet lips did redound.

[5] For his portrayal of threatening lust the playwright had also at hand the prototypical scenes of Hellenore among the Satyrs (3.10) and Serena among the cannibalistic Savages (6.8).

Finally, Marina brings Pericles back to happiness as Una accompanied the Redcrosse Knight through his discipline in the House of Holiness.

Without reasonable doubt the brothel scenes in *Pericles* are Shakespeare's, as appropriately so as Una's peril among the "Faunes and Satyrs" had been Spenser's. How otherwise than in such disfiguring circumstances could we see at work the holy nature and the humane dealing of this young sister of Una and thus understand the only power able to clean out the brothels of an unholy time?

Cymbeline

Spenser's Archimago not only shared his nature and, possibly, his name with Shakespeare's Iago, but also may have supplied with both name and nature that other archdeceiver, Iachimo (*Archimago*). *Cymbeline* is the counterpart of and answer to *Othello;* here at last the forces for evil will be confronted and defeated by equally powerful forces for good. Iago's villainy has prevailed—though the disclosure of it transforms Othello for a brief moment from a jealous husband into an equitable governor of Cyprus—but Iachimo's evil plot fails to destroy those whom he has imperiled. He is mischievous, but not so basely vicious as are Cymbeline's queen and stepson, who carry on the machinations of Spenser's Duessa and her minions, notably the Witch and her monstrous son of the seventh canto of the Book of Chastity. "O dissembling courtesy!" says Imogen of the Queen, as a hint from Shakespeare of the kind of plot we must anticipate. The evil at work in *Cymbeline* is as intense as that concentrated against Una or Florimell or Amoret in the Books of Holiness and Chastity; but the spiritual energies already in action to preserve the heroine are earlier mobilized than in *Othello*.

Posthumus Leonatus, son of Sicilius, is such a one as the Knight of the Red Crosse, that earlier defender of Britain, St. George himself. Like him and like Scudamour, Posthumus has been deceived and made jealous for reasons that are ostensibly sufficient. All three atone for their credulity in prison: the Knight of the Red Crosse in Orgoglio's dungeon, Scudamour in the House of Care, and Posthumus in a British prison (1.8. 37–41; 4.5.34–45; V.i, iii, iv). All are courtly; but like the Knight of the Red Crosse Posthumus is somewhat "vnfitte through his rusticity for a better place." Like Scudamour, whose learning and courage were unusual, Posthumus has been bred to "all the learnings that his time / Could make him the receiver of" (I.i.43–44). The injury he has done to his beloved reduces him to despair like that of Timias, self-rebuked for his one slight to Belphoebe.

Of all Shakespeare's heroines Imogen most resembles Belphoebe, the phoenix to Timias' turtle dove. Iachimo says, "She is alone th' Arabian bird" (I.vi.17), and he observes that her chimney piece is "chaste Dian bathing" (II.iv.82). In Pisanio's judgment she undergoes the assaults upon her in a manner "more goddess-like than wife-like" (III.ii.8). Even Cloten dubs her maids "Diana's rangers" (II.iii.74); and, when "Phoebus 'gins arise," he brings songsters to serenade her with "Hark, hark! the lark at heaven's gate sings"—in the tradition of the Witch's son bringing young birds taught to sing to another heavenly lady, Florimell. References to her as fairy, angel, paragon, divineness, when she appears under the name Fidele to her brothers and Belarius seem to list again the traits in the "heauenly portraict" of Belphoebe coming upon Braggadochio or Timias (2.3.22–23; 3.5.35). Belphoebe's eyes "two liuing lamps did flame . . . / And darted fyrie beames"; when the Shakespearean father, brothers, daughter, husband, mentor, have been reunited, Cymbeline exclaims (V.v.392–396):

> See,
> Posthumus anchors upon Imogen;
> And she (like harmless lightning) throws her eye
> On him, her brothers, me, her master, hitting
> Each object with a joy.

Even more probably than from Holinshed's *Chronicle*, from Spenser's "Chronicle of Briton kings" (2.10), which had furnished the names Leyr, Gonorill, Regan, and Cordelia, comes Shakespeare's designation of a "faire Imogene," Kimbeline, Claudius (Guiderius) and Arvirage (Arviragus). Also, Spenser's text offered for Belarius, Guiderius, and Arviragus their names when in disguise: Morgan, who "to those woodie hils did flie," Polidore, and Cadwal.[6]

As in its names, in its main situation *Cymbeline* duplicates the synthesis of events in the Book of Holiness. Imogen, pursued by Cloten after she has been repudiated by Posthumus, then finding asylum in a group of seeming rustics, should be compared with that archetypal pattern of Una repudiated by the Redcrosse Knight, pursued by Sansloi, and rescued by Satyrane. Imogen's trial when wandering to Milford Haven is still another trial of Una (1.7.28.7–9):

> Long tost with stormes, and bet with bitter wind,
> High ouer hils, and low adowne the dale,
> She wandred many a wood, and measurd many a vale.

The sister, unknowing and unknown, meets her brothers in Act III, where this playwright almost invariably shapes the form of things to come. The destinies of Britain are revealed to be in good hands; for here, away from the world, the education of the King's sons has gone on in the name of the goddess Nature under that most resolute of schoolmasters, Belarius. They have been taught to "Hail, heaven" (III.iii.9) and to "reverence . . . the wise" (IV.ii.95). Stimulated by the "mountain sport" in which they have been exercised, they are just ready to break from their tutelage in the oncoming emergencies of their coun-

---

[6] The name Fidele (and the name Hermione soon to be used in *The Winter's Tale*) occur in the anonymous old play, *The Rare Triumphs of Love and Fortune* (c. 1582–1589). Imogen-Fidele may also be compared with Spenser's Fidelia (1.10.4, 12).

try. After twenty years of gentle breeding, they prove themselves "princes born." Without them Cloten would not have been thwarted or the Romans resisted.

The destiny of Cymbeline's Britain is never in doubt; and a triumphant ending for Imogen and Posthumus is as implicit in the drama as in the allegory for Una and the Redcrosse Knight or for Florimell and Marinell—although not yet for Amoret and Scudamour and not yet for Timias and Belphoebe or Britomart and Artegall. Once the good fight is waged and won and the sighs of penitence have been breathed, the rarer action is concluded: "My conscience, thou art fetter'd / More than my shanks and wrists." Shakespeare knows supremely well how to fetter and unfetter the conscience. Whatever circumstances becloud or annoy the actual courts of great rulers, young men as bred by Belarius, young women persevering and faithful as Fidele-Imogen, and thoughtful young husbands thoroughly disciplined and penitent—"poor but worthy gentlem[e]n"—supply us anywhere in Faeryland and Britain with one quite credible sketch for a Court of the Faery Queen. In the words of Posthumus, such courtiers "shame the guise of the world." They will "begin / The fashion, less without and more within" (V.i.32–33).

The Winter's Tale

Another reassuring sketch for a Court of the Faery Queen would recruit its chief courtier and lady from Bohemia in the time of Polixenes I, that Bohemia with a seacoast not far from Sicilia. On the countryside where Perdita and the Shepherd, her foster father, and their friends the rustic Clown and the noble Florizel-Doricles graciously hold rustic court reappear Spenser's Pastorella, her foster father, Meliboe, and their friends Coridon and Calidore. The pictorial bounty evident in the Book of Courtesy seems now transformed into a human crisis. Green holiday prepares the agents of *The Winter's Tale* for a most rigorous final examination.⁷

Spenser's Bellamour and Claribell had found their lost daughter Pastorella without an ethically significant change of fortune. Before Leontes and Hermione should find their Perdita, how many discourteous acts must intervene! Yet it is the reference to courtesy and discourtesy which accounts for the gain in dramatic propulsion of the scenes in Sicily and Bohemia over those in the Forest of Arden, where there appear to be no slightest echoes of *The Faerie Queene*—even over those in the orchard at Messina, where Claudio exhibits so many romantic traits of Calidore, Spenser's Knight of Courtesy. Above all, how skillfully Paulina and Hermione are made to await the outcome of an ordeal which the Countess and Helena of *All's Well* had undergone with the long patience of Spenser's Glauce and Britomart.

In the economy of his plot Shakespeare bases the whole fourth act of *The Winter's Tale* on a Spenserian device. The bear from which Calepine saved the infant in the Book of Courtesy is, at the end of Act III of *The Winter's Tale*, rediscovered chasing Antigonus. Antigonus is expendable, but the infant he has exposed is saved by a shepherd and grows up to be the incomparable Perdita. In the revels at her sheepshearing (these are only mentioned in Greene's *Dorastus and Fawnia*, on which the playwright mainly depended for his story) Perdita exhibits many precious traits observed by Calidore in his first view of Pastorella among her companions. Pastorella as a "soueraine goddesse" and Perdita, queen "of the petty gods," "most goddess-like prank'd up," belong to a level of romance above the reach of artificial pastoral; moreover, the craft of the playwright, although relative to that of the allegorical poet, appears progressively more

---

⁷ Schofield (*Chivalry in English Literature*, pp. 243, 258) associates Perdita and Pastorella.

adroit as we watch Shakespeare's Clown and Shepherd emerging from rustics like Spenser's Coridon and Meliboe. Most notable change of all, Spenser's "lawlesse" pirates (6.10.39 ff.) and the "sort of merchants, which were wount / To skim those coastes" (6.11.9) have been masterfully concentrated into that superchapman and thief of thieves, Autolycus, for whom we gladly relinquish the whole tribe of Brigantes. This entanglement of pastoral revels with the episode of thievery in both the Book of Courtesy and *The Winter's Tale* might conceivably have been an accidental affair; but the way in which it helped both poets to their peripety suggests influence.

As the Brigantes "spoyld old Melibee of all he had," so Autolycus is in a fair way to despoil both Clown and Shepherd. To spare Perdita the agonizing attentions of such thieves and slavers as had persecuted Pastorella, Florizel intervenes like another Sir Calidore; he spirits her away on shipboard, where her seasickness en route from Bohemia to Sicily is a more merciful ordeal than the piteous "sickenesse" of Pastorella in Spenser's version. Also Florizel is spared the grief of Calidore in believing his Pastorella dead. That Shakespeare prefaces the reunion of the maiden and her parents with a metaphorical sea voyage may be a reminiscence of Spenser's "Like as a ship," used to begin the canto (6.12) in which Pastorella is restored to Bellamour and Claribell.

Then Shakespeare and Spenser, each in his characteristic way, advance to settle their account with the Blatant Beast, which in Leontes has taken the form of mad jealousy or jealous madness.

Whereas the Redcrosse Knight, Othello, and Posthumus have all been purposely deceived by Archimago, Iago, and Iachimo, and whereas Macbeth, Coriolanus, and Antony have been incited, enraged, or provoked by others, and even Lear has been helped into making his willful blunder by a misapprehension, Shakespeare's Leontes has no sufficient excuse. He is a completely autonomous and therefore responsible agent. Here is jealousy in its proper form, an inner action coiled about itself. Leontes as a psychological case study would have interested Shakespeare and his audience less than he does many modern interpreters; for his contemporaries he is merely another hero needing ethical discipline. This he will receive, at the instance of Paulina, during a sixteen-year residence in the equivalent of Spenser's House of Holiness. There, whither King Lear had been sent for a briefer but more bitter cure, Paulina (like Spenser's Caelia) and Hermione herself (like Spenser's Mercie, "auncient matrone") will restore and, in time, comfort him. He does not attain the heights of Contemplation, as did Lear, but he does accept the services of Humilta and Patience in a trial which goes far to compensate for the discourtesy done to the Queen in her public trial. Thus, the playwright avoids a tragic blazon for Leontes and a sentimental peripety for Hermione. Their reconciliation leads us to see in Perdita and Florizel the form of better things to come. Only with the parental scars healed can the younger generation be spared incurable heartache when sons and daughters take up their duties at the Court of the Faery Queen.

There Florizel and Perdita will be allied with Posthumus and Imogen and Ferdinand and Miranda—not quite yet a Round Table, to be sure; and for merriment Benedick and Beatrice, for music Orsino and Viola, will help; and sweet Anne Page with Master Fenton will not be far away, nor will Sebastian and a more civil Olivia, Helena and a less captious Bertram.

There, too, they will hear good doctrine, such pastoral discussions of the "gentleman born" as furnish the Clown and the Shepherd with their most delightful comic effects or such warnings as correct the pseudoaristocratic position taken by Polixenes regarding Florizel's marriage. For (6.Prol.5.8-9)

> vertues seat is deepe within the mynd,
> And not in outward shows, but inward thoughts defynd.

Then, should their inheritance from Adam incline them to foolish or willful behavior, they may avoid the disaster involuntarily provoked by the heedless Queen of Leontes if they will but listen to the good "counsell" of the Hermit (6.6.14):

> The best (sayd he) that I can you aduize,
> Is to auoide the occasion of the ill:
> For when the cause, whence euill doth arize,
> Remoued is, th' effect surceaseth still.

The Tempest

Our mere fancies provoke a serious question: What would have been the inner form of courtly life at the Court of Arthur and Gloriana? Failing help from Spenser's unwritten cantos, we may review Shakespeare's *The Tempest*. In it, the playwright gave us his own—and, it may be, Spenser's—answer. *The Tempest* is the Legend of the Liberal Artist. Prospero's uninhabited isle has its monster, its sprite, its uncorrupted maiden, its hero to be tested, and its magician able to save every situation. Caliban, Ariel, Miranda, Ferdinand, and Prospero, even the wicked usurpers, are in the line of descent from the giants and monsters and witches, the flying pursuivants, Una or Belphoebe or Florimell, the Knight of the Red Crosse, Arthur, Merlin, and the courtly or uncourtly rout of vicious or virtuous, lucky or luckless knights and ladies of *The Faerie Queene*. More than that, to Prospero has fallen the task of Timon, the education of the future ruler of Britain or Milan.

In a less otherworldly sense, it would seem that Prospero has learned from the Spenserian discipline of such as Artegall what Ferdinand, King of Navarre in *Love's Labour's Lost*, and the banished Duke of *As You Like It* did not know and what the moribund King of France in *All's Well* and the disguised Duke of Vienna in *Measure for Measure* were just painfully acknowledging—the high cost of good government. Moreover, Prospero reveals the growing conviction of Shakespeare that it is the scholar or tutor who redeems the state. Hamlet and Ulysses have both been readers of books; and now the exiled Duke of Milan must quell the revolt of a Caliban aware that the "first" step in overthrowing the liberal artist would be "to possess his books," "burn but his books." Although Prospero's "magic garment" is not an academic cap and gown, his art is similarly professional; it aims at order and happiness, not confusion and perdition. His urgent hour—"The hour's now come" (I.ii.36)—is the paradigm for a campus eight o'clock in history, in biography, and in psychology ("the dark backward and abysm of time," "such stuff as dreams are made on"); in political science; or in religion ("By Providence divine").

Not only the subjects but also the skills of the teacher come within the range of his magic. He has more compassion than "tutors not so careful." He knows the value of concentration ("obey and be attentive"). He can decide when to invite, welcome, or discourage questions. He insists on the practice of theories, on the responsibility for knowledge (I.ii.135-138):

> Hear a little further,
> And then I'll bring thee to the present business
> Which now's upon's, without the which this story
> Were most impertinent.

Supremely well he teaches by "majestic vision" the doctrine that otherwise might remain pallid and ineffective.

In the absence of evidence we can only guess that a later canto of *The Faerie Queene* would have touched on some such matter in a Legend of Timon, schoolmaster of Arthur and, like Prospero, "for the liberal arts / Without a parallel." Here we must return to *The Tempest*, which imitates the action in which a scholar, disregarding his responsibility as a ruler, learns at great cost the full meaning of scholarship in its relation to the arts (the discovery) and thereupon proceeds to rule his little island (the peripety).

His method of ruling emphasizes what in Shakespeare's plays has come to be their major constituent, the trial, ordeal, or test of the persons of the play—again permitting our cross reference to educational procedures. His own fundamental test begins with what looks to be the wreck of the metaphorical ship; but for this crisis he has prepared himself, and his review of the past, his synthesis of events, and his mastery of himself and his Ariel-like intelligence are beyond praise. Small wonder that his "old brain is troubled" and that he needs "a turn or two" of walking "to still [his] beating mind."

Ferdinand and Miranda, his pupils, are set upon the tasks of self-control and patience proper to their noble natures. The "vexations" of Ferdinand's examination day are "but . . . trials of [his] love." He "stood the test" and is thus seen to be another like Sirs Guyon and Calidore. When Prospero begins Act IV with a hymeneal charge to be temperate, we hear strong echoes of the Palmer and Sir Guyon; and the chess game played between the lovers is akin to the "courtesies" with which Sir Calidore entertained Pastorella, who had never yet been familiar "With such queint vsage, fit for Queenes and Kings." Shakespeare seems to make a point of Ferdinand's willingness to ask his father's permission for marriage, possibly to define a stricter code than was known by Florizel of Bohemia, who had been quite willing to dispense with the paternal blessing (*The Tempest*, V.i.190–191; *The Winter's Tale*, IV.iv.421–424).

The ignoble and vicious statesmen of Naples and Milan, along with Gonzalo, who means well but is ridden by impractical theories of government, are shocked out of their sins and errors, permitted to forget, and then allowed to remember their better selves by a device comparable with that of Dante, although more rudimentary in its workings. For Caliban chiefly, the method of trial, discovery, and reversal comes close to the demands of actual experience in the very world. More shrewd than are any of Spenser's monsters, he can account for his painful journey from brute to man. "You taught me language," he says; "and my profit on't / Is, I know how to curse." Yet he struggles toward the right distinction between earthly and "celestial liquor"; and, finally, he comes out of his "foul confederacy" with a sound deduction about asses who take drunkards for gods and worship dull fools.

As a result of this whole representative ordeal, the disclosures made are all reassuring: "Tell your piteous heart / There's no harm done" (I.ii.14–15); the villains may escape wrath by "heart's sorrow / And a clear life ensuing" (III.iii.81–82). In Miranda's "brave new world" there is hope also for Caliban if he will be "wise hereafter, / And seek for grace" (V.i.294–295). The crisis of the action ("Now does my project gather to a head") brings about a change for the better even in the schoolmaster ("Yet with my nobler reason 'gainst my fury / Do I take part"). Therefore the ship of whatsoever metaphorical state (V.i.224–225)

> Is tight and yare and bravely rigg'd as when
> We first put out to sea.

Whether or not he was aware of Spenser's management of ethical and political allegory, a mature Shakespeare could not fail to articulate his own dramatic events into a promise of hope and dignity for any who are willing to seek for grace. *The Tempest* in its entirety is the expressive equivalent of the archetypal test. For making it clear that all who know must also do, language cannot be more explicit nor doctrine more cogent than what may be found in the lines of this play. When knowledge and deeds, theory and practice, science and art, are in fruitful relation, all of us find ourselves "when no man was his own." This is the right tutorial action.

Accounts of the wreck of Sir George Somers in the Bermudas, which reached England in the fall of 1610, and the lively contemporary interest in new worlds will meagerly account for

Miranda's brave new world of men and women unless we also reconsider those voyages up and down Faeryland which it has been the aim of this book to associate with the poetic adventures of the Master Playwright. Whatever overtones are heard as readers or auditors undergo and overcome this mightiest literary tempest, students of drama will be listening in it for echoes of a theory of dramatic action; and hence they will not be disappointed when they hear Prospero announce that the rarer action is in virtue than in vengeance.

For the ways of good conduct and good government and good teaching are also the ways of good playwriting. All are archetypal actions, not artificial activities; however much they differ in tactics, their strategy is one and the same. All are representative; all forego self-assertion and dictatorial procedure for the orderly process of delegation; all are subtly persuasive rather than pontifical and homiletic; all appeal primarily to the imagination—witness Shakespeare's kind of forensic and ritual and Spenser's tourneys and ceremonies. And, most important, the patient operations of all must be as unyielding in essentials as they are endlessly resilient in externals. Or so at least we may assume to be true at the Court of the Faery Queen.

In this and the preceding chapters the reader will have gone swiftly over an investigation which has busied the writer for many years. The result of my review of certain plays in the light of a certain allegorical narrative has been to incline me to the belief, even the strong conviction, that there was Spenserian influence upon Shakespeare's dramaturgy in the period 1599–1604, and less distinctly thereafter. Like other beliefs, this in the realm of literary form is a matter of observations outside the scheme of proof by induction and deduction, and hence it is not reducible to a clear and authoritative statement of proof. I should myself be the more willing to challenge it, except that in following the same tentative method of comparison I have been unable to detect in the action or agents of the plays preceding *Much Ado* anything analogous to the action or agents of *The Faerie Queene*. Readers who cannot spare time to trace allusions or weigh evidence, however, will by now have been furnished, or so I dare hope, with an authentic picture of what is alike in the literary art of two great poets—their ethical action. Such similarity as exists has been carefully recorded. Meanwhile, the literary historian who must still, and rightly, question every hypothesis, is bidden to continue his search for those facts which may validate or invalidate mine.

CHAPTER XI

Conclusion: Of Forms and Shapes

WHEN beginning this study of Shakespeare's dramatic poetry we sought in his text for his own idea of action. Now, and in conclusion, we may briefly investigate his idea of form. Dramatic action and dramatic form (*praxis* and *mimesis*) would have been deduced by him from basic concepts, or at least would not have been alien to them. What, then, did Shakespeare understand by "form"?

Here and there, for instance in "plain form of marriage," he used the word to mean a conventional act or ceremony. Sometimes the "form" that is "set . . . upon" a "shapeless" "indigest" or gives meaning where otherwise there would be mere apprehension of "a world of figures" (*King John*, V.vii.25–27; I *Henry IV*, I.iii.209–210) implies a logical or rational procedure on the part of an individual. "Complots" to be digested "in some form" or battles for which "the form and model" must be drawn (*Richard III*, III.i.200; V.iii.24) call for a sort of tactical pattern or a habit in manners or customs. Such a pattern could be a guide to bring "a wild Kate to a Kate / Conformable as

Conclusion: Of Forms and Shapes 235

other household Kates" (*The Taming of the Shrew*, II.i.279–280), or it could be the fashion of a headdress or hairdress which Constance disarranges in her grief (*King John*, III.iv.101–102):

> I will not keep this form upon my head
> When there is such disorder in my wit.

Viola's disguise becomes "the form of [her] intent" (*Twelfth Night*, I.ii.54–55). Agamemnon and the Greek lords will "put on / A form of strangeness" (*Troilus and Cressida*, III.iii.51).

Form is not a concept merely. Macbeth's dagger of the mind has a "form as palpable" as the dagger he draws from the harness at his side. Nor is it a mere fancy; it bears a relation to the world of objects. Looking on little Arthur's dead body, the Earl of Salisbury asks (*King John*, IV.iii.44–45):

> Could thought, without this object,
> Form such another?

Form is "form of the thing" as well as "form" suited "to [a] conceit" (*Hamlet*, I.ii.210; II.ii.582–583); so Hamlet had learned at Shakespeare's Wittenberg. And at Shakespeare's Alexandria Cleopatra was familiar with the doctrine of forms, nature's forms and fancy's forms. Although "Nature wants stuff / To vie strange forms with fancy, . . . Antony," she says, is "nature's piece 'gainst fancy" (*Antony and Cleopatra*, V.ii.97–99). Finally, like Antony for Cleopatra, Ferdinand for Miranda is a masterpiece; on that insular campus where scholarship and teaching were nevertheless at their best her imagination could not "form a shape, / Besides [himself], to like of" (*The Tempest*, III.i.56–57).

Such a review of the usual connotation of the word in Shakespeare's plays has seemed necessary before we discuss his ideas about dramatic form. One early passage reveals his understanding of comic form; in *Love's Labour's Lost* (V.ii.520–521) the Princess begs that the play of the Nine Worthies may go on, and of its overzealous actors she says:

> Their form confounded makes most form in mirth
> When great things labouring perish in their birth.

As with comic form—"form in mirth"—so it is with tragic form, what might be called form in sorrow. Drama begins at form confounded, deals with great things laboring, about to survive or perish. Through her "blinding tears" the Queen of King Richard the Second (II.ii.14–27) sees a "confusion" of woes which, she is told, must be "ey'd awry" (obliquely or from a special angle, as through a perspective glass) before their true "form" can be "distinguish[ed]." The tragic poet here drops a hint that he also views the falls of princes in a certain perspective the better to seize their formal truth. These shapes of grief, these "things imaginary" for which the Queen weeps, are, says Bushy to comfort her, "nothing but conceit, my gracious lady." In her rejoinder may be spelled out the playwright's problem, too (II.ii.34–40):

> 'T is nothing less. Conceit is still deriv'd
> From some forefather grief. Mine is not so,
> For nothing hath begot my something grief.
>
> . . . . .
>
> But what it is that is not yet known what,
> I cannot name. 'T is nameless woe, I wot.

Here in the Queen's "unborn sorrow" we have another version of those "forms of things unknown," the "airy nothing," and the "name" given to it by the poet's pen in the contemporary *A Midsummer Night's Dream*.

Shakespeare, however, can name what it is that the anxious Queen does not yet know. In the garden of the Duke of York (III.iv) she is allowed to overhear the Gardener and his men talking about form in horticulture. They wonder why they should "in the compass of a pale, / Keep law and form and due proportion" when the land as a whole is full of weeds, "her knots disordered" in a "disordered spring." Through the per-

Conclusion: Of Forms and Shapes 237

spective glass thus furnished by the playwright the pending deposition of King Richard is given a meaning, and the shadowy woes of the Queen become one actual grief; their true "form" is at last "distinguish[ed]." Later, bidding the King farewell on his journey to the Tower and Pomfret Castle, she recognizes that he is "both in shape and mind transform'd." She cannot help him back into form; and he himself at Pomfret acknowledges his error in a musical trope of discord and "time broke in a disordered string." Thus the play is furnished with its quasi-tragic discovery, although its change of fortune still lacks the complete reversal of Shakespeare's mature tragedies. The King is permitted only a scant moment of frantic self-defense—less comprehending and much less satisfactory for tragic effect than is Othello's avowal of error in a final gesture of self-retribution—and the Queen will tell good old folks sitting by the fire the "lamentable tale" of "the deposing of a rightful king." But the point of form as order has been made unmistakably clear for his readers and auditors by the playwright. Across the shadowy confusion of history we have looked awry in his perspective glass to get a glimpse of the true form of royalty, the king who should be.

As in *Richard II*, so in both parts of *Henry IV:* Shakespeare is preoccupied with form as confusion to be brought into order. Hotspur "apprehends a world of figures," "but not the form of what he should attend." He will prove an unwise leader. Westmoreland speaks of "the ugly form / Of base and bloody insurrection," and the Archbishop of York gives as excuse the "misordered time" which "doth . . . / Crowd us and crush us to this monstrous form." The noble speech of Warwick (Pt. II, III.i.80–87) probes deep into "necessary form"; but, like Falstaff bidding, "Let time shape, and there an end," he, too, depends for action on "the hatch and brood of time." The dying King prophesies that "a time has come to mock at form." Is it the not-quite-yet tragic flaw of these great Englishmen that they cannot conceive of form in temporal and local matters as the playwright conceives of dramatic form in the ideal world? When his agents come to share his knowledge and responsibility, the actions in which they are involved will be properly tragic.

The Chorus of *Henry V* says in its epilogue that the "rough and all-unable pen" of the "author" has pursued a "story, / In little room confining mighty men." The perspective toward form in this play, we note, is apiculture—honeybees—and tennis. which serve the playwright as horticulture served him in *Richard II* and bodily surfeit and disease in *Henry IV*. When King Harry gathers "honey from the weed," or "distil[s]" the "soul of goodness" out of "things evil," under his metaphors we guess the procedure of an author, too. His speech on Ceremony, like the Bastard's on Commodity in *King John*, is still another device to make clear what would otherwise be a "confusion" of events or dim shadows of "place, degree, and [outward] form." Every soliloquy in the plays is this kind of help toward the discovery of inner form: it puts the play in order for the reader or auditor.

After he had finished his experiment with dramatic form in the histories, it remained for Shakespeare to elicit from his reading or experience what his knowledge of Holinshed or Stow or North could not supply, a belief that tragic form proper is more than fact or fate, more than political survival or civil order, and hence that in his actions-to-be-imitated he must ally it with spiritual purpose. The great tragedies were still unwritten; but they would come free of history, and whatever the waste or failure in responsible conduct, his agents would be led on their way to acknowledge a kind of order superior to tidy arrangements in this world. Hamlet, Othello, Lear, Macbeth, Coriolanus, and Antony are no dupes of circumstance. They are the indisputable evidence of ideal order.

Meanwhile, we may assume that the poet's definition of poetry through the words of Theseus at the beginning of Act V of *A*

Conclusion: Of Forms and Shapes

Midsummer Night's Dream details what he understood to be the steps in dramatic composition.

> As imagination bodies forth
> The forms of things unknown, the poet's pen
> Turns them to shapes, and gives to airy nothing
> A local habitation and a name.

If we read these lines backward, as it were, and more prosaically, we learn that identifiable poems are shapes recorded in script from forms; that these forms are forms of things; that these things without these forms would be unknown; and that the forms themselves are filial bodies or creations of the parental imagination. Thus the form mediates between the imagination of the poet and the final shape of poetry; it is indeed the mimetic implement.

Therefore let us here reconsider that middle step in storytelling or playwriting, the form bodied forth, the form of an unknown thing, the imitated action not yet become the text of the Book of Temperance or *Hamlet*.

To this end some further light is cast upon "form" by Shakespeare's use of "deform," "transform," "reform," even "perform." In *Much Ado* and *Twelfth Night*, the earliest plays in which we have distinct traces of Spenser's thought and expression, we first find form implied as that ideal pattern from which actual life may deviate and to which it may be returned. "What a deformed thief this fashion is," says Borachio; and the watchmen of Dogberry at once personify the remark: "I know that Deformed" (*Much Ado*, III.iii.131, 133, 182, 185; V.i.317). Sebastian's friend Antonio is disturbed when Viola-Cesario seems not to know him and disavows his loan of a purse. This is ingratitude, he assumes (*Twelfth Night*, III.iv.401–403):

> In nature there's no blemish but the mind;
> None can be call'd deform'd but the unkind.
> Virtue is beauty.

Such Platonic assumptions pro and con were not hard to come by, but they were never more conveniently furnished than in Spenser's *Hymne in Honour of Beautie:*

> For of the soule the bodie forme doth take:
> For soule is forme, and doth the bodie make.
>
> . . . . .
>
> Yet oft it falles, that many a gentle mynd
> Dwels in deformed tabernacle drownd,
> Either by chaunce, against the course of kynd,
> Or through vnaptnesse in the substance fownd,
> Which it assumed of some stubborne grownd,
> That will not yield vnto her formes direction,
> But is perform'd with some foule imperfection.

Would a dramatist not be likely to agree? The formal beauty of drama is, and must always be, beauty of an imitated action-toward-virtue.

Generally in Shakespeare's text "transform" connotes a change for the worse; in remembering Spenser the playwright would not forget Ovid. Thersites and Florizel both comment on the metamorphoses of gods into beasts. Cassio regrets "that we should . . . transform ourselves into beasts." Philo says that Antony is "transform'd into a strumpet's fool," and Enobarbus, rebuking Antony's maudlin sentimentality, begs him, "Transform us not to women." Richard II has been "transform'd and weak'ned." On the other hand, Shakespeare rarely mentions "reform" and "reformation"; once at the "reformation" of Henry V, who bids Falstaff also "reform" himself, and once with artistic relevance when Hamlet disapproves of players who imitate humanity abominably and hears that his visiting troupe "has reform'd that indifferently": "O, reform it altogether!"

If we approve Prospero's belief that the rarer action is in virtue than in vengeance, we shall expect from Shakespeare's mature plays no mere disclosure of guilty events and persons, no stark record of deformity as such, but the unfolding in the

Conclusion: Of Forms and Shapes

mind of his agents of the operative form of virtue correcting vice; and thereafter we are willing to forego retribution if we may watch the ultimate and necessary change of fortune, the *peripeteia*, into penitence and—granted time—into a better life.

> Things base and vile, holding no quantity,
> Love can transpose to form and dignity.

In this view the playwright is himself a lover; and as instances of dramatic form his later plays are bodied forth in doings or deeds to be done toward the "virtue [which] is beauty," otherwise unknown to human life or lost out of human experience. Arousing our appropriate feelings vicariously, their outer shape helps to clear our vision of dim forebodings and to satisfy our vague or frustrate desires. This is the form which is function.[1]

When, next, we ask by what technical agency Shakespeare's dramatic forms become plays, there is ample evidence to indicate that he first imagines or bodies forth a disciplinary action leading up to and onward from a revelatory ordeal.[2] This form of a thing, this instance of discipline in its triple sense of learning truth and doing right and thus relieving discomfort or guilty woe, provides his drama with what Aristotle called *anagnorisis*, *peripeteia*, and *katharsis*—all three.

Whether or not he owes this strong formal predilection in large part to his reading of Spenser, it is germane to the evidence to point out that Spenser's narrative form is also a disciplinary form. *The Faerie Queene* is a repetitive series of disciplines, for

---

[1] The Duke in *Twelfth Night* (II.iv.3-4) echoes Aristotle when he says that an "old and antique song . . ./ . . . did relieve [his] passion much."

[2] The process of playwriting as Hamlet describes it to the players accords with the process of composition set forth by Theseus: An excellent play is "well digested in the scenes." Cf. Aristotle's σύνθεσις τῶν πραγμάτων or ἡ τῶν πραγμάτων σύντασις where πραγμάτων is not adequately translated by "incidents" but rather by "deeds" or "doings." Cf. also συντάσεως τοῦ μύθου as the procedure which transforms action into plot—what Shakespeare calls "form" bodied forth and shaped.

the Redcrosse Knight, for Sirs Guyon, Artegall, and Calidore, for Scudamour and Marinell, and for the Virgin Knight Britomart. What formal use could a playwright make of Spenser's narrative poem?

Like those "Briton moniments" which Prince Arthur read in the House of Alma, *The Faerie Queene* ends "abruptly" (2.10.68.2–6),

> Without full point, or other Cesure right,
> As if the rest some wicked hand did rend,
> Or th' Authour selfe could not at least attend
> To finish it.

We may not, therefore, speak of its form as a complete poem. Yet the first six Books of it as shorter narratives have definite structure; there is a pattern shared among them and evident in each of them. In sequence it sets forth: (1) a villainous deceit and repeated instances of villainy; (2) minor successes of the hero, fostering pride; (3) a physical ordeal and mighty overthrow; (4) the spiritual testing toward new vision and penance; (5) the mission of the hero accomplished with the defeat of the villain or villains and the rescue of the beloved maiden or the besieged country. In this sequence Spenser composed the story of the Redcrosse Knight, of Sir Guyon, of Sir Artegall; of Sir Calidore and Sir Calepine somewhat less distinctly; and, in an action extended through Books III, IV, and V, of Britomart, Marinell, and Scudamour, three knights whose destiny is more elaborately entangled.

Such a quintuple sequence is also characteristic of Shakespeare's formal actions, most clearly so in the plays after 1599. Troilus loses Cressida but saves his military repute; Hamlet loses Ophelia but saves Denmark; Othello loses Desdemona but in his last word and gesture certifies his governorship of Cyprus; Lear's reunion with Cordelia is one kind of salvation, and his Britain is saved by those who avenge him; Macbeth loses self

Conclusion: Of Forms and Shapes 243

and Lady Macbeth, but Scotland is safe at last; Coriolanus saves his ladies and his country at the cost of his own life; and Antony as husband precedes his lass unparalleled into a new heaven quite different from the good new Roman earth united under Octavius. In every case, however, there has been deceit and villainy, prideful success and chastening overthrow, ultimately the revelation of and penitent regard for the form of human destiny. With Shakespeare the personal cost has been mightily increased to lend weight and significance to the discipline.

In the comedies, too, heroes and heroines alike partake of the arrogance which subjects them to villainy or untoward circumstance, and—ludicrously if less painfully—are restored to play their proper parts in formal courtship or formal officialdom. Benedick, Beatrice, Claudio, Olivia, Orsino, Bertram, Helena, Isabella, Angelo, and, in a slightly different mode, Posthumus, Leontes, Pericles, and Prospero himself are all formal agents. Granted the humor, wit, or charm with which Shakespeare has endowed them, the passionate and insistent natures through which none but he might bring them so completely alive, under the dark conceit we can still eye the form.

This roughly estimated likeness between Spenser's narrative and Shakespeare's drama is further corroborated when we note that the Spenserian and Shakespearean discovery occurs usually within the third or fourth stage of the formal action as we have detailed it. In what we might call the "Houses," Spenser's "goodly frames" of holiness or temperance, the Hut of the Hermit or the Palace of Mercilla or the Hill of the Graces, the appropriate life is recognized. On the other hand, the villainy is hatched or the deformity exhibited in dens and caves and castles: witness Errour's Den, the postern of the House of Pride, the Dongeon of Orgoglio, the Cave of Despaire, the Castle of Medina, the Cave of Mammon, the Bowre of Blisse, Castle Joyous, the Castle of Malbecco, the "greene-wood" of the Satyres, the Castle of Busirane, the shore on which the Gyant of the Scales holds forth, the Castle of Radigund, Briana's Castle of the Beards, the Cave of the Brigantes. The lovers of the interlocked Books of Chastity and Friendship must continually suspect treachery even in the tourneys and the Masks of Cupid which invite them—and us—to rest between their wanderings. Such static "frames" and "castles" are, of course, inherited from the medieval tradition, where they formalize the helpful or baneful aspect of doctrine or adventure; but Spenser uses them with supreme skill, not for pictorial beauty alone, or for ethical significance alone, but more successfully than ever before to orient his action.

Just here the dramatist has a great advantage over the romancer and allegorist. He may convert Spenserian Houses and Dens into stage settings, and ethical doctrines into persuasive argument and language, thus characterizing the persons to be tested and enlightened and, further, enriching their thought and diction.

If Shakespeare conceivably transformed in this way those cantos of *The Faerie Queene* which are mainly locodescriptive and schematic, he did what any good dramatic writer has always done to the stories he adapts. When he called for such settings as the "pleached bower" hiding Beatrice or the orchard encompassing the Trojan lovers or Herne's Oak in Windsor Forest, the "dark house" of Malvolio or the prisons and brothels of Vienna or the confining Court of the King of France, the formal pertinency of such scenes would be suggested to Elizabethan spectators who knew Spenser's poem. Hamlet's "mother's closet" or the Palace of Priam would be cross-referred to infamous places where Malecasta and Acrasia imperiled the unwary. And where have we, too, observed more significantly than in *The Faerie Queene* dangerous isles testing the self-command of generals and exiled dukes? That desperate heath in Gloucester's realm and that Castle of Inverness so fair without and so unholy within—we have been there, or thereabouts, before. All that panoply of Rome and all that luxury of Alexandria are familiar. We who have read Spenser's allegory are at home in the bedchamber of Imogen, the Cave of Belarius, even on the shore of the sea where Timon is trying to balance the scales between "this beggar" and "that lord." The Temple of Diana, which served Pericles and Marina better than the Temple of Venus served Scudamour and Amoret, speaks without words; and even without its banter and verbal music the scene of merry-making for Perdita and Florizel would lead us to expect the best because it recapitulates the good fortune of Pastorella and Calidore. We can trust what is beneficently determined in the Cave of Prospero because we have visited the cave of another magician, Merlin.

So plausible an argument by analogy cannot prove indebtedness; but it locates the wide country of Shakespeare's drama very near Faeryland. He is a veritable as well as an actual contemporary of Spenser.

Again, a maker of tragic or comic plots cannot afford to depict error or deformity through repetitious episodes like those which furnish the early stanzas of the romancer. Shakespeare, or any other dramatist dealing with the jealousy of a Moor, will telescope or abbreviate the many perils from Turks such as Sansfoi and Sansloi; for his play of Troy he must put more compactly the defeats of such as Furor, Pyrochles, and Cymochles and the characteristic seductions of such as Duessa, Phaedria, and Acrasia; Marinell's rebellions and Scudamour's suspicions need not be so elaborately amplified in a Bertram and a Claudio.

In brief, Acts I and II of a five-act play will concentrate what is set forth in the early cantos of a Spenserian Book of Holiness or Temperance or Courtesy. Thus barely half of an allegorical action like those of *The Faerie Queene*—the part of it veering toward or exhibiting the ordeal, the discovery, and the effortful final struggle—will suffice for a tragedy. Or, for a comedy in the vein of *Much Ado, Twelfth Night,* or Act V of *The Merry Wives,* what serves the romance writer as an episode can be lifted out and amplified into a comic action according to the familiar pattern of ordeal, discovery, repentance. Here in the patient study of structure resides the workaday magic of playwriting, of forms bodied forth.

What actual shape, then, will the second half of the Spenserian Book, its final cantos, take in drama? Giants to be overthrown, dragons to be killed, lustful bowers to be destroyed, threatened maidens to be rescued, tyrants to be slain, brigands to be dispersed, are romantic statements of the deed to be done. The dramatist, whose imperative pattern is not less grim, will rather emphasize the preparation of the hero to do his deed. Here of all the romancers Spenser is the best guide. And here the evidence seems well-nigh incontrovertible. Spenserian romance and Shakespearean drama are both characterized by the test, trial, ordeal, or other shape of outer struggle or inner strife suiting the inherited fable or the invented plot. All possible refinements and applications of what the *Tractatus Coislinianus* calls βάσανος, (βασανίζειν now and again in the plays of Aristophanes) [3] are employed to lend both shape and shapeliness to the Books of Faeryland and to the dramatic canon of the greatest of Gloriana's playwrights.

Verbal hints of this are not lacking in the text of the plays. Hamlet asks that his sanity be brought to the test, Angelo begs that a test be made of his metal, Ferdinand has strangely stood his test. Even to the bearing of logs and the playing of chess *The Tempest* is a long trial of love for Ferdinand and a longer trial of wisdom for Prospero. More particularly, Pistol calls "A trial, come" for Sir John Falstaff, and Dame Quickly applies the trial fire. Lafeu expects a trial for Parolles, which comes off with great skill on the part of the playwright. Leontes will give his Queen a just and open trial, little conceiving what in-

[3] Consult Cooper, *An Aristotelian Theory of Comedy,* pp. 269–279.

ner discipline is in store for himself. Lear imagines Goneril and Regan at their trial even as he himself is wrung into shapes of agony. Wrestling matches, fencing matches, trials in court, trials by joust, trials by war, all those "protractive trials of great Jove / To find persistive constancy in men" which great sieges at Troy and great campaigns at Actium illustrate are the visible facets of Shakespeare's dramaturgy.

Before what we have assumed to be his study of *The Faerie Queene* at the turn of the century, such comic ordeals as those planned for the lovers in *A Midsummer Night's Dream* or the melodramatic trials of Shylock and Antonio in *The Merchant of Venice* or the farcical abuse of Katherine in *The Taming of the Shrew* are managed by fairies with potent herbs or by arbitrary weather gods or by incredible roustabouts with cracking whips. In the early tragedies we call to witness the magic or deadly vial and the "infectious pestilence" of *Romeo and Juliet*, which arbitrarily bring on the painful but unfruitful agony. Without the suggestion from Spenser of the need for ethical testing, an Orlando must again and again be matched with a Charles in an encounter for which the playwright as umpire fixes the outcome; Rosalind and Celia would again and again join the Duke in an exile whose hardships are carefully manipulated not to ruffle the unvarying holiday mood. The battles, treasons, assassinations, and tortures that wring the souls of kings and princes in the histories would continue, as they do in fact from that day to this, to leave actual life unchanged and very little tempered or refined. What progress is made other than the traditional falls of princes and deaths of kings and Caesars shows but dimly in the regrets of Richard II, the reformation of Prince Hal, and the mistaken patriotism of Brutus. None of these agents thoroughly understands or explains himself; music and soothsayers and ghosts are called in to help interpret the "evil spirit" or to compensate for the lack of any real glimpse of godhead.

In *The Faerie Queene*, on the other hand, the ordeal of knights and ladies, however palpably bodied forth in jousts and wanderings, is a spiritual matter, a trial and test for the soul. The central concern of Spenser's Books is the discipline proper for credulous, languorous, or inconstant behavior. Such discipline is not episodic, introduced capriciously or for pictorial effect alone; it is the main form of his narrative action. In the Cave of Despaire and the House of Holiness the Redcrosse Knight has been prepared for his fight with the Dragon. In the Cave of Mammon and the House of Alma Guyon has been inwardly tempered for his outward task of destroying the Bowre of Blisse. In the Cave of Merlin Britomart has been commissioned for her rescue of Amoret from the House of Busirane. Scudamour is chastened at the Cottage of Care so that he may be fit to seek for a lady won too easily in the Temple of Venus. Artegall earns in the Prison of Radigund the power later effecting his victory over Grantorto. And it is during his humble chores in a shepherd's cot that Calidore finds the motive prompting him to dare the Cave of the Brigantes and to muzzle the Blatant Beast.

Like Spenser, then, the mature Shakespeare of the years 1600–1611 might well imagine the form of his action as an ordeal. This he locates in the shape of his Act III. Although the protensity of his action carries us by due degrees from Act I to Act V, the form of his action is established at its center; and almost without exception Act III takes on the characteristics of the *basanos*. Witness the great third acts of the tragedies. The third act of *Hamlet* is an essential "mouse-trap" with its alarming disclosures and its purgatorial testing of Gertrude—and Hamlet—as the first indication of Hamlet's regenerated will. In Act III of *Othello* the essential housewives' "skillet" is put on the head of the uxorious Moor, who fails in the test no mere military tactician can ever meet. King Lear and the Duke of Gloucester are in the third act sent out upon the open heath into the sort of chastening destined for all who are willful and blind. It is in the third act of Macbeth's regicide that Banquo's ghost appears at the royal banquet to tell truth and exact payment; and it is in the third act of that other tyrannical action, *Coriolanus*, that the arrogant general Caius Marcius fails to meet his test and is exiled to "a world elsewhere" for his further civic reformation. Finally, such an imperial test as proves the full strength of the "triple pillar of the world" inadequate for the support of his third of the Roman Empire dictates the shape of Act III of *Antony and Cleopatra*. The moment of self-knowledge varies from play to play, but throughout Shakespeare's last decade in no tragic situation, not even in that of Timon, does the hero fail to understand himself and the reason for his change of fortune or to pronounce his own doom in terms appropriate to his fault.

To give ethical meaning and hence dramatic validity to this form of discipline of the third act, the second and fourth acts deal respectively with deformity and reformation. The function of Act II, to reveal indisputably what is deformed, wayward, or evil, is often foreshadowed in Act I; and the function of Act IV, to wring from faulty or mistaken agents the hidden vestiges of wrongdoing and to set them on the way to a new and happier life, must often be extended into Act V. On either side of the central *basanos*, the form of discipline is temporally and logically buttressed.

There can be little doubt that in Act I the playwright will handle informative matters necessary to his plot, those suggestions of pertinent code, those commissions, vows, wishes, and characteristic opinions which arouse expectation or dread and ally our sympathies with whatsoever hero or heroine is to represent us vicariously. We have misgivings when we hear Othello vow that housewives shall "make a skillet of [his] helm" if ever his "disports corrupt and taint [his] business." Lear's wish, "O, let me not be mad, not mad, sweet heaven!" aims at the terrible deformities of Act II and the revelatory ordeal of

Act III of this mightiest of English tragedies. Macbeth knows that "We still have judgment here," but he willfully disregards the royal code. In his early triumph, even as he is named "Coriolanus," Caius Marcius jokes without understanding when he says, "The gods begin to mock me." And the initial choices of that other Roman, Antony, rest most forebodingly on his frank estimate of himself: "Things that are past are done with me." Macbeth would "jump the life to come"; Antony has no loyalty to the past. If we might some day read an analysis of Shakespeare's use of the imperative and optative mode, we should be further enlightened as to the adjurative constituent in his form of discipline.

Then in Act V, for which previously plays of the Nine Worthies or Pyramus and Thisbe have performed their ritual or ceremonial function, along with romantic and reconciliatory episodes at Belmont and in the Forest of Arden, wedding breakfasts without great distinction and sylvan revels galore, the playwright must now devise a "performance" of a rarer sort. This will be freighted with a more universal joy or regret, but it will arise out of the new life of the individual hero merrily, as in *Much Ado;* with graceful and melodious civility, as in *Twelfth Night;* ironically, as in *All's Well;* with bitter riddling on human nature and human destiny, as in *Troilus and Cressida;* and in *Measure for Measure* with an ostentatious celebration of the *status ad quem,* rewards and punishments given with as steady a hand as life or art ever allows. Similarly, in Act V of the tragedies earlier discussed as forms of unholiness to be disciplined into holiness our assumption is borne out that Shakespeare bases his "performance" on renewable hope and on what is therefore dignified or fitting in human destiny. Witness in *Antony and Cleopatra* (V.ii.328–330):

> —Charmian, is this well done?
> —It is well done, and fitting for a princess
> Descended of so many royal kings.

Conclusion: Of Forms and Shapes

Caesar "himself [comes] / To see perform'd" the dreaded act he has sought to hinder; in the Roman view Antony and Cleopatra have both done well. At the end Coriolanus shows "all like" himself, a patriot of Rome. Those forms of British and Scottish discipline which supply the third acts of *King Lear* and *Macbeth* point toward characteristically British and Scottish "performances" in their fifth acts. The emergence of a champion from the heralded tourney even as the "gods themselves throw incense" upon the "sacrifices" of Lear and Cordelia is not less comforting a performance for Britain than the sagacious behavior leading to the coronation of the young King Malcolm of Scotland (V.ii.27–29):

> Meet we the med'cine of the sickly weal;
> And with him pour we in our country's purge
> Each drop of us.

Although Macbeth will not "play the Roman fool, and die / On [his] own sword," as a reformed Caledonian he disavows the "juggling fiends." Even more willingly, Othello, at last a rightful general of the Venetian state and no mere uxorious Moor, takes the metaphorical "skillet" from his head and does justice upon himself. In all five tragic instances the form of discipline has been thoroughly performed.

Moreover, in Act V of the late romances the playwright performs for us a kind of theophany to validate the gods above without devaluing the human agents below. Witness Diana of Ephesus in *Pericles*. Witness also in *Cymbeline* Jupiter opening his "crystal window" in order to peep through his "marble mansion" or descending upon an eagle to announce, "Whom I love I cross." *The Winter's Tale,* presided over by the oracle of Apollo, if not a theophany, is an exhibit of resolute womanhood; Hermione, like Thaisa, has been formed into something of a divine nature previously unrecognized. And when *The Tempest* intensifies the magical nature and restorative powers of

Prospero into one total performance, the discovery of Ferdinand and Miranda playing chess would seem to symbolize the proper royal game in a brave new world for which only the courtly constellations provide an adequate pattern.

Readers will think of the exceptions and modifications which such a dogmatic analysis always rightfully provokes; but they will be well advised to give its due weight to the symbolic form of disciplinary action from which Shakespearean drama is shaped. The ritual nature of the final act and the relation of the whole action to the *agon* and *sparagmos* of Greek cultural forms have been helpfully investigated by scholars,[4] but the heroes of Spenser and Shakespeare are more than a succession of scapegoats; they are conscious agents in an ethical world, agents whose choices and trials are voluntarily related to Christian procedures by poets who understood the Christian mysteries, although neither cared to Christianize his writing outwardly.

The dramatic rhythm of religious action oscillates between free choice and willing sacrifice, and for this analogy, too, Shakespeare gives us many suggestions. His agents are almost never victimized. Portia chooses to obey the will of her father, knowing that she "stand[s] for sacrifice." Orsino almost "sacrifice[s]" Viola, the lamb that he loves; and she, "most jocund, apt, and willingly, / To do [him] rest, a thousand deaths would die." Romeo and Juliet are "poor sacrifices" of civil enmity and strife, yet not entirely without fault in their heedless choices. The sacrifice at Delphos but faintly symbolizes, although it rebukes, the sacrifice of Hermione in Sicilia. The imprisoned Cordelia and Lear, glad to be together at last in spiritual communion, are "sacrifices" upon which "the gods themselves throw in-

---

[4] For instance, recently by Burke, Wheelwright, and Fergusson, as hitherto cited, and by C. L. Barber, "From Ritual to Comedy: An Examination of *Henry IV*," in *English Stage Comedy* (Columbia University Press, 1955).

cense." Both pagan and Christian rites [5] underlie this aspect of the ordeal.

Now it may be that the sacraments of a culture rooted in the free will and dignity of the individual man or woman are the best analogies for Shakespearean dramatic forms, even though they, too, are forms of things as yet darkly seen and imperfectly known. Apollo's oracle, "kin to Jove's thunder," did not have the last word in an action taken over by the redemptive agency of Christendom, nor is *The Winter's Tale* its chief record of human courage and patience. Yet Shakespeare's drama is for the best of reasons a lay drama, as Spenser's legends were lay poems; both poets were humble in the face of religious revelation and sacrifice. Here, then, as Spenser and Shakespeare did, we shall invoke a lay rather than a religious symbol for this review of forms becoming shapes.

The Greek word ἡ βάσανος is literally "the touchstone by which gold is tried," "a test to try whether a thing be genuine or not." With Shakespeare's "less Greek" we cannot assume that he had Ben Jonson's knowledge of the *Poetics,* nor could he know the *Tractate.* Nevertheless, his actions are all attempts to prove the gold in humanity. Beyond the ludicrous whippings associated with the comic *basanos* and within the ills that flesh is amply and endlessly heir to, his drama assumes the worth of men and women.[6] What we have earlier, in the first chapter of this book, called "dramatic urgency" is more than a mode of

---

[5] The cultural loyalties of Shakespeare's agents become evident to readers in the many lesser shapes or devices familiar to playwrights: codes, laws, or rules according to which choices are to be made; characteristic beliefs as expressed in the maxims and opinions of those who choose or who persuade others to choose; and the particular choices themselves or the compacts that ratify the choices.

[6] In *King John* Constance says she has been
  "beguil'd . . . with a counterfeit
  Resembling majesty, which, being touch'd and tried,
  Proves valueless."

excitement driving through suspense to anticipated retribution or rescue in time and space. We, the spectators of the play, not only share in the double vision, the irony, permitted us in common with the gods on high who wait to see truth revealed and goodness rewarded; we have our urgent hour, too. We do not leave the theatre of this playwright without the chance to pay our own debts of stupidity or guilt as we undergo vicariously the penitential sufferings of heroes reformed to the point where they have found themselves again. Like them, in our proper form we may still do our proper deed.

Thus Shakespeare's forms of discipline can be associated with the greater archetypes, the archetypes of beneficent action. From our very earliest times we make believe that we can be heroic and doom ourselves into hardship and adventure—we put ourselves to the test. But however often we are deceived as to what is gold and what is gilt a little dusted over, men and women mean business; even when traitorous, they are makers rather than aesthetes, doers rather than victims. From the *basanos* of Aristophanes to the martyrdom of Eliot's Celia, as from the *agon* of antiquity to the athletic contest of today, our zeal bears witness to an indestructible form of a thing deep within us. Like the richly human agents of Shakespearean action, our actors and audiences—and that means all of us—crave a touchstone.

That is why there will never again be an effective drama without a contemporary literary or actual *basanos*, obvious or subtle. Physical and mental torture, whippings, goadings, unendurable sorrows, and bestial vices, anything which dejected playwrights invoke to debase or victimize their merely pitiful persons for sadistic or pseudoaesthetic ends do not make drama. Without the concept of and faith in human value or the illustration of human worth a play has no mode of logical structure, does not itself serve as touchstone.

To separate the spurious from the genuine has been the function of poetry in both antiquity and Christendom; to estimate what in poetry is spurious or genuine must remain the duty of the critic. If for scholarship and criticism the *basanos* is fundamental, in a very real sense *The Faerie Queene* has served as our *basanos* for a fresh understanding of Shakespeare's plays, and for new proof of their value.

Index

[Mention of Shakespeare, of *The Faerie Queene*, and of the terms "action" and "agents" is so frequent in the text that these items are omitted from the Index. Spenser is listed as author only when his other writings are concerned. The plays of Shakespeare are indicated by title and the books of *The Faerie Queene*, 1-6 respectively, as the Book of Holiness, of Temperance, of Chastity, of Friendship, of Justice, of Courtesy. Main agents of poem and plays have been individually named; where there might be uncertainty as to persons with the same name, the entry is followed in parentheses by an abbreviation of the title of the play or the numbered book of the poem.]

Achilles, 88, 96-97, 101, 101n, 107, 109, 113, 118n, 121, 126, 216-217
Acrasia, 110, 112-114, 116, 135-136, 204, 244-245
Adams, Joseph Q., v, xi, 7n
Aeneas, 86, 89, 93n, 114
Aesculapius (1), 189
Agamemnon, 86, 93n, 96-98, 107, 112, 126, 235
Agamemnon (Caxton), 125n
Agon, 4, 106, 252, 254
Aguecheek, Sir Andrew, 17, 54-56, 58-59
Ajax, 97-98, 113, 117n, 121
Albany, Duke of, 180-182

Alcibiades (*Tim.*), 214
Alice (*H.V*), 77
Allegory, 6, 10-11, 17-18, 34-35, 80, 108, 110, 112, 127, 154, 162, 175, 178, 181, 185, 190, 196, 201, 205, 212, 217, 224, 231, 245
All's Well That Ends Well, 10, 24, 34, 64-76, 82, 106, 176, 216-217, 225, 228, 250
Altick, Richard D., 88n
Amidas, 166
Amoret, 20, 47, 51, 61-62, 65, 72, 78, 142, 173n, 180n, 221, 224, 245, 248
Amyot, Jacques, 204

Anagnorisis, see Discovery
Angela, 72, 151n
Angelo, 20, 150-173, 176, 243, 246
Angus, 191
Antigonus, 225
Antiochus, 220
Antiquity, 5, 13, 17, 27, 106, 254
Antonio (*Merch.*), 26, 36, 247
Antonio (*Twel.*), 59-60, 239
Antonius (1), 192
Antony, Mark (*Antony*), 177, 192, 195, 199-206, 209, 217-218, 226, 235, 238, 240, 243, 248, 250-251
Antony, Mark (*Caesar*), 34
Antony and Cleopatra, 11, 177, 195, 199-207, 235, 247-248
Apemantus, 213
Apollo (3), 68-69
Apollo (*W.T.*), 251, 253
Arachne (2); Ariachne (*Troi.*), 119-120
Archetype, 4, 4n, 10n, 83, 115-116, 174, 190, 207, 231-232, 254
Archimago, 143, 175, 177-178, 180, 180n, 199, 206, 221, 226
Argante, 75-78
Ariel, 1-2, 228, 230
Ariosto, 205
Aristophanes, 246, 254
Aristotle, 6n, 10n, 11n, 12n, 13, 68, 152-153, 241n; *Nichomachean Ethics*, 216-217; *Poetics*, xi, 3, 10n, 11-12, 13n, 14-15, 18, 19n, 68, 241, 253; *Tractatus Coislinianus*, 13n, 246, 246n, 253
Artegall, Sir, 20, 33, 39, 71, 129, 134, 137, 148, 153-155, 153n, 158, 160-162, 161n, 164n, 165-171, 173n, 212, 224, 228, 242, 248
Arthur, Duke of Britain (*John*), 235
Arthur, Prince, 53-54, 57, 59, 110, 112, 121, 129, 131, 134-135, 141, 147-148, 179, 189, 191, 202-204, 206, 208-209, 208n, 213, 218, 228-229, 242
Arviragus, 223

As You Like It, 9, 34, 37-38, 54, 215-216, 225, 228
Astraea (5), 134-135, 168, 212
Ate (4), 42n, 51
Ate (*Much*), 42, 65
Atin, 113-114
Aufidius, Tullus, 193-194, 198
Autolycus, 226
Aveugle, 180, 184

Bacon, Sir Francis, x
Baker, George P., v
Bakwin, Ruth M., xii
Baldwin, T. W., ed., 86n
Balthasar (*Much*), 52
Bandello, Matteo, *Novelle*, 44, 54
Banquo, 188, 248
Barber, C. L., 77n, 252n
Bardolph, Lieutenant (*Wives*), 83
Barnardine (*Meas.*), 152, 163-164
Basanos, 246-255
Bassanio, 26
Batchelder, Merritt C., 127n
Beatrice, 40-44, 49, 51, 53-54, 56, 67, 227, 243-244
Belarius, 222-224
Belch, Sir Toby, 54-55, 58-59
Bellamour, 225-226
Belphoebe, 20, 51, 62, 65, 74, 165, 173n, 222, 224, 228
Bembo, Master Peter, 87, 92-94, 93n, 100, 104-105
Benedick, 40-44, 49-54, 56, 227, 243
Bergen, Henry, ed., 124n
Bertram, Count, 65, 67, 176, 216, 227, 243, 245
Bianca (*Oth.*), 179
Bianca (*Shrew*), 27
Bible, 5, 16, 26, 27-28
Blake, William, 188
Blandamour, 29, 42, 74
Blandina, Lady, 58
Blatant Beast, 32, 39, 43, 45-47, 64, 226, 248
Boccaccio, 66
Boethius, *De Consolatione Philosophiae*, 123n, 210

Index

Bolingbroke (*R.II*), 29
Bonfont-Malfont (5), 213
Book of Chastity, 64-82, 148, 221, 244
Book of Courtesy, 39-40, 44, 46, 48, 50n, 54, 59, 224-225, 245
Book of Friendship, 32, 64-82, 148, 244
Book of Holiness, 16, 143, 174-208, 220-221, 223, 245
Book of Justice, 9, 29, 32, 33n, 74, 80, 150-173, 210
Book of Temperance, 49, 108-109, 112, 117, 121-123, 128, 130, 132, 136, 140, 204, 239, 245
Borachio, 46, 239
Bowers, Fredson T., 149n
Bowre of Blisse, 106-122, 135, 204, 243, 248
Brabantio, 178, 217
Bracidas, 166-167
Bradbrook, M. C., 11n
Braggadochio, 51-54, 73-75, 79-80, 83n, 133-134, 136-137, 154, 158, 165-166, 173n, 222
Briana, 20, 55-56, 59, 62
Brigantes (6), 226
Britomart, 20, 44, 54, 62, 65-68, 70-75, 78, 140, 142, 154, 160-162, 170, 224-225, 242, 248
Brooke, Tucker, xi
Brower, Reuben A., 13n
Bruin, Sir, 59-61
Brutus (*Caesar*), 247
Brutus (*Cor.*), 199
Burke, Kenneth, 2n, 10n, 13n, 86n, 252n
Burlesque, 80
Bush, Geoffrey, 59n
Bushy (*R.II*), 31, 236
Busirane, 72
Butcher, S. H., 10n
Bywater, Ingram, 10n

Caelia, Dame (1), 177, 179, 227
Caesar (1), 192
Caius, Doctor (*Wives*), 77
Calchas, 109, 119-120
Calepine, Sir, 58-59, 225, 242
Caliban, 228-231
Calidore, Sir, 19, 28, 32, 39, 48, 54-56, 60, 62, 224-226, 230, 242, 245, 248
Camillo, 4
Campbell, Oscar J., xi, 112n
Captain (2), 65
Captain (6), 65
Captain, Sea (*Twel.*), 57
Carter, A. H., 70n
Cassandra, 113
Cassandra (Caxton), 125n
Cassio, Michael, 179, 240
Castiglione, Baldassare, *Book of the Courtier*, x, 84-105, 126
Castle of the Beards, 56, 244
Castle of Briana, 55-56
Castle of Busirane, 243
Castle of Inverness, 244
Castle Joyous, 140, 173n, 243
Castle of Malbecco, 243
Castle of Medina, 243
Castle of Orgoglio, 189-190
Castle of Radigund, 154, 162, 244, 248
Catharsis (katharsis), 10n, 68, 68n, 83, 241, 241n
Cave of Belarius, 245
Cave of the Brigantes, 244, 248
Cave of Despaire, 181, 184-185, 243, 248
Cave of Mammon, 118-120, 158, 243, 248
Cave of Merlin, 72, 245, 248
Cave of Prospero, 245
Caxton, William, *Recuyell of the Historyes of Troye*, 124, 124n, 127
Cerberus, 118n
Cesario, 54-58, 61, 67; see also Viola
Chapman, George, *Iliades*, 127n
Charmian, 205, 250
Chaucer, Geoffrey, 25; *Boece*, 210;

Chaucer, Geoffrey (*cont.*)
  Troilus and Criseyde, 91-93, 91n, 106, 108, 123, 123n, 127
Chekhov, Anton, 11n
Cherefulnesse, 44
Chief Justice (2 *H.IV*), 32
Choice (*proairesis*), ix, 6n, 10, 12, 17-18, 26, 36, 39, 84, 98, 108, 153, 174, 205, 207, 252, 253n
Christendom, 5, 14, 27, 253-254
Christian sacrifice, 252
Cinthio, Giraldi, *Epitia*, 151n, 153; *Hecatommithi*, 153, 177
Claribell (2), 49, 225-226
Clarinda (5), 162
Claudio (*Meas.*), 152, 154-160, 162-165, 164n, 165n, 167-170, 173n, 217
Claudio (*Much*), 20, 42-43, 47-53, 50n, 109, 176, 225, 243, 245
Claudius, King, 86, 99-100, 122, 130-131, 133-135, 136n, 138, 141, 144, 145n, 147-148, 149n, 176, 217
Clemens, H., ed., 102n
Cleopatra (1), 192
Cleopatra (*Antony*), 2, 20, 192, 195, 199-206, 209, 235, 243, 251
Cloten, 221-224
Clown (*Antony*), 2
Clown (*W.T.*), 224-227
Code, x, 6, 13, 20, 34, 67, 108, 108n, 207, 249, 253n
Comedy, 3, 18, 20, 35-63, 66, 76, 77n, 112, 215, 245-246, 252n; of humors, 7, 31, 35-37, 37n, 54, 63
Comedy of Errors, The, 9, 21, 215
Cominius, 194-196, 199
Commedia dell' arte, 22
Concord (4), 65, 144
Conrade, 46
Constance (*John*), 235, 253n
Contemplation (1), 187, 227
Cooper, Lane, xi, 10n, 13n, 19n, 246n
Corambis, *see* Polonius

Cordelia, 176, 181, 186-188, 219, 242, 251-252
Coridon, 48, 54, 224
Coriolanus, 11, 177, 192-200, 207, 248
Coriolanus, 20, 176-177, 192-199, 217-218, 226, 238, 243, 248, 250-251
Cormoraunt, Gyant, 61
Cory, Herbert E., 8n
Cottage of Care, 248
Court of Faery, 20, 227
Court of Mercilla, 154, 170, 213
Courtly code, 37, 60, 84-105, 108, 112, 116, 126
Craft cycles, 5, 13, 16
Craig, Hardin, xi, 33n, 86n, 155n
Cresseid (Henryson), 125
Cressid (*All's W.*), 75
Cressida, 20, 85-95, 109-110, 112-120, 126, 176, 242, 244
Criseyde (Chaucer), 123
Croll, M. W., ed., 102n
Crudor, Sir, 55-56, 59
Cupid (3), 66
Cupid (*All's W.*), 65-66
Cupid (*Much*), 40-41
Cupido (*Ham.*), 135
Cymbeline, 11, 173n, 218, 221-224, 251
Cymbeline, King, 222, 224
Cymochles, 53, 108n, 112-115, 121, 245
Cymodoce (Cymoent), 65-66, 68, 138, 143-145
Cynthia (Henryson), 126n

Dante, *Divine Comedy*, 13, 16, 230
Daunger (3), 145
Dauphin (*H.V*), 4, 29
Decetto, 46
Defetto, 46
Delay (4), 147
Desdemona, 20, 176, 178-180, 217, 219, 242
de Selincourt, E., ed., xi

Despaire (1), 129, 138, 141, 184-185
Despetto, 46
Desyre (3), 145
Diana, 66
Diana (1), 220
Diana (*All's W.*), 69, 72-73
Diana (*Cym.*), 222
Diana (*Troi.*), 119
Diana of Ephesus (*Per.*), 251
Dianoia, 18, 153, 244
Diction (*lexis*), 3, 104, 153, 244
Diomede (Lydgate), 124n
Diomedes, 87, 90, 94, 96, 110, 113, 115-116, 118, 120-121, 126
Discipline, 5, 24-25, 62, 83, 85, 96, 151, 154, 176-177, 183, 206, 211, 216-217, 221, 227-228, 241, 243, 247-249, 254
Discord (4), 65
Discovery (*anagnorisis*), 4, 10, 13-15, 19-20, 26, 34, 67, 82, 109, 118, 150, 159, 212, 229-230, 237, 240-241, 243, 245-246
Disdaine, 40, 53, 57-58, 118, 120
Disdaine, Ladie, 40, 44; see also Mirabella
Dogberry, 45-46, 216, 239
Dongeon of Orgoglio, 203, 222, 243
Doran, Madeleine, 6n, 153n
Doubt (3), 50, 145
Dowden, Edward, 70n
Downer, Alan S., 10n, 13n
Dragon (1), 181, 194, 196-198, 248
Dragon (*Cor.*), 193
Dramatic irony, 14-15, 209, 254
Dramatic urgency, 14-15, 209, 229, 253-254
Dramatis personae, 17, 35-39, 54-55, 62, 107, 112-117, 157-158, 254
Draper, R. P., 212n
Duessa, 20, 47, 66, 142, 175, 180-181, 188-191, 199-201, 206, 213, 221, 245
Duncan, King, 188-189

Dwarfe (1), 183, 189, 191
Dwarfe (6), 55

Edgar (*Lear*), 181, 182, 184-186
Edmund, Bastard, 180-182, 184
Eiron, 14
Eliot, T. S., *Cocktail Party*, 254
Elissa, 193
Elizabeth, Queen, as Gloriana, 77
Ellis-Fermor, Una, 108n
Elyot, Sir Thomas, 33
Enobarbus, 205, 217, 240
Epic, 14, 18
Erasmus, *Praise of Folly*, 86n
Errour, 178
Errour's Den, 243
Escalus, 152, 157, 159-160
Ethos, 11-12, 18-19, 21, 29, 54-63, 153
Evans, Sir Hugh, 76, 79, 215

Falstaff, Sir John, 30, 32, 76-83, 83n, 209, 237, 240, 246
Fancy (3), 145n
Fate, 35, 108
Faulconbridge, Philip, Bastard (*John*), 33, 238
Feare (3), 145n
Fenton, Master, 78, 80-81, 227
Ferdinand (*Temp.*), 227-228, 230, 235, 246, 252
Fergusson, Francis, 11n, 12n, 13n, 252n
Feste, 54-58, 62, 215
Fidele, *see* Imogen (Fidele)
Fidelia (1), 223n
Florimell, 20, 32, 47, 66, 69, 74, 143, 221-222, 224, 228
Florimell, the false, 47, 66, 142
Florizel, 3, 224, 226-227, 230, 240, 245
Fluellen, 76
Fool (*Lear*), 181-183, 215, 217
Ford, Mistress Alice, 63, 67, 76-78

Ford, Master Frank, 76, 78-80, 82
Form, ix, 4, 6, 17, 30, 54, 112, 150, 207, 228, 234-255, 241n; comic, 21-22, 38-39, 58, 80, 209, 235-236; "Deformed," 46-47, 54, 239; dramatic, ix, x, 13, 84-86, 238, 241, 243; epic, x, 13; narrative, 242-243, 248; tragic, 194, 201, 205, 209, 238
Fortinbras, Prince of Norway, 105, 137
Fortune, 35, 37-38, 108, 205
Francis, Friar (*Much*), 45, 216
Fregosa, Sir Frederick, 88, 101, 102n, 103
Fregosa, Lord Octavian, 96
Frye, Northrop, xi, 2n, 13n, 16n, 37n
Furness, H. H., 42n
Furor (2), 50, 113, 245

Garden of Adonis, 138-139, 148
Garden of Proserpina, 111, 139, 139n
Gardener (*R.II*), 236
Genius, the (2), 116
George, St. (1), 188, 195, 198, 202, 204, 221; *see also* Redcrosse Knight
George, St. (*John*), 27
George, St. (*R.II*), 28
Gerard of Narbon (*All's W.*), 68, 71, 216
Gertrude, Queen, 86, 99-101, 102n, 103-105, 122, 126n, 131, 135, 138, 143-144, 146, 148, 176, 244, 248
Ghost (*Ham.*), 86, 100, 122, 131, 135, 145n, 146, 148
Glauce, 66, 71-72, 74-75, 225
Gloriana, 15, 20, 54, 66, 108, 121n, 127, 129-130, 142, 180, 202, 206, 208-209, 218, 224, 227-228, 232, 246
Gloucester, Earl of (*Lear*), 180-181, 183, 186, 244, 248
Goneril, 180-183, 247

Gonzaga, Lord Cesar, 88
Gonzaga, Lady Elizabeth, 88, 91
Gonzalo, 230
Gower, John, *Confessio Amantis*, 218-220, 218n
Grantorto, 248
Gratiano, 26
Gravedigger (*Ham.*), 4
Green (*R.II*), 31
Greene, Robert, *Dorastus and Fawnia*, 225
Greenlaw, Edwin A., ed., xi, 8n, 12n
Griefe (3), 144-145
Grill (2), 113, 135-136
Guiderius, 223
Guildenstern, 86, 101n, 102, 138, 140, 147-148
Guyon, Sir, 19, 28, 32, 51, 66, 108-110, 108n, 112, 115-122, 128-130, 132, 134-136, 140, 148, 216, 230, 242, 248
Gyant with the Scales (5), 32, 137, 168-169, 212-213, 243-244

Hal, Prince, 29-32, 215, 247
Halle, Edward, 17
Halliwell, James O., ed., 15 1n
Hamlet, 4, 12n, 64n, 85-88, 87n, 88n, 98-105, 101n, 106, 121-122, 126, 150, 216-217, 239, 248, 255; first quarto, 128, 131, 135, 136n, 139, 139n, 145, 148; second quarto, 10, 67, 104, 128-149, 176
Hamlet, King, 87, 103, 135, 136n
Hamlet, Prince, x, 3-4, 17, 20, 67, 85-88, 87n, 98-105, 102n, 108n, 121-122, 121n, 128-150, 176-177, 184, 217, 229, 235, 238, 240, 241n, 242, 246, 248
Harsnet, Samuel, *Declaration of Egregious Popish Impostures*, 185
Hate (4), 144
Hector, Prince, 96, 107, 110-112, 119, 121, 216-217
Hecuba, Queen (*Ham.*), 131

Hecuba, Queen (*Troi.*), 122
Heilman, Robert B., 4n
Helen (2), 111
Helen (*Troi.*), 76, 86, 90, 96, 111-113, 116-117
Helena (*All's W.*), 20, 62, 65-76, 70n, 176, 216, 225, 227, 243
Helenus, 96
Hellenore, 73, 76, 79, 220n
Henderson, W. B. Drayton, 84n, 86n, 87, 87n, 105n, 108n
Henry IV (Dering version), 33n
Henry IV (Meres), 9, 21, 29
Henry IV, Part I, 29-30, 76, 77n, 81, 234, 237-238, 252n
Henry IV, Part II, 9, 29, 31-33, 33n, 76, 77n, 81, 237-238, 252n
Henry IV, 29-32
Henry V, 9, 33, 76, 238
Henry V, 5, 29-30, 32-33, 240
Henry VI, Parts I, II, and III, 9
Henryson, Robert, *Testament of Cresseid*, 125, 125n, 127
Hercules, 195-196, 203, 206
Hermione, Queen, 5, 20, 176, 223n, 225, 227, 246, 251-252
Hermit (6), 45, 227
Hermitage of Contemplation, 187
Herne's Oak, 244
Hero, 40, 43-48, 50, 109, 176
Hillebrand, H. N., ed., 86n
History plays, 9, 27-35, 247
Hoby, Sir Thomas, tr., *Book of the Courtier*, x, 84-105, 126
Holinshed, Raphael, 17; *Chronicle*, 138, 190, 223, 238
Holofernes, 215
Homer, 88, 108
Hopkins, Vivian C., xii
Horatio, 100-101, 105, 131, 145n, 148, 217
House of Alma, 65, 112, 132, 133n, 134-135, 140, 242-243, 248
House of Busirane, 65, 78, 248
House of Care, 222
House of Holiness, 177, 181, 221, 227, 243, 248

House of Pride, 140, 181, 183, 189, 192, 199, 220, 243
Humilta (1), 227
Humors, 7, 28, 31, 36-37, 39, 63, 66, 76
Hut of the Hermit, 243

Iachimo, 221-222, 226
Iago, 177-180, 180n, 199, 221, 226
Ibsen, Henrik, 111n
Idle Lake, 109
Ignaro (1), 143, 190-192
Imitation, 3, 13
Imogen (Fidele), 20, 62, 176, 221-224, 223n, 227, 245
Impatience (2), 135
Impotence (2), 135
Infant (6), 225
Irony, 182, 205
Isabella, 152, 154, 156-158, 161-163, 164n, 167-170, 173n, 176, 217, 219, 243
Isbel (*All's W.*), 75
Isis, 169-170

Jaques, 38
Jessica, 26, 217
Jesus of Nazareth, 13, 15-16, 19, 28
John, Don (*Much*), 46-47
John, Friar (*Romeo*), 36, 215
Jones, H. S. V., 12n
Jonson, Ben (Jonsonian), 10, 16, 32, 36-37, 37n, 54, 63, 76, 253; comedy of humors, 11, 36-37; *Cynthia's Revels*, 76n, 112, 114; *Every Man in His Humour*, 36-37; *Poetaster*, 76n, 112, 112n
Jove (5), 160, 170
Jove (*Ham.*), 136, 145n
Jove (*Oth.*), 179
Jove (*Wives*), 78
Jove (*W.T.*), 253
Julia (*T.G.V.*), 22-25
Juliet, 252
Julietta, 152, 157, 162, 167
Julius Caesar, 1, 9, 34-35, 215
Jupiter (*Cor.*), 194

Jupiter (*Cym.*), 251
Jupiter (Henryson), 126

Katharsis, see Catharsis
Katherine (*H.V*), 77
Katherine (*Shrew*), 27, 234-235, 247
Keats, John, *Sonnet to Spenser*, 18
Keepdown, Mistress Kate, 158
King John, 9, 21, 27-28, 33, 234-235, 238, 253n
King Lear, 11, 177, 180-188, 185n 198, 200, 207, 215, 217, 248, 251
King of France (*All's W.*), 67, 69, 70n, 72, 75, 228, 244
Kittredge, George L., v, xi, 25, 34, 185n
Knight of Courtesy, *see* Calidore, Sir
Knight of Holiness, *see* Redcrosse Knight
Krasis, 11n, 68

Laertes, 86, 99, 103, 131, 133n
Lafeu, 67, 72, 74-76, 246
Langbaine, Gerard, Jr., 49
Langer, Susanne K., 2n, 59n
Lascelles, Mary, 153n, 155n
Laurence, Friar (*Romeo*), 215
Lavache, 67, 75
Lawrence, W. W., 70n, 151n
Lear, King, 20, 176-177, 181, 193, 218, 226-227, 238, 242, 247, 249, 251-252
Leech, Clifford, 153n
Legend, 25-26, 28, 30, 35
Lennox, 189-191
Leonato (*Much*), 47-49, 53
Leontes, King, 20, 177, 225-227, 243, 246
Lewis, C. S., 108n
Lewis, Count of Canossa, 88, 103
Lexis, see Diction
Liagore, 68-69
Ligarius, Caius, 1, 4
Litae (5), 170

Lodge, Thomas, *Rosalynde*, 54, 216
Lorenzo, 26
Love (4), 144
Love's Labour's Lost, 9, 21-22, 25, 35, 215, 228, 235
Love's Labour's Won (Meres), 9, 25, 66
Lucian, *Timon the Misanthrope*, 210-211, 213
Lucifera, 142, 181-183, 192, 199
Lucio (*Meas.*), 152, 153n, 154-157, 165, 172, 173n
Lucy (5), 166-167
Lydgate, John, *Troy Book*, 123-124, 124n, 127
Lyly, John, 22, 35; *Euphues*, 102n
Lysimachus, 220

Macaulay, G. C., ed., 218n
Macbeth, 11, 12n, 177, 188-192, 200, 207, 248, 251
Macbeth, King, 12n, 20, 174, 176-177, 188-192, 200, 217-218, 226, 235, 238, 242, 248, 250-251
Macbeth, Lady, 20, 188-192, 243
Macduff, 189-191
Macduff, Lady, 189
Machiavelli, *Prince*, 86n
Malbecco, 74, 76, 78-80, 82
Malcolm, Prince, 176, 188-189, 251
Malecasta (3), 146, 244
Maleffort, 55-57, 59
Maleger, 134-135
Malvolio, 49, 54-58, 62, 216
Mammon, 109-111, 119-120
Man (human activities), 26-28, 33, 38
Marcius, Caius, *see* Coriolanus
Margaret (*Much*), 40-41
Maria (*Twel.*), 54, 58
Mariana, 152, 157, 161, 166-167, 170, 173n
Marina, 218-221, 245
Marinell, 65-70, 74, 138, 143-145, 147, 224, 242, 245
Mars (*Ham.*), 136, 136n

Index

Mars (Henryson), 126
Mask of Cupid, 50, 52, 65, 138, 142, 144-145, 145n, 148, 244
Measure for Measure, 10, 29, 38, 67, 126, 150-173, 176, 217, 228, 244, 250
Medicis, Lord Julian de, 94n, 96
Medina, 193
Medway (4), 142
Meliboe, 48, 224, 226
Menelaus, 113
Menenius, 193, 196, 199, 217
Merchant of Venice, The, 9, 21, 24-28, 215, 247
Mercie (1), 186, 227
Mercilla, 170, 173n
Mercury (*Ham.*), 136
Mercury (Henryson), 126
Meres, Francis, *Palladis Tamia*, 9, 21, 25, 66
Merlin, 71-72, 228
Merry Wives of Windsor, The, 10, 34, 67, 76-82, 106, 176, 215, 246
Merson, Janice C., xii
Messenger (*Much*), 43, 48, 51
Metamorphosis, 11n, 240
Metaphor, 3, 22, 27, 30, 38, 87, 97, 99, 104, 114-115, 151-152, 158, 162-163, 166, 183, 230, 238
Meyer, George W., 107n
Midsummer Night's Dream, A, 3-4, 9, 21, 25, 27-28, 35, 38, 76, 215, 236, 239, 247
Milton, John, *Paradise Lost*, 133
Mimesis, 3, 4n, 10n, 15, 68n, 229, 234, 239
Mirabella, 40-41, 54, 57
Miracle plays, 16
Miranda, 20, 227-228, 230, 235, 252
Mishap (3), 41
Monster (3), 142-143
Monster under the golden idol (5), 213
Montaigne, Michel de, 18; *Essais*, 86n
Morality plays, 5, 16, 35

Much Ado about Nothing, 8n, 9-10, 21, 24, 32, 34, 37-54, 39n, 49n, 50n, 62, 67, 109, 109n, 111, 126, 176, 216-217, 225, 233, 239, 246, 250
Munera, Lady (5), 212
Mysteries, see Craft cycles
Myth, 3, 11, 24-26, 62, 177, 193, 196, 198, 200, 207, 210-213
Mythos, see Plot

Nares, Robert, 138
Narrative poetry, 12
Nature (*Antony*), 235
Nature (*Cym.*), 223
Nature (natural phenomena), 25-28, 30, 35-38
Neill, Kerby, 50n
Neptune, 69, 116
Nerissa, 26
Nessus, shirt of, 195-196, 203
Nestor, 97, 124-126
Nicolson, Marjorie H., xi
Night, Grandmother, 189
Nine Worthies, 25, 250
Nomoi, 84
North, Sir Thomas, tr., Plutarch's *Lives*, 17, 86n, 192-193, 217, 238; Life of Alcibiades, 208n, 209-210; Life of Marcus Antonius, 200, 202, 204-206, 209-210
Novella (e), 17
Nym, Corporal, 31, 76, 83

Occasion (2), 113, 134
Octavia, 200
Octavius, 176, 200-201, 205-206, 243, 251
Oedipus Tyrannus, 12n
Olivia, 20, 54-62, 227, 243
Ollyphant, 72, 75-78
Olson, Elder, 13n
Ophelia, 4, 20, 85-86, 102-103, 102n, 105, 130-131, 138, 142-143, 145, 148, 176, 242

Ordeal, 4, 13, 18, 20, 37, 44, 67, 77, 86, 88, 92, 94, 98, 108-109, 117, 125, 148, 150, 156, 163-164, 168, 176-181, 187, 195, 206-207, 218-219, 226, 230-231, 241-242, 245-246, 249
Orgoglio (1), 188-192
Orlando, 36, 38, 215, 247
Orsino, 54, 59-62, 176, 227, 241n, 243, 252
Osric, 86, 101n, 131, 133
Oswald, 180-181
Osyris, 169-170
Othello, 4n, 11, 12n, 177-180, 199-200, 207, 221, 248
Othello, 12n, 20, 150, 176-177, 218, 221, 226, 237-238, 242, 248-249, 251
Overdone, Mistress, 157, 160
Ovid, *Metamorphoses*, 25, 240

Padelford, F. M., 7n
Page, Mistress Anne, 78, 80-81, 176, 227
Page, Master George, 81-82, 176
Page, Mistress Meg, 63, 67, 76-77, 80-82, 176
Painter, William, *Palace of Pleasure*, 66
Palace of Mercilla, 243
Palace of Priam, 76, 86, 106-122, 244
Pallavicin, Lord Gaspar, 94, 97
Palmer Reason, 33, 53, 66, 109, 112, 115-116, 120-121, 130, 132, 136, 216, 230
Pandarus, 75, 86-87, 89-94, 98, 110, 113, 115-117, 125
Paridas, 73
Paridell, 42, 73-74, 76
Paris, Sir, 73
Paris (2), 111
Paris (*Troi.*), 76, 86, 96, 110-113, 116
Parius, 73
Parolles, 65, 67, 72-74, 246
Pastoral, 25, 37, 225

Pastorella, 47-48, 65, 224-226, 225n, 230, 245
Patience (1), 179, 186, 227
Patroclus, 97, 101n, 113, 217
Paul, Henry N., 188n
Paulina, 177, 225, 227
Pedro, Don, 42, 48-53
Penaunce (1), 186
Perceval le Gallois, 56
Percy, Hotspur, 29-31, 237
Perdita, 224-227, 225n, 245
Pericles, 11, 218-221, 251
Pericles, 218-221, 243, 245
Peripeteia, see Reversal
Peripety, see Reversal
Perissa, 193
Petruchio, 215
Phaedria, 44, 109-110, 112-113, 115, 117, 245
Phebe, 38
Phedon, 49-50, 109
Philemon, 49-50
Philo (*Antony*), 240
Philotime, 109-111, 119-120
Philtera, 166-167
Phoebus (*All's W.*), 71
Phoebus (*Cym.*), 222
Phoebus (*Ham.*), 135
Phoebus (Henryson), 126
Phrynia, 213
Pia, Lady Emilia, 91
Pinch, 215
Pistol, Ancient (*Wives*), 79, 83, 246
Plato (Platonic), 152
Plautus, 21
Pleasance, 44
Plot (*mythos*), 1, 3, 6n, 10, 12, 17-19, 22, 25, 29, 36, 38, 88, 98, 107, 109, 179, 207, 225, 241n, 245
Plutarch, *Lives*, 17, 86n, 192-193, 217, 238; Life of Alcibiades, 208n, 209-210; Life of Marcus Antonius, 200, 202, 204-206, 209-210
Pluto (2), 117-120
Pluto (*Troi.*), 109-110, 117n, 118n

Index

Poet (*Tit.*), 213
Polixenes, 224, 227
Polonius, 86, 101-103, 102n, 138, 143, 143n, 148, 149n
Pompey (1), 192
Pompey (*Antony*), 201
Pompey (*Meas.*), 152, 157, 165, 167
Pope, Elizabeth M., 153n
Porter (*Macb.*), 190
Portia, 2, 26, 177, 252
Posthumus Leonatus, 177, 221-224, 226-227, 243
Potts, Abbie F., 8n, 78n, 109n, 112n, 121n
Potts, L. J., 19n
Pragmata, 6n, 241n
Prat, Mother (*Wives*), 78
Praxis, 3, 4n, 6n, 153, 234
Presson, Robert K., 127n
Priam, King (*Ham.*), 131, 148
Priam, King (*Troi.*), 96, 107, 110, 217
Priest (*Twel.*), 61
Prince of Verona, 27
Princess of France (*L.L.L.*), 235
Proairesis, *see* Choice
Proserpina, 118n
Prospero, 1-3, 5, 10n, 20, 107, 169, 214, 228-232, 240, 243, 246, 252
Protensity, 15, 20, 248
Proteus, 22-25, 68, 143, 215
Prouty, Charles T., 8n, 49n
Provost (*Meas.*), 154, 163-165, 167
Pryene, 49
Psyche of drama, 6n, 10n
Puck, 25-26, 215
Pyramus and Thisbe, 25, 250
Pyrochles, 53, 112-113, 121, 131, 245
Pyrrhus, 131, 148

Queen (*Cym.*), 221
Queen (*R.II*), 236-237
Queen of the Fairies (*Wives*), 77, 80

Quickly, Dame (*Wives*), 79-83, 246

Radigund, 74, 130, 154, 161, 163
Recognition, *see* Discovery
Redcrosse Knight, 19, 28, 47, 51, 129, 134, 138, 140-142, 148, 171, 177-181, 183-189, 192, 194-198, 200-201, 203, 205-206, 208, 220-224, 226, 228, 242, 248
Regan, 181-183, 247
Remorse (1), 186
Renwick, William L., 8n
Repentance (1), 186
Reproach (6), 146
Revelation, *see* Discovery
Reversal (*peripeteia*, peripety), 10-11, 10n, 13-15, 20, 25, 34, 37, 65, 76, 81-82, 95, 100, 110, 122, 150, 162, 176, 201-202, 212, 225-227, 229-230, 237, 241, 249
Reynaldo, 102n, 143n, 148
Richard II, 9, 21, 28-31, 33, 236-238
Richard II, 28-29, 31, 151, 215, 240, 247
Richard III, 9, 234
Riche, Barnabe, *Of Apolonius and Silla*, 54, 59-60, 216
Ritual, 4-5, 30, 77n, 81, 83, 250, 252, 252n
Roderigo, 179
Romance, 5, 17-18, 20, 148, 176, 225, 251-252
Romeo, 36, 252
Romeo and Juliet, 8n, 9, 21, 25-27, 215, 247
Rosalind, 38, 177, 247
Rosencrantz, 86, 101n, 102, 138, 140, 147-148
Rossillion, Countess of, 67, 69-73, 216, 225
Rouse, W. H. D., 84n
Ryence, King, 71

Salisbury, Earl of (*John*), 235
Saluage man (6), 45, 47

Sansfoi, 178-180, 245
Sansjoi, 178-179, 180-181, 189
Sansloi, 178-180, 184, 223, 245
Saturn (Henryson), 125
Satyrane, 74, 78, 179, 220, 223
Satyrs (1), 220
Satyrs (3), 220n
Savages (6), 220n
Schofield, William H., 29, 225n
Sclaunder, 42
Scorne, 40, 53, 57-58
Scudamour, 51, 61-62, 65, 132, 147, 180n, 221-222, 224, 242, 245, 248
Sebastian, St., 59-60
Sebastian (*Twel.*), 54-56, 59-62, 216, 227, 239
Sedgewick, G. G., 14n
Seneca, 18, 134-135
Serena, 44-47, 54, 58, 220n
Servant (*Troi.*), 116
Seven Deadly Sins, *see* Virtues and vices
Shame (6), 146
Shepherd (*W.T.*), 224-227
Shylock, 26, 36, 151, 217, 247
Sicinius (*Cor.*), 196, 199
Sidney, Sir Philip, *Arcadia*, 184
Silvia, 22-23, 25, 215
Smith, J. C., ed., xi
Smith, Robert M., 153n
Socrates, 159
Somers, Sir George, 231
Sommer, H. Oscar, ed., 125n
Sonnets of Shakespeare, 33
Sparagmos, 252
Spectacle (*opsis*), x, 153, 244
Spencer, Theodore, 85n, 86n
Spenser, Edmund, *Amoretti*, 133; *Daphnaida*, 208n; *Hymne in Honour of Beautie*, 240; Letter to Sir Walter Raleigh, 5, 208
Spurgeon, Caroline F. E., 87, 87n, 88n
Stearns, Marshall W., tr., 125n
Stephano, 83n
Steward (*All's W.*), 73
Stow, John, 33, 238

Stuart, King James, 188, 190
Symbol, 3, 26, 34, 252
Syntaxis, 6n, 241n
Synthesis, 6n, 241n
Sypher, Wylie, 151n, 153n, 173n

Talus, 33, 137, 154, 165, 167, 212, 214
Taming of the Shrew, The, 9-10, 25-27, 215, 235, 247
Tempest, The, 11, 107n, 218, 228-232, 235, 246, 251-252
Temple of Diana (*Per.*), 245
Temple of Isis, 154, 169-170
Temple of Venus, 65, 138, 144, 147-148, 245, 248
Tennyson, Alfred Lord, *Princess*, 162
Terpine, Sir, 154-155, 163-164, 164n
Terwin, Sir, 185
Thaisa (*Per.*), 218, 251
Thaler, Alwin, xi, 8n, 49, 187n
Thematic literature, 18
Thersites, 67, 75-76, 86, 94, 97-98, 113, 117n, 119, 217, 240
Theseus, 3, 238, 241n
Thomson, J. A. K., 14n
Timandra, 213
Timias, 65, 173n, 222, 224
Timon (1), 208-211, 208n, 228-229
Timon (Lucian), 208n
Timon (Plutarch), 208n, 209
Timon (*Tim.*), 210-214, 212n, 228, 245, 249
Timon of Athens, 210-214
Titus Andronicus, 9
Todd, Henry J., 83n
Touchstone, 38
Tragedy, 3, 17-18, 20, 39, 174-207, 209, 217, 245; Greek, 10n, 13-14
Trevisan, Sir, 185
Trinculo, 83n
Tristram, 59-61
Troilus, Prince, x, 20, 85-99, 90n, 104, 107, 108n, 115n, 129, 150, 176, 216-217, 242, 244
Troilus (Caxton), 124

Troilus (Chaucer), 123
Troilus (Lydgate), 124n
Troilus and Cressida, x, 10, 24, 67-68, 76, 76n, 83n, 85-98, 85n, 86n, 87n, 88n, 93n, 101n, 104, 106-129, 107n, 108n, 117n, 127n, 150, 164n, 176, 216-217, 235, 247, 250
Trompart, 79-80, 165
Turpine, Sir, 58, 134, 147
Twelfth Night, 10, 24, 34, 37, 39, 54-63, 67, 176, 215-217, 235, 239, 241n, 246, 250
Two Gentlemen of Verona, The, 9, 21-25, 215
Tybalt, 36

Ulysses, 67, 86, 88, 91n, 94-97, 101, 109-110, 113-115, 118n, 119-120, 122, 126, 164n, 216-217, 229
Una, 20, 47, 54, 141-142, 176-178, 180, 185-186, 189, 200, 202-206, 219-221, 223, 228
Unico Aretino, 94

Valentine, 23, 215
Valeria, 193, 198
Vanitie (1), 181
Venus, 66
Venus (2), 111
Venus (Henryson), 126

Vincentio, Duke, 67, 151-160, 155n, 162-165, 164n, 165n, 167-173, 173n, 177, 217, 228
Viola, 19-20, 54-56, 61, 176-177, 227, 235, 239, 252; *see also* Cesario
Virgil, 25, 108n, 124
Virgilia, 193-194
Virtues and vices, 7, 11, 19, 22, 31, 37, 108, 130, 157, 175, 181-183, 193, 198-199, 241
Volumnia, 192-194, 196-199
Vulcan, 110, 136n

Watkins, W. B. C., 8n, 83n, 108n, 173n, 180n
Wheelwright, Philip, 2n, 10n, 13n, 68n, 252n
Whetstone, George, *Promos and Cassandra*, 151n, 153-154
Whirlepoole of decay, 116
Whitaker, Virgil K., 5, 5n, 16n, 108n
Wimsatt, W. K., Jr., 77n
Winstanley, Lilian, ed., 7n
Winter's Tale, The, 4, 11, 15n, 218, 223n, 224-227, 230, 251, 253
Witch (3), 221
Witches (*Macb.*), 1, 174, 177, 217
Wordsworth, William, xi
Wright, Ernest H., 210n, 211
Wright, W. A., 42n

SCHEELE MEMORIAL LIBRARY
3 6655 00000617 1
PR2955.S6 P6 1969
Potts, Abbie Findla/Shakespear

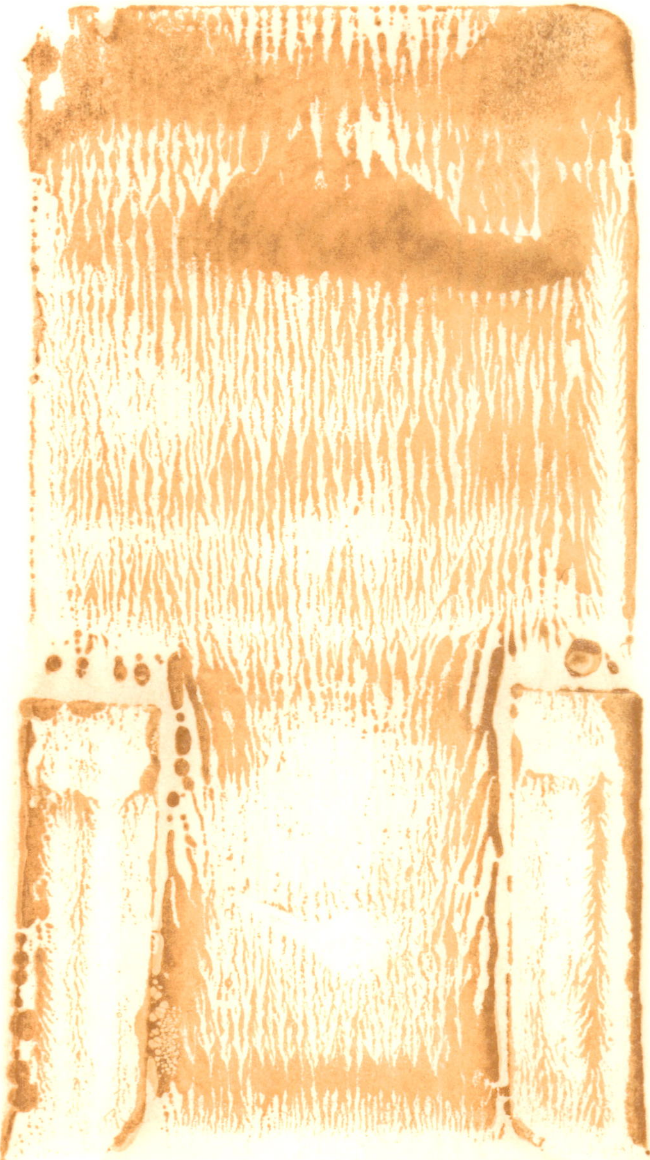